# A Clergy Guide to Child Abuse and Neglect

# A Clergy Guide to Child Abuse and Neglect

Cynthia Crosson-Tower

Cleveland

*For*
*Lois Buchiane,*
*who inspired and challenged me as a mentor*
*and became my caring and valued friend*

The Pilgrim Press
700 Prospect Avenue
Cleveland, Ohio 44115-1100
*thepilgrimpress.com*



Printed in the United States of America on acid-free paper

10 09 08 07 06 5 4 3 2 1

**Library of Congress Cataloging-in-Publication Data**

Crosson-Tower, Cynthia.
A clergy guide to child abuse and neglect / Cynthia Crosson-Tower.
p. cm.
ISBN-13: 978-0-8298-1595-5
1. Church work with children. 2. Child abuse – Religious aspects – Christianity. 3. Children's rights. 4. Church work with families. 5. Pastoral theology. I. Title.
BV639.C4C76 2006
261.8′3271 – dc22

2006017775

ISBN-13: 978-0-8298-1595-5
ISBN-10: 0-8298-1595-3

# Contents

# Acknowledgments

This book might not have become a reality without the many people who both believed in the project and cared about children and families in churches. My thanks to two area ministers of the United Church of Christ who have helped me at various stages along the way: Laura Lee Kent of the Central Area and Peter Wells of the Western Area of the Massachusetts Conference. My appreciation goes to all the clergy who completed my questionnaire to give me background and anecdotal material early in the project. Although you are too numerous to mention individually, please accept my thanks. And to Natalie and the late Herb Maynard, Paul Ferrin, and Gordon Tate, who started me on the journey toward ministry that would give rise to this book, my gratitude. Thanks also to Harold (Skip) Lloyd, who took the time to read over and comment on the manuscript, and to Randy Kafka, who helped with the Jewish perspective. My sincere thanks to Sharon Thornton, Dean Allen, Ben Valentin, Julieanne Hallman, and Mick Comstock, who each provided me with pieces of insight that became woven into the text.

I am always indebted to my research assistant, Peggyann Prasinos, who like Sancho of Don Quixote fame is ever ready to start off on the next adventure in the pursuit of some obscure fact that I need (yesterday!) for my writing. In addition, she is always willing to listen to my ideas and offer valuable insight. My thanks to my son, Chay, who offered me his literary and editorial talents, and to his wife, Becky, who kept him fed and sane while the drama of mother-and-son collaboration unfolded. My appreciation goes to my editor, Ulrike Guthrie, who was willing to suggest to the folks at The Pilgrim Press that they take on this project.

When one writes a book there are always those people who have listened to the ideas, commiserated with the setbacks, shared in the excitement, and given encouragement from the sidelines. I found such friends in Kate Martin, Lois Buchiane, and Ellen Woodbury, and owe them special recognition and thanks. To my family, Jim, Chay, Becky, and Andrew, who have stood by me while I was in "writing mode," thank you: I could not have done it without you!

I offer this book in memory of my son, Jamie, and my mom, who spurred me on but did not see its completion. Their deaths within a month of one another stimulated another passage in my own spiritual journey and no doubt added to the content and tone of the words written here.

And finally, thanks to the many ministerial colleagues who expressed their interest in the subject and, I hope, are still waiting eagerly to buy the book!

# Introduction

"A parishioner came to me maintaining that her husband was sexually abusing her daughter. So what *am* I to do?" my clergy friend asked me. Should he support the mother and the child and risk breaking up the family? What role should he play with the father — alleged by his wife to be a perpetrator? And where should he look for additional help on such an issue?

In my role as an educator, consultant, and counselor in the area of child victimization, I am often asked for such advice from a variety of professionals. But a clergyperson's dilemma seems especially unique. He or she is seen as someone who is expected to give comfort, but must also make difficult decisions within that role. As more and more states include clergy among those mandated to report child abuse and neglect, the need for knowledge and understanding about child maltreatment becomes vital.

The majority of people who are in trouble go first to clergy for help. Yet clergy are typically ill prepared by their seminary training to address issues of child abuse and neglect. This book is a step toward rectifying this lack of information and preparation.

## Why We Must Be Involved

Carol Adams and Marie Fortune, in their *Violence against Women and Children,* echo my concerns about the need to train clergy to recognize and intervene in abusive situations. They contend that maltreatment issues not only fall within the realm of pastoral care, but are "also hermeneutical, exegetical, liturgical, theological, ethical, and historical issues because . . . [they] profoundly affect the lives of congregants and students."[1]

To fully address our role in responding to child maltreatment, we clergy must:

- understand and accept our legal mandate (in many states) to report child maltreatment situations
- become familiar with the dynamics of abuse and neglect

- learn about the community resources available to respond to abuse and neglect
- consider our unique position for intervention as clergy

## Clergy as Mandated Reporters: Helpful or Hurtful?

Every state in the United States requires that those in certain professions who know about or suspect child abuse and neglect report this abuse to a particular state agency. Some states include domestic violence in this mandatory reporting law. In many states, clergy have recently been added to the list of mandated reporters, while other states have included them for some time (see Appendix 1 for listing of states in which clergy are mandated to report).

Yet there has been a considerable outcry in some areas about this mandate. "There is no reason that I should tell a child protection agency about someone in my parish!" a minister told me recently. "This is better handled within the church community. I don't want those children snatched out of their homes by some social worker!" Though I tried to explain that removal of children is the absolute last resort when all other attempts to protect them from the abuse have failed, unfortunately this clergywoman did not want to be swayed. Though some valid criticisms exist for having clergy designated as mandated reporters, there are also some important arguments in favor of the legislation that are discussed throughout this book.

## Knowing the Dynamics of Maltreatment and the Community Resources

Among the most frequent concerns I have heard from clergy is that they feel they do not know enough about the dynamics of abuse situations to be good judges of when to report. This very apprehension has stimulated the writing of this book. It is crucial that all professionals work together in the interest of children and their families. Toward this end, it behooves clergy to learn more about child abuse and neglect.

For many years, I worked as a social worker with families who abused or neglected their children. I remember several cases in which well-meaning and concerned clergy actually impeded the help that the families so desperately needed. I have seen clergy, sometimes unknowingly, contaminate evidence, withhold vital information, discourage a family's cooperation with the child protection agency, and give families false hopes. Here is one such case:

> *Child Protection Services (CPS) first became involved with the Heralds when eight-year-old Dorie was brought to their attention by the parochial school that she attended. Dorie's teacher, noticing that the child was dressed in long sleeves on a rather warm day, had urged her to remove her sweater. The child's fear as she cringed and refused to remove the garment set off an alarm for the teacher. The teacher eventually discovered that the child's arms were covered with bruises, and the situation was finally reported to Child Protective Services (CPS).*
>
> *The parish priest, who happened to be at the school that day, knew the Herald family and immediately called Dorie's mother. Before CPS even had time to screen the case, Myrna Herald was at the school, angrily accusing anyone she could. When the CPS worker arrived, he tried to talk with the hysterical mother, who was in the priest's office. Together, clergyman and parent faced the CPS worker and insisted that Dorie had simply fallen and that CPS had no right to be involved. At no time did the priest disclose that he was well aware of Paul Herald's problems with alcohol and his vicious temper, or that in fact Myrna had called him to the house on several occasions when she too had been beaten by her husband. The priest had talked with Paul twice and felt that the man was doing better. Surely, he reasoned, the situation could be worked out through pastoral counseling. In an attempt to protect the husband, and preserve the relationship he felt they had, the priest never disclosed certain critical facts.*

Had the priest and the social worker been able to work together, the ending might have been quite different. The mother might have been helped to disclose the family's secret of abuse and to seek help for her daughter and her husband. Instead, assuming that Dorie might be in danger from her mother, the CPS worker was forced to remove the child from the home for what he considered to be her own safety. So irate was the priest by this outcome that he counseled the parents not to talk with CPS and to seek legal counsel. He connected them with an attorney within the church, who, after meeting with Myrna Herald, told her that the only way her daughter would be returned was to reveal her story and cooperate with CPS in seeking help. This mother was both frightened and later embittered by the turn of events.

How much different the scenario might have been if the clergyman had spoken of his concern with the mother before CPS arrived and had prepared her to cooperate with the worker. The father might have been approached in a manner that enabled him to recognize that he needed help, rather than enabling him, through secrecy, to continue his destructive patterns of behavior. Moreover, had the professionals worked together in the family's interest, a little girl might have been spared a painful separation from home.

Through understanding and working with social service agencies you can aid families in accessing all the helping networks available to them. The few negative experiences I encountered as a social worker are offset by the positive relationships I have had with ministers, priests, and rabbis who with me have worked in the interests of the victims and those close to them. We learned from each other, and the clients/parishioners benefited.

One criticism I often hear from clergy is that reporting destroys the relationship that a clergyperson has with a parishioner or causes the family to leave the church. Although this is certainly possible, there are ways to sustain a relationship with a family once the report is made. First, the manner in which the family is told of the report may make a difference in whether they maintain contact with the clergyperson. (For more information, see Chapter 5.) Second, families need support during this difficult time of disclosure. Offering to support them through it is often enough to encourage them to maintain the relationship. Our faith reminds us that God will be there for us through whatever trials come our way. Who better than God's representative to be the sustainer of the victims and perhaps the family in this crisis?

## The Unique Contribution of Clergy

Your role as a clergyperson or church leader puts you in a unique position to become involved with child abuse and neglect situations. Like the prophets of biblical times, church leaders have a prophetic role when it comes to child maltreatment, a role that many people would prefer not to own. Yet each year thousands of children become victims of abuse and neglect. Preventing it is a matter of justice. As those called by Christ to live in community with one another, caring for our neighbor and ministering to those who are in need, it is also our task to care for both perpetrators and victims of abuse.

## What This Book Will Do for You

A church community that is safe for and caring of its "children" large and small does not just happen. It requires careful preparation and tending. The pastor has an integral role in beginning or encouraging this process. This book will help you move toward involving your congregation in the important work of addressing abuse and neglect issues.

There are several steps to this process. First, you must *arm yourself with the knowledge* that you require to educate your congregation and move them to action. *A Clergy Guide to Child Abuse and Neglect* is a primer on child maltreatment, and additional resources are listed in the Appendixes. Many colleges now offer courses on child abuse and neglect, victimization, violence, and a variety of related topics. The more you learn, the better you will feel, both prepared when intervention is necessary and able to guide others in their learning.

A second step is to *open the door for discussion* within the church and the community. People in the pews need permission to discuss difficult subjects like violence against children. They need a prophetic leader who is willing to talk about and respond to a difficult situation. Such prophetic leadership and permission to discuss often come through sermons that address violence; they are also shared through working at a shelter or on a crisis hotline. But you must take the initiative, for until people know that it is not only permitted but expected that abuse will be discussed and responded to, they will avoid discussion at all costs. One way I have found to open a difficult discussion is to say, "Let me tell you about a book I am reading"; *A Clergy Guide to Child Abuse and Neglect* can be just such a book.

No matter how you do it, going public about child abuse and neglect not only gives people permission to talk about what was previously taboo, it also makes it easier for victims to seek help. An adult survivor once told me that it was a sermon that helped her to recognize that she could seek help with the residual scars of her childhood abuse.

Third, this book will inspire you to *learn more about community resources*. What is available in your community to help children and families? Where is the Child Protective Services office, and what are its hours of operation? Is there a crisis hotline? What agencies in the area provide treatment for families who abuse or neglect? For perpetrators of sexual abuse? Such fieldwork requires that you make a point of researching and visiting these agencies to discover the resources that your congregation will need in a crisis. Before the crisis hits, become known as someone in the community who is interested in abuse issues and wants to work in conjunction with other professionals to help families, victims, and perpetrators. In addition to learning the policies and procedures of agencies and how to refer to them, you might also want to create a resource directory for the church or community. Perhaps the whole church might join in this mission.

And finally, I hope that this book will *inspire you to want to learn more* about this important subject and become more involved in community efforts for change, perhaps by joining a community team of professionals who work together to improve services within the area. May this information and these resources give you the confidence to respond to abuse when you encounter it.

## Outline of This Book

Chapter 1 describes the various types of child maltreatment and provides a list of symptoms that one might observe. Chapter 2 looks at how a clergyperson can recognize the various types of abuse and neglect. The characteristics of abusive and neglectful families are given special attention in Chapter 3, while the focus in Chapter 4 is on the sexual abuser whether within or outside the family.

There are many myths about the reporting of child maltreatment and about how other professionals interface with the child protection system. Chapters 5 and 6 provide guidelines about how to report abuse and neglect, outline how the social service system responds to those reports, and suggest what role a clergyperson or church leader might have in helping that system to be more effective. Chapter 6 looks specifically at the family where there is domestic violence and how a pastor might intervene. Intervention in child maltreatment can often be difficult for families, and the pastor can be an important resource in helping them through the process, for which I offer guidance in Chapter 7. In Chapter 8, I discuss the congregation's role when one of its members/families is the subject of that intervention. Who counsels the family in which abuse or neglect has been discovered? What can a clergyperson expect from the congregation in such a situation? Chapter 8 offers more specific guidance in helping clergy to identify for whom and by whom counseling is best offered.

Discovering that a fellow clergyperson is an abuser, of course, is most difficult. Chapters 9 and 10 guide the congregational leader who suspects or knows that a fellow leader is an abuser. And what of the congregation scarred by such events? Chapter 11 suggests how healing may take place in these congregations.

Children are not the only ones affected by abusive situations. Many adults have suffered maltreatment as children and come to church still wounded by those events. Chapter 12 addresses how their needs might be met within a church community.

The best way to address child abuse is to prevent it from occurring in the first place. One way to do this is to develop a church protocol that stops abuse before it starts and that responds to any abuse that might be happening. Chapter 13 guides the clergy and their congregations through the development of such a protocol.

Addressing the needs of children and families who are affected by maltreatment requires a great deal of energy on the pastor's part. Chapter 14 emphasizes the necessity of clergy self-care. And finally, Chapter 15 speaks of the future and offers further suggestions to more actively address the difficult topic of child maltreatment.

Throughout, I speak not only of the logistics and process of intervening in dysfunctional family situations, but also take seriously the role of clergy as spiritual guides, offering them advice, reassurance, and companionship.

## Chapter 1

# Maltreatment Comes in Many Forms

*The most striking thing I noticed about Dona was her huge brown eyes staring at me from a dirty face that had seen too much for its seven years. She watched my every move with studied suspicion as I climbed the creaking outside stairs of the tenement that was home to Dona and her two brothers and three sisters. The baby she had slung on her thin hip slipped and she hiked him up, his disinterested expression already betraying his approach to life.*

*"She ain't home," drawled Dona with practiced authority as I started up the stairs. Two toddlers, possibly twins, sat on the top step, their frail legs dangling over the ground far below. Another child, slightly younger than Dona, stared at me from behind an open door at the top landing.*

*"She ain't home," repeated the child more insistently.*

*"Who's taking care of all you kids?" I asked.*

*"Me!" announced Dona with seeming finality as if challenging my questioning that she could do so. It was my first introduction to the Peras, a family that came to church occasionally and one to which it had been suggested I pay a pastoral call.*

*"They need you," I was told. "That family has a lot of problems."*

*I could only guess at how understated those words actually were. What followed that visit and my attempts to ensure that the children were safe involved our entire congregation in a world of social services that was entirely new to me despite my years as a pastor.*

Most of what has been written in the last decade about child abuse and the role of the church and the needs of the community describes abuse of a sexual nature, particularly the abuse of children by clergy and its cover-up by many church organizations. As observed by a veteran pastor (above), the maltreatment of children is much more diverse than this. Behind closed doors, children are being neglected; their basic needs are left unmet, they are abandoned for long periods, and are asked at a very young age to care for younger brothers and sisters. Like Dona, these children are expected to function as best they can in a world of adults who do not have the emotional energy to respond to their needs.

And then there are the children with physical scars that attest to the abuse they have suffered — children who fear talking about the beatings lest these intensify. Behind these same closed doors are the children who have been led into a world of sexuality long before they have the knowledge, understanding, or authority to consent to such acts. And what of the children whose lives are punctuated by harsh words that make them feel worthless and unloved? Or those who watch, often silent and terrified, as their parents engage in a drama of domestic violence? These children are in our congregations and our communities, yet we are usually unaware of their trauma.

How can we recognize and understand what goes on in the lives of such children so that we might begin to help them? Perhaps the first step for clergy is to become familiar with the different types of maltreatment that children suffer.

When we discuss child maltreatment, it is important to distinguish between what a social agency might define as abuse or neglect and what each of us values as adequate child rearing. We hope that all parents value their children and nurture them in ways that guide them into healthy adulthood. Given the rich cultural mix in the United States, each culture with its own customs and values regarding how to raise a child, it is difficult but essential, in order to protect them, to arrive at some standards of treatment of children. These standards for child rearing do not so much govern what you can do as a parent as what you cannot. For example, a child has the right to be protected from harm and given a healthy environment in which to grow. When the parents' actions rob the child of these basic rights and fail to provide for the child's most basic needs, our society says that we have an obligation to intervene. But for each culture, what constitutes harm and health differs widely. As one social worker explained:

> *We have laws about how people can treat children. When those laws are broken, we must address it for the child's sake. But, with increased training in cultural awareness, we workers have learned to fully assess the situation before we act. We might have to say, "I know that you used to beat your child in your country, but here we do not do that. It is all part of learning the customs of your adopted land." We try*

*to frame it in the context of the many new and different things they will have to learn in order to live in the United States. Most families need only a bit of education and support.*

How then does one distinguish abusive behavior from cultural mores? One social worker recounted how she felt sure that an immigrant family's severe physical punishment of a male child was a cultural behavior, but after educating herself discovered that boys were never hit and rarely disciplined before the age of five in that culture. So education in cultural diversity is now part of a social worker's training.

How do the standards under which we operate in the United States define the various types of child maltreatment?

## What Is Child Neglect?

When we think of neglected children, we may imagine parents who are so caught up in their careers or other pursuits that they have little time for their offspring. While such families are certainly in trouble and may be candidates for counseling, theirs are not typically the children who come to the attention of agencies that deal with child maltreatment. *Neglect* is *not meeting a child's basic needs for food, shelter, clothing, medical care, educational instruction, protection from harm, and supervision.*

The definition of neglect varies a great deal from culture to culture. For example, it is common for many Native American groups to allow children the freedom to roam within a neighborhood, much as they would on the reservation. Such parents assume that the community will care for the child when he or she is not within the parents' view. This logic breaks down when the Native American family comes to live in a large city where not all the residents consider it their responsibility to protect that child.

Some theorists divide neglect into several additional categories according to what need is not being met.[1] *Physical neglect* refers to failing to provide adequate food, clothing, and shelter for a child. Notice the word "adequate." Child protection regulations require that parents provide only adequate care. "Adequate," defined in the regulations of agencies state by state, may not fall within the range of what we find acceptable, but protective agencies can only expect what the law requires.

*Hygiene* also falls under physical neglect. Many children are not required to have adequate hygiene and are never bathed or taught how to keep themselves clean, which often creates problems for them when they interact with the outside world.

Some theorists separate *emotional and developmental neglect* from physical neglect. Emotional and developmental neglect are about denying children the right to adequate stimulation, development of language, and the development of gross and fine motor skills. For example, a child left tied in a playpen without human interaction for hours on end would be considered neglected.

*Medical neglect* involves denying medical or dental attention for children when needed. *Educational neglect* refers to not allowing children to receive an adequate and appropriate education. Some parents are neglectful by not sending their children to school, others by hampering their ability to gain knowledge. For example, the child with younger siblings who is kept home for days to care for these children is being prevented from getting an education. And finally, *supervision* is part of a parent's job when dealing with children. Children who are not adequately supervised may come to harm in a variety of ways.

Over the last two decades considerable controversy has ensued over what constitutes prenatal abuse. An expectant mother's inhaling of cigarette smoke can result in babies with low birth weight and breathing complications. There is a known correlation between drinking alcohol to excess and fetal alcohol syndrome and fetal alcohol effects, both of which have an impact on a child's development, intelligence, and personality. Various drugs likewise create an array of physiological and psychological problems for infants. Yet we are not always clear about how accountable a mother should be held. Is such behavior abusive or neglectful? Some states recognize prenatal abuse/neglect while others do not.

Neglect poses a difficult problem for those who consider intervening, especially protective services workers. Because neglect is less dramatic than other forms of abuse and sometimes not as easy to see and pinpoint, it can be hard to define. Sometimes neglect and poverty are erroneously grouped together as one. Although poverty can contribute to child neglect, all poor families are certainly not neglectful. Furthermore, once neglect is uncovered, the process of intervention for child protection is not always easy. Neglect has often been part of the family's history for several generations. Changing deeply ingrained values and behaviors requires persistence and intervention, usually involving long-term involvement of social service agencies.

## What Is Physical Abuse?

The identification and recognition of the physical abuse of children has an interesting history, marked with distinct signposts and unlike the history of any other type of maltreatment. It is worth recounting.

Throughout history, children have been seen as the property of their parents to do with as the parents saw fit. Beating children was not uncommon in earlier times, supported by such adages as "spare the rod and spoil the child." By the later 1880s, in this country, there were some who felt that children should not be harmed by adults, yet there were still no laws to protect these small individuals. Then in 1894, the case of one little girl changed the course of the history of child advocacy.

Mary Ellen Wilson was an eight-year-old child living in a section of New York City. Mary Ellen's own parents had died, and she was left to the mercy of a stepparent and that stepmother's new spouse. The neighbors began to hear the cries of little Mary Ellen when she was being beaten or left outside in the frigid temperatures. Since there were no laws about such things, no one knew how to intervene. Finally Etta Wheeler, a neighborhood worker whose role it was to attend to the needs of the poor (adults) of that area, was alerted. In desperation, Wheeler brought Mary Ellen's situation to the attention of Henry Bergh, then head of the Society for the Prevention of Cruelty to Animals. Wheeler's plea was that animals were treated better than this child. Bergh helped Wheeler to begin the process of removing Mary Ellen from the abusive home, prosecuting the stepmother, and forming a new agency that could intervene on behalf of abused and neglected children. The Society for the Prevention of Cruelty to Children still exists today.[2]

Physical abuse was further recognized in 1946 when a radiologist named John Caffey discovered that a number of the children he saw had old breaks and injuries that had not been previously reported to medical personnel. After some exploration, Caffey postulated that these injuries had been caused by abuse from adults, and for a time these types of instances were known as Caffey's Syndrome. In 1961, a physician named C. Henry Kempe, along with his colleagues at the American Academy of Pediatrics in Denver, sought a catchy phrase that would bring to the public's attention the physical abuses perpetrated against children. Adopting the term "the battered child syndrome," Kempe and his group heightened the attention given to physical abuse and stimulated numerous studies that enhanced the treatment provided for abused children today.[3]

It was a shocking eighty years from the time that little Mary Ellen shivered in the cold until 1975, when a law was passed that designated certain professionals as mandated reporters, thereby legitimating the importance of intervention in the maltreatment of children.

Still today, it is often difficult to determine where discipline leaves off and physical abuse begins. So, to clarify: "discipline" is designed to give direction to children so that they develop in a healthy manner, whereas "physical abuse" refers to *nonaccidental injury of a child that is perpetrated at the hands of a caretaker.* This definition contains two important pieces: that the injury is intentional on the part of the adult and that a physical injury results.

When child protection agencies define the limits of abuse, they usually say that the nonaccidental injury must have left some type of mark. It actually requires quite a bit of force to leave marks on some parts of the body. Most of the children whose cases are "screened in" (the term used when a report is accepted as a case) by child protective services have the easily recognizable injuries that are discussed further in Chapter 2.

## What Is Sexual Abuse?

Sexual abuse may not be as obvious as other forms of abuse or neglect, and yet it can be just as devastating to a child. We define "sexual abuse" by referring to the *sexual involvement imposed upon a child by an adult or one who had greater power and resources.* In recent years, states have included *the production of or exposure to pornography* in the definition of sexual abuse. The fact that sexual contact between adults and children is not acceptable may seem obvious to some, but others argue that, if a child consents to the activity, he or she should be allowed to participate. There are organizations such as the North American Man Boy Love Association (NAMBLA), the Rene Guyon Society, or the Childhood Sexuality Circle that actually promote sexual activity between children and adults. Although these organizations are illegal, they continue to flourish, especially in recent years since contact with like-minded individuals has become easier through the Internet.

Most adults would agree that sexual contact with children is abusive, but few have likely considered why, except that it is "morally wrong." The "why" rests in the value held in our culture that sexual contact is between consenting individuals. Researcher and child advocate David Finkelhor proposes that in order to consent, one must have the knowledge of what is being consented to and the authority to make that choice, yet children have neither the knowledge nor the authority to consent to sexual relations.[4]

The most pervasive myth that still exists is that sexual abuse against children is perpetrated by strangers. In fact, between 75 and 85 percent of the sexual molestation of children is committed by someone who is known to and usually trusted by the child, such as a family member, caregiver, or neighbor. Another myth is that girls are the primary victims of sexual abuse. Admittedly, reports of abuse of girls are widespread. It is estimated that one in three girls will be sexually abused or at least approached prior to the age of eighteen.[5] Yet statistically, the figure for boys who have been sexually abused is one in five, though these estimates may be deceptive for several reasons. First, boys are less likely to report being abused. Our culture often sees boys who become victims as "sissies" or less masculine. Boys also fear being labeled as homosexual, especially if the abuser is an adult male. In addition, a boy may feel that he must have somehow attracted the abuse and therefore is himself homosexual.

If the boy is abused by a woman, he may not recognize that it is abuse. Boys, along with the rest of us, often buy into what I call the "Summer of '42 Syndrome," the distorted attitude that girls are abused when involved sexually with an adult while boys are initiated. *The Summer of '42* was a movie years ago that followed several teen boys during a summer when the country was deeply involved in World War II. The boys became enamored of a young wife whose husband was overseas. She was at first amused by them but in her loneliness, she gave them her time and attention. When, at the end of the movie, her husband was killed, the young woman took one of the teens to her bed with all the lights, music, and romantic overtones that Hollywood could muster. The movie was fairly popular, and it occurred to few that this was sexual abuse. Instead, the boy's "education" by an older woman was seen as part of his "rite of passage." Sadly, many people still feel this way. But take a teenage girl and an older man, and few would fail to call their sexual relationship abusive.

Despite this disturbing societal attitude, many boys are adversely affected by relationships with adult women. Rodney spoke tearfully of his experiences as an altar boy.

> *Our minister had this woman who helped him with altar boys. She was pretty enough, and we all liked her. I think that some of us had a crush on her. I remember one time when she came in and I was changing out of my robe. I was only about nine or so. It was really hot, and I had taken off my pants and shirt and just had the robe on over my underwear. She told me what a good altar boy I was and started rubbing my back. Then her hand moved down to my butt. I*

*guess that's how it started. I felt aroused when she was rubbing me, and I was kind of attracted to her. She took me out for ice cream, telling the minister she'd take me home. We went by her apartment, and she invited me in. She lived alone, and she had pictures of boys like me all over her bedroom. Before I knew it I was going over there regularly, and she was having me do things to her... sexual things. I knew there was something wrong, but then I thought that I must be queer or something. Here was this neat lady doing stuff for me, and I wasn't sure I liked it. I didn't tell anyone until I was an adult. I now wonder if she abused other kids too.*

If a boy tells his parents that he is being abused, it is quite likely that his activities will be curtailed. In a culture where boys are given much more freedom than girls, such restriction provides a significant deterrent to boys admitting that they have been abused.

## What Is Psychological Abuse?

Psychological/emotional abuse can be as devastating as any other type of abuse, but it is very difficult to isolate and prove, and it is equally difficult to know how to intervene in response to it. The magnitude of child protection caseloads often means that psychological abuse cases are not investigated. Still, by recognizing the symptoms of psychological/emotional abuse, we may be able to help the child cope and even refer the family to other helpful resources.

At one time, the abuse of children that involved words rather than physical assault was referred to as "emotional abuse." More recently with the recognition of the intense psychological impact that words can have on children, this type of abuse is more often referred to as "psychological abuse." In fact, psychological abuse is present with any other type of abuse but can stand alone as well. The attempt to define this type of abuse has caused a long-standing debate, partially because it can seem quite intangible. It is not an isolated event but rather *a pattern of psychologically destructive words and behaviors*. Most theorists divide this type of abuse into five categories: rejecting, isolating, terrorizing, ignoring, and corrupting.[6]

*Rejecting* is when a parent refuses to recognize a child's needs or worth. The parent may belittle the child ("You stupid jerk! Can't you do anything right?"), shame the child ("Stop that blubbering! Do you want people to think you're a baby?"), and publicly humiliate him or her ("Have you ever seen such an ugly kid?").

When *isolating* a child, a parent cuts him or her off from forming normal relationships with peers, and makes the child feel alone in the world. The parent may restrict the child's freedom so severely that the child is unable to meet his or her socialization needs at all.

> *I knew that the Gebhards had a child, but I had never seen her. One day in church, I asked them about her. "She doesn't go out much," I was told dismissively. On a pastoral call, I found a very withdrawn child of about twelve who would hardly talk to me. When she was out of the room, I asked Mrs. Gebhard why I had never seen her.*
>
> *"We like to keep Vivienne at home," she told me. "Her older sister got in trouble, so we decided it was better just to keep Vivienne here. We home-school her, too."*
>
> *"Doesn't she have any friends?" I asked, wondering when this mother would feel I had overstepped my bounds. But she didn't seem to and went on.*
>
> *"Vivienne doesn't need friends. She has us. We are a close family."*
>
> *What I later discovered was that the Gebhards were a very dysfunctional family, and it was poor Vivienne who had suffered the most.*

*Terrorizing* a child is when parents use verbal assaults and threats of frightening things that will happen to the child. The threat of violence may be something the parent proposes that he or she will do to the child, or the fear may be induced by suggesting that there is an outside, often unseen, entity. What is considered psychologically abusive may differ from culture to culture. For example, some African groups and some Native Americans threaten their children with the equivalent of the bogeyman when they see the need to do so. In many cases, these practices date back to the roots of the culture, and determining if they are actually abusive is difficult. Similarly, the degree of pressure put on children to "save face" in many Chinese and other Asian families would seem to those from outside the culture to be abusive.

*Ignoring* deprives children of basic stimulation that leads to healthy growth. A parent may ignore a child's attempts to interact or to get her or his attention, or fail to express any affection to the child.

By *corrupting* a child, the parent encourages the child to learn antisocial or destructive behavior that will later clash with the rest of society. For example, the parent who teaches his or her child to steal or to get what the child wants through aggressive behavior may be setting the child up for future trouble with the law.

There are other acts that are emotionally abusive that may not fit neatly within these categories. Some authors add that any parental behavior that is *detrimental to mental health* may be categorized as psychological abuse. For example, the destruction of a beloved object, especially in front of the child, fits into this definition. Bobby's set of much-beloved and devotedly collected baseball cards were viciously burned before his eyes by his father. Evie's class ring that she had saved for months to buy was deliberately thrown into the woods by her angry parent when the girl did not finish her chores. These incidents can have a lasting impact on the child.

## What Is Domestic Violence, and How Does It Impact Children?

Ideally, the home should be a haven, a place where one can go to be safe. But for some families, this is not the case. There is no clear definition of spousal or partner abuse. Fighting differs from family to family. If such a definition had to be proposed, one might say that spousal abuse involves *intentional acts of violence imposed upon one partner by the other, or between adult partners, usually resulting in harm.* Abusers use coercion, deception, manipulation, and humiliation to gain power over their intimate partners.

One of the most tragic aspects of domestic violence is the impact that it has on the children in the family. A recent Boston City Hospital (now Boston Medical Center) study reported that the majority (75–87 percent) of the children who live in violent homes have observed this violence at least once.[7] Many of these children have watched as their fathers brutally beat their mothers or their parents attacked one another. There also seems to be some correlation between domestic violence and child abuse. Of the families in which partner violence is an issue, 40 percent to 60 percent also abuse the children in the home. Even when families do not intend to abuse children, small bodies are often injured when parents or other adults are attacking one another.

Several myths surround domestic violence. One assumption is that very young children are less affected by their parents' battles, yet cases have been reported in which infants demonstrate many of the classic anxiety reactions to witnessed violence that are present in older children. Another myth is that violence in families is an urban issue. While such violence is often reported in urban areas, it can and does happen anywhere from the largest city to the most rural countryside setting. Finally, domestic violence is often thought to be an ethnic issue primarily affecting Hispanic and African American families, but studies show that poverty has more of an influence on such violence than race or ethnic origin.[8]

Whenever one mentions domestic violence in a religious context, someone invariably brings up the issue of submission. Doesn't the Bible say that wives should submit to their husbands? Miles points out that those who quote this scripture neglect to recognize other scriptures which point to a husband's need to submit to his wife, such as Ephesians 5:21, which says, "Submit to one another out of reverence for Christ" (NIV).[9] The bottom line is that children should never be harmed in this debate over the ownership and quality of submission.

Understanding what constitutes abuse and neglect is an important part of recognition. In Chapter 2, we consider the variety of symptoms found in child victims of maltreatment.

# PART ONE

# When a Child Is Abused in the Home or Community

## Chapter 2

# Recognizing Child Maltreatment: Symptoms and Suspicions

In the previous chapter, we considered different types of child maltreatment. What would these look like if one saw them in the context of the life of the church community? This chapter pinpoints specific symptoms that one might recognize as indicators of abuse and provides charts for their easier identification. It is important to look not only for one isolated symptom in a child, but rather for clusters of symptoms that suggest abuse or neglect.

### Children Who Are Neglected

Most of us believe that we could recognize a child who was being neglected. Yet issues like poor hygiene may seem indicative of neglect when they are merely part of a family's lifestyle. Children who are victims of actual parental neglect demonstrate recognizable symptoms. Very young babies who have not been given a sufficient amount of nurturing may appear listless and uninterested in their environment. Some show the telltale signs of parental inattention like flattened heads from lying too long in their cribs or severe rashes from long-unattended diapers. In the extreme, a neglected baby can turn inward and become so uninvolved with life that she refuses to eat or interact. When this happens, she may fall below the fifth percentile in height and weight (used by pediatricians to determine a healthy child's normal growth) and therefore demonstrate what is referred to as Nonorganic Failure to Thrive (NFTT), a condition that can, if left untreated, result in death.

Normally, babies who are nurtured sufficiently begin to develop a characteristic cry to fit every need. Caretakers and babies learn to communicate through these differentiated cries, but babies who do not receive consistent attention in having their needs met do not develop differentiated cries. Instead, their rage at not being cared for in any way manifests itself in a shrill cry that can be quite unnerving.

*My hospital chaplaincy sometimes took me into the pediatric unit. I will never forget the first day that the Rivers baby was there. When I came onto the unit, I was greeted by several frazzled nurses trying to tend a baby whose cry went right through me. He was a tiny, wizened thing whose dark skin almost seemed to hang on him.*

*"Found alone in an abandoned apartment," one of the nurses explained, shaking her head.*

*"The police think Mom's into drugs. We don't know the last time this baby ate. But we can't get him to take a thing. I think he forgot how to eat, the poor little thing!" That was my first introduction to a failure-to-thrive baby and to the cry that let the world know of his anguish and despair.*

As neglected children grow older, they begin to develop a kind of self-sufficiency which often takes the form of a dulled affect and a manner of doing things that seems quite listless and matter-of-fact. Their malnutrition is also obvious in the dullness of their hair and eyes and the poor condition of their teeth and skin. They may also appear tired, a result of inadequate sleep. Their hygiene may be poor, and may elicit remarks from others.

It is not uncommon for neglected children to develop habit disorders like constantly rocking, whining, picking at scabs, or banging their heads. This may actually be a form of self-stimulation that helps them to stay in touch with reality. Some neglected children crave the attention that they are not able to get at home, often inviting negative responses from adults or peers rather than getting no attention at all. These children may exhibit a suspicious wariness of adults. Their relationships with peers are often problematic as well, possibly due to their hygiene, but more likely a result of their depressed negative attitudes.[1]

Neglected children often appear to have a great deal of freedom, yet this is more the result of adult inattention than permissiveness. Even at the age of five, six, and seven such children are sometimes expected to care for younger children for inordinate amounts of time in their parents' absence. Some neglectful parents remain away overnight or for days at a time, leaving their children alone or in the keeping of children who are hardly old enough to care for themselves.

Stealing or hoarding is common in neglected children. Vandalism is something they know well, for since they have little regard for objects, they often place no value on the possessions of others. Because neglect is pervasive, the disorganized lifestyle that these children have lived prevents them from learning how to organize their thoughts or possessions.

## A QUICK REFERENCE TO NEGLECT SYMPTOMS

*Children who have been neglected may exhibit a cluster of the following:*

- appear listless and tired, due to little energy or no routine or structure about bedtimes
- always seem to be hungry, hoarding or stealing food
- report caring for younger siblings when the child caretaker may be only five to eight years old
- demonstrate poor hygiene, or dirty or decaying teeth; may smell of urine or feces
- be emaciated or may have distended stomach, indicative of malnutrition
- appear in soiled clothing, significantly too small or too large for them and often in need of repair
- may not be adequately dressed for the weather
- appear to have unattended medical or dental problems such as infected sores
- have head lice

*Behaviorally, these children may:*

- steal, vandalize, or exhibit other delinquent behaviors
- have few relationships with peers, perhaps because of hygienic problems or a depressed, negative attitude
- be withdrawn
- crave attention, any attention — even negative; may act up to get this attention
- be destructive or pugnacious, showing no apparent guilt over their acts
- appear to have low self-esteem
- appear to have lower overall intelligence (often due to lack of stimulation)
- have difficulty coping or problem solving
- be reported to have trouble in school

Teachers find that such children are often unable to conceptualize on more complex levels, making learning difficult.

> *"I told the children to take out their workbooks, find colored markers that they like, sit back in their seats, and get ready for me to start the lesson," explained a teacher of a large first-grade Sunday school class. "But Shona just sits there staring at me. I tell her again, but she still does not do any of what is asked of her."*

This teacher had to be helped to recognize that Shona, used to a household in which "Shut up!" "Get lost!" and a variety of other one-command statements were the mode, had never learned to mentally process complex commands. Faced with them she froze, unsure of how to respond. Breaking such commands down into smaller parts was helpful, and after the child complied, another direction could be given. This worked for Shona, and eventually she was able to respond to several requests strung together.

Teenagers in neglectful homes can be especially difficult to reach. Many leave their homes early through an emancipation that is more like a drifting away. They may be at home one minute, then out for several nights, and eventually the parents realize that the teen no longer lives at home. Some fall into substance abuse or delinquent behaviors. Neglected teens who can be engaged by caring adults, however, may so appreciate the attention that they will respond. The most significant challenge may be to gain their trust; life has not inspired trust in them, and trusting is therefore something that is not easy for them to do.

If reading about neglected children has made you feel depressed and hopeless, then you can understand how the social workers who deal with such families feel. The lack of energy that pervades the whole household saps hope and makes dealing with such families a challenge. But the caring individual who can see past his or her hopelessness often can make a difference for the parents and children.

## Children Who Are Physically Abused

The most obvious manifestations of physical abuse are the observable signs. Bruises, especially those in areas of the body that are not as prone to natural bruising, like the face, the upper arms, the upper legs and the back, are suspect. Especially on lighter skin, bruises change colors over time, going from red to black and blue to greenish yellow. An abundance of bruises in various stages of healing should cause concern. Bruises may also give clues to how they occurred. For example, if a child is struck hard enough with the palm of the hand, the bruise that results will be an identifiable handprint. Or when a child is hit with a rope or electrical cord, the bruise that encircles the body attests to this fact. Bruises on multiple parts of the body may tell that a child has been hit from different directions.[2]

Fractures are also prevalent in abuse situations, but may only come to the attention of the church community secondhand. Yet in the total context, information that there have been fractures over time can raise red flags for those in contact with the child. One youth worker noticed that nine-year-old Roosevelt had limited range of motion with his right arm. When Roosevelt mentioned that he was unable to do a task because of it, the leader asked its cause. The child hesitated and finally said that he had fallen. In later conversations, Roosevelt mentioned that he had broken other appendages. Slowly a picture began to emerge when it became obvious that many of these had not healed properly. Having learned in a training session that several improperly healed fractures may point to abuse, the youth worker spoke to a church elder about his concerns that the current bruises that the boy had might be more than simple falls. In fact, it was later discovered that Roosevelt was being beaten and had been a victim of such abuse for years. Fearful of the response, his family had not been willing to take him for medical attention.

There are also types of fractures that lead one to explore the possibility of abuse. Spiral fractures are indicative of the bone being twisted, an action that can be nonaccidental. Dislocations may also result from a child being grabbed and pulled or dragged. Be aware that some innocent behaviors can cause dislocations. For example, swinging a child by the arms in play or lifting an infant by the arms or hands can actually dislocate arms or shoulders in some children. If you become aware of such injuries, the child might be asked the cause (if he or she is old enough to tell you). If they are in fact the result of abuse, many children will not disclose this out of fear of retribution or out of loyalty to the abusive parent. But a child's affect when giving an explanation can also be a clue. If the explanation seems plausible and the affect indicates no guilt or fear, but you still have concerns about abuse, the chart later in this section may help to rule out other factors or behaviors that indicate abuse.

It is not uncommon for children to be burned as a form of abuse, the most common type of burn being from cigarettes. These telltale burns are so characteristic that they are difficult to miss. Burns in the shape of other objects like irons or radiators may indicate how the abuse was inflicted. Glove-like burns point to a hand being immersed in hot liquid, whereas a

## A QUICK REFERENCE TO PHYSICAL ABUSE SYMPTOMS

*Visual clues to physical abuse may be:*

- frequent bruises around the head or face, the abdomen, or midway between the wrist and elbow (areas less likely to be bruised normally)
- bruises in specific shapes such as handprints or clothes hanger marks
- marks that indicate hard blows from an object such as an electrical cord or other whip-like object that makes a burn around the body
- bruises on multiple parts of the body indicating blows from different directions
- spitting up or passing blood that could indicate unexplained internal abdominal bleeding
- complaints of soreness and stiffness or awkward movements, as if caused by pain
- bald spots from severe hair pulling
- adult-sized human bite marks
- burns, especially from objects such as cigarettes and irons

*Behaviorally, children may demonstrate that they are being abused. They may*

- be overly aggressive, pugnacious, or defiant
- demonstrate fear of adults
- exhibit destructiveness to self or others
- not seem to want to go home
- display extreme risk taking, seem fearless
- be described as accident prone
- cheat, steal, lie (may be related to too high expectations at home)
- not achieve in school (to learn, children must convert aggressive energy into learning; children in conflict may not be able to convert this energy)
- not have peer relationships
- often wear clothing that covers the body and that may be inappropriate in warmer months (be aware that this may be cultural as well)
- seem very immature for age
- avoid or express dislike of physical contact (e.g., may not tolerate physical praise such as a pat on the back)

burn that is more intense in the middle and radiates outward speaks of hot liquid being poured on the skin.

Sometimes abusers will grab hold of a child's hair for punishment or to induce compliance. Such an action can create a bald spot, as we see here with Gretchen.

> *I didn't give much thought to why thirteen-year-old Gretchen wore a kerchief on her head when she came to junior youth group. But when it slipped off during a game we were playing, I could not believe the bald spot that it had covered. A large chunk of her hair had been ripped from her head. Concerned, I asked what had happened. At first she passed it off, quickly replacing the bandana. But when I persisted, she finally broke into tears and blurted out that her father, in a fit of rage, had grabbed her by the hair, pulling some out.*

The Shaken Baby Syndrome has been much publicized in the news over the last few years. In fact, shaking a child of any age can cause considerable damage to the brain, the skull, and the eyes. Violent shaking can cause blood to form around the brain, a condition known as a subdural hematoma. If not caught in time, this condition can result in death. Shaking may also result in fractures to the skull or in the detachment of the retina from the eye. Both have the potential to be extremely serious. A child who complains of head pain or eye difficulties, especially if he or she reports being hit in that area or shaken, should receive immediate medical attention.

Behaviorally, children exhibit clues to their abuse in several ways. Some children become especially withdrawn or fearful. Still others mirror what they see by striking out against others.

> *Mrs. Davis complained about Sally, a girl in her Sunday school class.*
>
> *"She's always hitting everyone," the young teacher complained. "She can't keep her hands to herself." We later learned that Sally had been the victim of her mother's beatings for years. Although she felt powerless to resist these, she had reacted by striking out against other children.*

Other children choose to wear clothing that covers their bruises and prevents the world from knowing their secrets. For example, a child who wears long pants and long sleeves consistently when the weather dictates something cooler might be hiding the evidence of being abused. It is important here to note the cultural background of children who are dressed in such a manner; some traditions require that young girls' arms and legs be covered in public, for example.

Although these are not observable, internal injuries may also be indicators that a child has been abused. For example, a child might vomit or pass blood, which can come to the attention of an adult. Obviously such indicators should be taken seriously, no matter what their cause.

When one suspects that physical abuse might be involved, it is important to determine how well the explanation of an injury fits the injury itself. For example, children do not usually (there is always the exception) break bones by falling off a bed — unless it is a second-tier bunk bed. By listening to the reported cause of injuries one can often tell that this is a fabrication and may be covering a different or abusive event.

Within the last few decades, another form of abuse has been seen more and more. This is known clinically as Munchausen-by-proxy Syndrome. This results from the pathology of a parent (usually the mother) who, seeking attention from the medical community, inflicts upon her (or his) child substances that will cause illness. For example, children who are victims of Munchausen-by-proxy Syndrome may have been given large doses of ipecac, causing them to vomit repeatedly, may have been injected with substances that affect blood sugar, or have been given something that causes diarrhea. Fortunately, the syndrome is relatively rare and usually only uncovered in medical facilities, but an increasing number of cases have come to the attention of the protective services agencies.

The extreme pathology of these parents (discussed further in Chapter 3) puts their children in real danger. It is often difficult for professionals to discern what is actually happening until the child has suffered severely or even died.

## Children Who Are Sexually Abused

When children are sexually molested they exhibit symptoms, but many of these are not specific to sexual abuse and therefore may not be recognized. Unlike physical abuse and neglect, there are few physical symptoms of sexual abuse that are readily observable. For example, children may have bruising or tearing in their genitals; have sores, rashes, or a discharge; or they may contract venereal disease, but it is unlikely that anyone other than a parent or medical personnel would be in a position to detect these symptoms. Frequent urinary tract infections or yeast infections, often common to adults, are suspect in children. But these too might go unnoticed. Wetting the bed (called enuresis), soiling (encopresis), nightmares or night terrors (coming awake in fear), or suicide attempts might be observed in the privacy of the home but would probably not be that apparent outside of the home.

Sexually abused children may sometimes cry for help with their behavior in ways that shed more light on the sexual nature of the problem. Even overly secretive children are, on some level, hoping that someone will discover their secret. When a child is introduced at an early age to sexuality, his or her ability to process it may become impaired. Thus, such children may act out sexually in several ways: sexual self-stimulation, sexual interaction with peers, sexual aggression toward peers, sexually accosting adults, and seductive behavior or promiscuity.

Sexually abused children may self-stimulate by exhibiting compulsive masturbation. While masturbation is normal in children, conflict may cause them to increase the frequency of this activity often without attention to where or when it is being done. This might create issues for teachers or those who observe the child masturbating openly in church settings. The behavior may become so intense that the child actually injures himself or herself.

The child who has more sexual knowledge than his/her years would suggest or who acts out sexually with peers might be equally obvious. It is common for many children to "experiment" with peers by mutual explorations of anatomy or even touching one another. The difference between this and acting out sexually is usually that experimentation is age-appropriate with both parties exhibiting about the same knowledge. On the other hand, when one child has considerably more knowledge than the other and especially when that information is not usually part of the repertoire of someone that child's age, then there is cause for concern.

*Josh and Gerry were in the first grade Sunday school class. When the two boys both asked to use the bathroom at the same time, the teacher, busy with several other children at the time, allowed them to go. After all, it was just across the hall from the classroom. When they were gone a bit longer than she expected, she went to investigate. What she discovered was a crying Josh, who insisted that Gerry had been "sucking his pee pee" and had hurt him. Upset by this and sure that this was not typical six-year-old behavior, the teacher reported it to the minister.*

Some abused children are sexually aggressive toward those younger than themselves.

## A QUICK REFERENCE TO SEXUAL ABUSE

*Children who have been sexually abused exhibit a variety of symptoms including the following:*

- painful urination
- excessive bathing
- frequent vomiting
- excessive sore throats (may be indicative of gonorrhea)
- chronic or excessive masturbation
- reports of frequent urinary tract infections
- difficulty in walking or sitting
- evidence or reports of genital/anal itching, rashes, pain, swelling, or burning
- reports of frequent yeast infections
- other symptoms of venereal disease such as vaginal or penile pain or discharge, genital or oral sores, genital warts
- early pregnancy
- frequent psychosomatic illnesses

*Behaviorally children may exhibit:*

- exceptional secrecy
- more sexual knowledge than is appropriate for the child's age (especially in younger children)

*Four-year-old Darlene was in the nursery class at our church. We, the parents, took turns. I had been there for only one Sunday when I observed Darlene with a younger child. She was on top of him and rubbing herself on him. I was horrified. I got her off immediately and asked her what she was doing. She would not answer me and ran off to play. After church I asked another mother if they had noticed anything about Darlene. This mother finally told me that she had observed similar behavior in the child. We didn't say anything at first, but when I caught her taking a little boy's pants down, I knew that I had to tell the pastor.*

- evidence of in-depth sexual play with peers (in younger children, different from the common "playing doctor" form of exploration)
- approaching or accosting adults sexually
- promiscuity, especially at a young age
- withdrawal or overaggressiveness
- inordinate fear of males (or females)
- extreme seductiveness
- disinclination to participate in activities with others, especially if they involve undressing (e.g., changing into swimsuits)
- reported sleep problems or nightmares
- crying without provocation
- sudden fear or phobia about certain things or situations
- expressions of little self-worth and talking of being damaged
- pseudo-maturity, appearing much older and more worldly than peers
- suicide attempts or expressing ideas of wanting to kill self
- running away from home excessively
- extreme cruelty to animals (especially those that would normally be pets)
- setting fires
- symptoms of an eating disorder
- cutting, scratching to draw blood, or self-mutilation in other ways

The pastor, in turn, sought the advice of a social worker in the parish. What they found was that little Darlene had in fact been sexually abused and was acting out her trauma on other children.

Sexually abused children may also act out by approaching or accosting adults. Although we sometimes encounter teens who appear quite seductive, we do not usually expect it from younger children. When children approach adults in a particularly seductive manner, it is usually something they have learned—and something that should be investigated.

Although many teens are sexually active at an earlier age, some can be observed to be especially promiscuous. It is interesting that, in this culture, it is usually girls and not boys with numerous sexual partners that we label as promiscuous. Promiscuity is usually linked to self-concept and is often a way for the teenager to prove to herself that she is desirable. If she has been initiated into sexuality early, she may also have adopted sex as a manner of relating to the opposite sex. Whatever the reason, this behavior hampers her ability to form meaningful relationships with her peers. Boys too, having experienced sexual abuse, may move from partner to partner unable to chance real intimacy and unsure of the actual meaning of sex.

Sexually abused children may also exhibit a variety of nonsexual problems. These may include physical issues like the bladder, bowel, and sleep problems mentioned above; emotional problems like hyperactivity, depression, anxiety, phobias, or fear and general preoccupation; school problems like a dramatic drop in grades or poor peer relations; or behavioral issues like destructiveness, aggression, or vandalism. Although not guarantees of sexual abuse, any type of concern about a child should include alertness to the possibility of sexual abuse. Problems that correlate strongly with the exposure to sexual abuse are cruelty to animals and fire setting.

## Children Who Are Psychologically Abused

How might one know if a child is being psychologically or emotionally abused? Certainly the interaction between the parent and child may give an indication of this type of maltreatment. But if one does not observe this interaction, the problem becomes less obvious, partially because the symptoms can be indicative of other dysfunction as well. Children carry the scars of psychological abuse in different ways. Some anesthetize themselves by denying that there is a problem, joking when they are in pain and putting on a "happy face" for the world. Underneath is an emotionally bleeding child who may not be able to reach out for help. Other children turn their pain inward and withdraw, are self-destructive, or self-stimulate by rocking, thumb sucking at inappropriate times, soiling or wetting themselves, or developing an eating disorder. Some develop psychosomatic ailments like asthma, ulcers, severe allergies, and so on.

Instead of turning inward, children who are victims of psychological maltreatment may also strike out against the world by being violent, destroying objects or vandalizing, cheating or stealing, or other types of delinquent behavior. It becomes fairly obvious as we consider this laundry list of symptoms that many are related to other issues as well, but it is well to keep the possibility of psychological abuse in mind.

## A QUICK REFERENCE TO PSYCHOLOGICAL ABUSE

*Children who are being psychologically abused may:*

- always joke about negatives and laugh when in pain
- exhibit extremes in behavior — manically happy or very depressed
- withdraw from others
- be self-destructive
- be destructive to objects or cruel to others
- exhibit compulsive attention to detail
- steal, cheat, vandalize
- demonstrate self-soothing behaviors like rocking, thumb sucking, head banging
- wet their pants (enuresis) or soil after an age when such behavior is inappropriate (encopresis)
- abuse drugs or alcohol
- exhibit an eating disorder
- exhibit psychosomatic ailments like asthma, ulcers, or severe allergies
- exhibit other types of delinquent behavior

## Children Who Witness Violence

Children who witness violence between their parents may respond in different ways. One child will be fearful that he or she will also be hit and may try to withdraw from the situation. This child feels helpless to either prevent the abuse or to intervene. Another child may have attempted to intervene at some point and, after being hurt, withdraws and no longer tries to be of any help to the parent being abused. Some children do attempt to intervene on a regular basis; male children especially may feel that they want or need to protect their mothers, and in so doing often get hurt themselves. Going up against a much stronger adult whose strength is often enhanced by anger can become extremely hazardous to the child

## A QUICK REFERENCE TO CHILDREN WHO WITNESS VIOLENCE

*Children who have witnessed violence between their parents (or other adults in the home) can exhibit a variety of symptoms including the following:*

- extreme aggressiveness
- fear or worry about being safe
- hypervigilance (always looking for the threat)
- depression
- sleeplessness at night
- sleepiness during daytime due to lack of sleep at night
- somatic complaints (headaches, stomachaches, etc.)
- anxiety
- reluctance to explore physical environment
- poor self-concept
- withdrawal, timidity
- difficulty paying attention, distraction
- regression (reverting to a younger age in behavior)
- irritability, especially in infants
- feelings of powerlessness, hopelessness
- seeing the world as a dangerous place
- being easily frightened
- being violent, acting out violently

who attempts to protect. Older children recognize the futility of trying to intervene on behalf of an abused parent, but they are often able to protect their younger siblings. It is not uncommon for the oldest child to corral his younger brothers and sisters and keep them out of harm's way.

For some children, going against the abuser at all is just too threatening. Instead this child chooses what seems to be a less dangerous path. He or she sides with the abuser against the abused parent in a syndrome referred to as identification with the aggressor. Such children construct an internal mind-set that says that the abused parent deserves what happens to her or him. Sometimes the child will join in the abuse of the parent by the batterer. When the abuser leaves the home, these children will often take up the abuse where the batterer left off.[3]

Some children, particularly girls, who as children have witnessed violence, in later life confuse love and the abuse that they saw between their parents. As adults, such individuals are quite likely to find partners who will replicate the (abusive) behavior with which they are familiar. Boys also may have learned that violence and intimate relationships are synonymous and therefore go on to abuse their mates.[4]

Children who witness violence experience various symptoms of trauma. They may be fearful and worry about being safe. Children may feel powerless and helpless in the face of the everyday world. Because they are kept awake at night, either because of the fighting between their parents or because they are fearful of being hurt themselves, these children are often listless and sleepy during the day.

It is not always obvious that children have come from homes where there is domestic violence. But sometimes little clues will point to the family's secret and the life that this child has endured.

The symptoms of children who are abused and neglected manifest very differently from child to child. The quick reference charts provided in this chapter should give you some tools to determine when abuse or neglect is an issue. Remember that it is not just one symptom that necessarily indicates maltreatment; it is more likely to be a cluster of symptoms that one needs to consider.

## Between the Suspicion and the Report

After reading this chapter, you may recognize that there were situations over the years that required intervention, but at that time you might not have recognized what was needed. We cannot live by hindsight. Hopefully those children came to the attention of some other professional or concerned layperson. What is necessary is to look ahead and be prepared for the children of the present and future who need our help.

If you suspect abuse or neglect, the child and his or her family need help. Help comes in many forms and from many different sectors. Help may begin by making a report to child protective services (referred to from now on as CPS). It is not up to a reporter to prove that there is abuse or neglect. (We discuss this in more detail in Chapter 5.) One need only have a *suspicion* that there is abuse or neglect in order to get help from CPS. It is the role of CPS to prove or disprove whether maltreatment is an issue. The child and family are much better served if you provide the help that is within your ministry, while CPS workers do what they have been trained to do. The end result is, hopefully, a group of concerned professionals who can work together in harmony so that a child's life will be improved and a family can get the help it needs.

## *Chapter 3*

# A Look at the Dysfunctional Family

*I don't remember how I first discovered that a member of my church was sexually abusing his daughter. I was horrified. The gentle man I knew could not be guilty of doing that to his own child! It was to be the beginning of a painful learning period for me as I began to recognize that parents who abuse their children may look like anyone else and that they are not the monsters that I had once imagined.*

If you have never known abusive or neglectful parents, you may find it difficult to understand what motivates them to harm their children. Yet once you comprehend the complex reasons behind their behavior, it may inspire a compassion that helps you to reach out to them despite what they have done.

Parenting is one of the toughest jobs there is. We rarely stop to consider that what prepares us to parent begins long before we ever consider having children. In fact, our parenting skills are often developed while we are still very young ourselves by modeling how we see our parents behaving. When one does not have positive models, especially when abuse or neglect is part of that childhood experience, there are two possibilities: one recognizes the deficiency of the parenting model and strives to improve on it, or one repeats the same mistakes and becomes part of another generation of a dysfunctional family.

Before we lay all of the responsibility for abuse and neglect at the feet of the abuser's parents, let me say that there are also variations in personality and experience that can affect later parenting and may not be entirely related to how one's own parents performed their roles. When siblings compare notes, they often see things in their childhoods quite differently. Research also tells us that the experience of each sibling is different from that of the others depending on what is happening in the family at the time of their childhood years. Whatever the cause, individuals who abuse or neglect children are influenced by factors that are often deeply rooted in their personalities. Studies with such parents have uncovered some reasons that they might have difficulty providing a safe and healthy environment for their children. In this chapter we consider dysfunctional families that abuse or neglect children through passive or aggressive violence, and in Chapter 4 we consider those who sexually abuse children.

## Parents Who Are Neglectful

*Honey remembers little of her own childhood. Maybe it is that she chooses not to remember. If pressed, she will tell you that her mother used drugs from the time she was quite young. She wasn't quite sure who her father was, but she believed that he was one of the men who lived with them off and on. When Honey was sixteen, she grew tired of caring for her six younger siblings. She wanted to be an actress. She used to cut out pictures of actresses from magazines she stole from the market. That was how she met Stub, a bagger who happened to see her push the magazine under her coat. He told her that he wouldn't tell if she'd have a drink with him after work. That was how it started.*

*Honey had only gone out with Stub a few times when she had a row with her mother and he offered to let her move in. He was twenty and had an apartment on his own. She jumped at the chance to have "her own place," even if it was really his. Stub treated her like a queen, told her how beautiful she was, and flattered her into believing that they would have an idyllic life together. He told her that when he made lots of money, he would help her get into acting school. She believed him.*

*Honey and Stub drifted into their life, and before she knew it she was the mother of two, Dwayne and Tamisha, ten months apart. Gone were her illusions that her pregnancy-strained body would ever appeal to anyone on screen. She began to feel like she was home again, taking care of kids and with no time for herself. Stub had bounced from job to job, and the money was never too plentiful either. Life stretched before Honey like a bleak desert with no mirages of hope.*

*There was a little church near her apartment that she discovered gave out free food sometimes. Honey started going there to see what they had. They also had bingo, and she enjoyed playing that. Nobody knew it, but she and some of the other women would spike the coffee and juice that they were offered. It helped when the kids screamed, which they did a lot. Her kids were so demanding, both of them. At least when she had cared for her brothers and sisters, her mother had been there sometimes. Now, there was no one but her. Stub was rarely home. No one ever told her that having kids could be so tough. They were always needing something, either to be fed or to be changed. It was so tiring.*

*Honey began going to church on Sunday too, hoping that maybe God could help her get out of the rut she was in. She'd leave the kids with Stub, who was usually sleeping, but she was sure they'd be okay. Usually when she came home, he was still sleeping and the babies were crying and dirty and hungry. Mechanically she'd feed them and wish she could have stayed away for the whole day.*

*When Honey wasn't at the church, she'd be home with the kids, dreaming about the plans she had had. What had happened anyway? Here she was: nineteen years old and with two children. Where had all her dreams gone? Depressed by what she saw as a hopeless life, she began to sleep whenever she could. This was where the pastor found her when he came to call one day — Honey asleep and the two children crawling around the filthy floor putting into their mouths whatever they could find.*

Honey was one of the many young people for whom life had moved too fast. Ill-equipped by her own upbringing to deal with the reality of responsibility, Honey opted out in the only way she knew how — by striving to meet her own needs at the expense of her children's needs. Were you to meet Honey, you would see a girl who looked old before her time, her deep-set dark eyes lacking luster or hope. It is difficult for someone like this young woman to nurture her own children when she has so little of herself to offer anyone. She would also seem immature and childlike, if you were to meet her, someone who lacked the positive experiences that bring most of us to maturity.

What creates the Honeys of the world? Garbarino and Collins, in their study of neglect, comment that child neglect "is a pattern of behavior or a social context that has a hole in the middle where we should find the meeting of basic developmental needs."[1] The neglectful parent is one whose own basic needs have gone unmet in childhood. Often victims of neglect themselves, they have not experienced having their own needs met consistently. Thus, they are in constant pursuit of ways to fulfill themselves and have little energy to give to others.

Usually the neglectful family consists of the mother who has had difficulty maintaining an intimate relationship. Sometimes she has a current partner. If there is a father or male who has been involved for any amount of time, he is often caught up in his own pursuits, and their relationship is one in which two individuals are just existing together. Unable to forge more than the most superficial relationships, the neglectful mother sees herself surrounded by unsupportive, uncaring people who give her little support. The irony is that because those in her past have rarely been psychologically available for her, she has never learned to be psychologically available for anyone else, including her children. And when she isolates herself, others find her unapproachable or too needy and she becomes further isolated.

Were you to talk with those who knew Honey, such a picture would emerge. Honey did converse with other women at the church center when she went for coffee or bingo, but she was unable to engage in anything more than the most superficial chatter. Many of the women saw her as odd, somewhat dirty, disheveled, and dull. Those who felt a bit more compassion said that she was so needy that they hesitated to become involved. The pastor, recognizing her depression and hopelessness, saw someone who was difficult to reach emotionally but obviously needed help.

How much of a correlation is there between poverty and neglect? It is certainly possible to be poor and not at all neglectful of one's children. Yet one often sees neglectful parents in the lower socioeconomic strata for several reasons. First, more affluent neighborhoods often do not tolerate the physical neglect of children. One would like to believe that those with more resources would reach out to families in trouble. Sometimes this is the case, but I have also seen middle-class neighborhoods that make life so difficult for those who neglect their children and their surroundings that residents literally force neglectful families out of the neighborhood.

Neglectful parents may also become poor because they do not have the energy to sustain themselves at any higher level. There are those who suggest that more adequate compensation in the form of public assistance programs would eradicate neglect. Yet studies have found that although it is difficult to subsist on assistance payments, money or resources alone do not solve the problem of neglect.[2] Neglect is a psychological as well as an economic issue, and the solution lies in psychological arenas.

Crittenden contends that the cause of neglect is in the manner in which neglectful parents mentally process information.[3] This author divides these into three types of families, those who exhibit *disorganized neglect,* families with *emotional neglect*, and families who demonstrate *depressed neglect.*

*Disorganized neglect* describes those usually considered multi-problem families. They are inconsistent in their parenting of their children and disorganized in their lifestyles, and they spend their time going from crisis to crisis. The Gagnes are such a family.

> *Mildred Gagne lives alone with her seven children. Her alcoholic husband disappeared several years ago. She has called her priest, as she frequently does, and asked him to come to see her, a task which, despite his sincere desire to help the family with its many problems, he usually finds frustrating and unnerving. When he is invited in, a rather emotional soap opera continues to blare from the television screen that covers half the wall. Mildred seems oblivious to it and makes no attempt to turn it down. Only five of the children are home, but from the noise, clutter, and confusion, Father John would have guessed that it was twice the number. The four-year-old is walking listlessly across the back of the soiled and torn couch. No one seems to notice. Two children, clad only in dirty T-shirts and short pants, are fighting over a metal truck and emitting screams destined to wake the neighborhood. The remaining baby lies in his dirty playpen mouthing a bottle with milk that is curdled. A radio with a heavy rock beat reverberates from an unseen room. The phone rings every few minutes. Mildred listens for a moment and then slams the phone down with a disgusted "More people wanting money!" Father John mouths his understanding about the ever-present telemarketer. Mildred looks at him strangely for a moment and then says in a matter-of-fact way, "No, it's something I was supposta pay."*
>
> *Mildred tells Father John that she has asked him to come over to help her "figure out what to do." She has just learned that her husband is in the county jail, but will be released only if he has a place to stay. The long-absent spouse has told Mildred that he is coming there to resume residence with the family.*
>
> *"I don't want him!" the mother complains. "He'll just steal from me and drink up all the money I have!"*
>
> *One of the children at war over the truck hits the other, and the victim wails loudly. Mildred looks at him fleetingly, determines he is not hurt, and yells, "Tommy, you stop that wailing. Harry, leave him alone!" and returns to the conversation with the priest, who by this time wants nothing more than to make a quick exit.*

Families like the Gagnes tax any professional. Despite their myriad needs, one is not always sure when these parents actually understand their issues or agree to address them. The issue here is that feelings motivate behavior. The immediate crisis gets the attention, while all others are relegated to the back burner. Affect is valued over cognition, making it difficult to promote any type of understanding.[4] Because the immediate crisis is attended to, parents often unknowingly reinforce their children's negative behaviors. For example, the children fighting over the truck were the only ones, in the short period mentioned above, who were rewarded with any type of attention by the mother. Later, when the four-year-old fell off the back of the couch and hit her head, Mildred only held her briefly until she stopped crying.

The inconsistency of attention displayed by this type of neglectful parent teaches the children that, unless one can create a real disturbance, one gets little or no attention. Even when their children are infants, these mothers are so inconsistent in their nurturing that the baby begins to feel vulnerable and distressed. He or she cannot predict when the attention will come. Some infants turn inward and do not thrive that well. Others learn with the first few angry cries that, if they are loud enough, they will get a response. Children learn that to be disruptive is to survive. Given this, it should not be a surprise that delinquent acts often become a part of these children's teen years.

When one is organized around feelings rather than thinking things through, it is obvious that little gets accomplished unless these tasks come with intensive messages. For example, a bill might be paid only if the bill collector is at the door or the power has been shut off. Children may be cared for only if their needs seem disturbing enough to attract attention. In short, the family constantly teeters on the edge of disaster. Since this is often the type of family in which the parents were also raised, they are hard pressed to see another way to live. Sometimes, it is only the child protection agency's threat to remove the children for neglect that promotes the desire for change.

Despite how frustrating these families can be, they need caring relationships with sufficient structure to protect the professional from being totally drained. They are usually much in need of tangible items and are frequently seen at food banks. But what is needed goes far beyond the tangible. These parents need acceptance, patience, and consistency. They often learn by modeling appropriate behaviors from others and may benefit from programs that provide ongoing parental support. The phrase often used by CPS workers is that one must "parent the parent so that she or he can parent the child."

*Emotionally neglectful* parents may provide for their children materially but fail to connect with them emotionally. Still other families can do neither for their children. The only way that these families can navigate through life is by surrounding themselves with a structure that leaves little room for emotion. Cognition is valued; affect is all but ignored. When children are young, the parent may attend to their physical needs in a mechanical manner while disregarding the children's needs to be cuddled or soothed, which in turn promotes children who feel empty and sad and who never learn the wealth of emotions that human beings are capable of feeling.[5]

> *I would never have thought of Dolores simply as a neglectful mother. How could she be? Her head for mathematical figures was unparalleled in the church, and she had served as the treasurer for several of the church organizations. Her husband, Stanley, was a paraplegic, and everyone talked about what excellent care she took of him. Her children, Milton and Frances, were quiet and polite, saying little in Sunday school. The teachers had mentioned them to me, feeling that they seemed quite depressed and would fall apart were they not sure of the rules or expectations. I wondered if the children were suffering the effects of their father's accident several years before. I knew that the family had little since the father had become incapacitated, but they seemed to make do. Dolores, although she never finished high school, supported the family as a bookkeeper in a small company. It was not until I visited the home that I saw a different picture of Dolores and her family.*
>
> *The apartment was organized to the point that I was almost afraid to put down my purse, lest it disturb the order of the room. The family had little furniture, but what they had was arranged in a manner that would be functional. Stanley sat, slumped in his wheelchair. Although he was neatly dressed and clean, he showed little interest in my arrival. There was a dullness in his eyes and a depression about him. I wondered if this too was a result of the accident. The children were doing their homework in one corner, regimented little beings who also paid little attention to me. As I observed during my visit, it became clear that this was a family that seemed to have little connection with one another. What I interpreted as Stanley's depression was the only real emotion I encountered during my stay. His care and the questions of the children were attended to with robotic precision. There seemed to be no room in this household for any type of emotion. I wondered how children survived in such a wasteland.*

Emotionally neglectful families also have deep needs, but they would rarely admit this. Pointing out to them that they are not meeting a child's affective needs will make them feel vulnerable and threaten their sense of structure, often resulting in hostility and withdrawal. They are often best approached from a cognitive level, tapping their knowledge or rationality and helping them to feel competent. Only then can they feel safe enough to consider the other aspects of parenting.

Neglectful parents who demonstrate *depressed neglect* are defending themselves against both affect and cognition. These parents have often withdrawn so far into themselves that they cannot respond to their children in any manner. They demonstrate neither hostility nor anger to professionals who try to help them. To them, life has little or no meaning, so they see no point in interacting with others. Their children's physical needs may be met, to some extent, but the contact is minimal and emotional nurturing is absent. The children, whose needs are hardly met, eventually shut themselves down and, as adults, often repeat their parents' lives of depression, poverty, and neglect.[6]

It is difficult to motivate anyone who has given up on life. Nonetheless that is the task of child protective workers who attempt to help such families learn how to parent their children. Years of experience have taught CPS that threatening to remove children elicits little in the way of change in these families. Sometimes a parent is suffering from clinical depression that can be remedied through medication. In other cases, one must begin to intervene with the children, and by helping to meet their needs hope to interrupt the future cycle of depressed neglect.

Professionals generally agree that the neglectful family is the most challenging, based on several factors. First, neglect tends to be generational in that children learn inadequate patterns of parenting from their parents. Interrupting this cycle usually requires creative responses. Second, because neglect is so deeply ingrained in families, intervention is a process, and sometimes a lengthy one. This type of process requires consistency and a variety of resources, and the ability to provide either may not be possible. Finally, the effect that neglect has on the helper can be profound. Even reading some of the cases provided here can elicit feelings of hopelessness and resignation. Working closely with some neglectful families can feel incredibly draining. In my work as a social worker, however, it was at the point when I was ready to give up that I would frequently begin to see changes.

I think often of one particular family when I am overwhelmed with the fact that working with neglect can be an uphill battle. The Dwyers lived in a particularly run-down section of the city where asphalt and decaying buildings were all that one could see for blocks. I had worked with

Mrs. Dwyer for some time and was feeling that I had done nothing to improve either her ability to provide a safe and relatively grime-free home for her children or her skill in adequately parenting them. But she seemed to have connected with me at long last and appeared to care how I felt about her. When I went to see her on what would be the last visit before I was to leave for graduate school, I was amazed at the transformation. At least the top layer of grime had been cleaned from her ancient floors and the children appeared relatively well dressed. Anyone else would have been put off by the remaining dirt and odor, but I knew that this was an improvement. And there in the middle of the kitchen table was a huge bouquet of lilacs. I did not dare question their origin given the Dwyers' vegetation-less yard. The fact that I am violently allergic to lilacs in close proximity did not even matter. What did matter was that this mother was trying to please me and show me that she had made progress. What a gift!

I began to call this my "flowers amidst the filth" story, which demonstrates that, with a great deal of perseverance, one can make a difference with some of the most difficult-to-reach families. Sometimes it seems that what is necessary is for someone to tap the spirit—the God-given core of these individuals—and, like flowers, water it with love and attention. The blooms that emerge can be unexpected and miraculous.

## Parents Who Are Physically Abusive

For some of us, hitting a child is easier to understand than psychological and physical neglect. Some parents hit children, although research now tells us that there are more effective ways of disciplining. Still, one wonders how anyone can hit a child to the degree that abusive parents do. There is no simple answer to this question. Rather, the etiology of such abuse can be found in complex societal, environmental, and psychological factors.

That we live in a society in which violence is accepted in almost every aspect of our lives is no longer remarkable. We cheer on sports teams that we hope will *beat* their opponents. Our children spend their time glued to video games in which some electronic force is destined to *obliterate* another. Crime and violent acts against people and property are rampant both in cities and rural areas. Competition — the battles of one power against another — drives both our work and our play. It is no surprise then that our violent attitudes may implode into arenas that are at the very core of society: families.

In addition to the values that shape our lives, the supports that were once there to protect us from feeling vulnerable are disappearing. Many of us no longer have the protection of large families with a variety of role models from which to choose. The high rate of divorce means that most children cannot be assured the stability of a united system of parents who live with them throughout their developing years. Mobility, economic stressors, and a variety of other issues put an undue strain on the well-being of many of us, including the parents who are attempting to perform the role most vital to the continuation of our culture — raising children. Despite all these pressures, many parents find ways to cope. But there are those who, for a variety of reasons, have a much more difficult time doing so.

Explanations for parental abuse of children abound.[7] Some point to mental disorders or substance abuse to explain abusive behavior. Others suggest that parents have learned inappropriate parenting models or are influenced by the violence that filters into their lives. But theories do not always give an entirely adequate picture of individuals and their behaviors.

A fair number of physically abusive parents are simply overstressed, isolated, and less tolerant of frustration than most people. One of the exercises I ask my college students to do in my child abuse classes is to recall the angriest moment they have ever had. Once they have recalled that, once they are pumped up with adrenaline by the memory, I ask them a series of other questions.

- What did you want to do about it (the situation that created the anger)?
- What did you do about it?
- At any point were you out of control?
- What helped you to regain control (if you had lost it) or maintain control (if you did not)?

I then ask them to reflect in hindsight. Most students are shocked to recognize that they were actually out of control at some point. The ways in which they regained or maintained control sometimes surprise them as well. So, when I suggest to them that all of them have the potential to be an abusive parent, some of them begin to see abusive parents quite differently.

The difference between the abusive and nonabusive individual may lie in the latter having a higher tolerance for frustration and stress, or having more ability to self-calm. These qualities are usually based on one's psychological foundation, as well as how much one's coping abilities are taxed by life's offerings. Certainly, factors that diminish the ability to cope, like the abuse of alcohol or drugs, can also have an effect as well.

Pediatrician Ray Helfer explains that some parents are not equipped by their childhoods to maintain control or cope with difficult situations. In particular, Helfer suggests, they have not learned five essential tasks.[8]

1. *Abusive parents have not learned the difference between feelings and actions.* Instead of recognizing that one must talk about being angry, for example, this individual will act out his or her anger physically by hitting out at someone or something.

2. *Abusive parents have not learned appropriate ways to get their needs met.* Children from dysfunctional families use extreme measures to get an adult's attention in order to get their own needs met. Helfer uses the example of a child trying to get the attention of a mother who is on the phone. This mother is busily involved in her call and ignores her child's repeated request for her attention. Therefore, his demands escalate in intensity until the frustrated child lies on the floor and has a full-blown temper tantrum. "I'll have to call you back," says the mother to the caller whom she can no longer hear, and she attends to the child. After several instances like this, the child learns that extreme reactions get quick results. As an adult, this child may continue to go to the most extreme end of a continuum of behaviors to express his or her needs. These are the adults who threaten suicide, for example, rather than being able to say "Hey, I need a hug!"

3. *Abusive parents have not learned to make decisions.* Abusers do not like to feel out of control.

4. *Abusive parents have not learned to delay gratification.* It is natural for children to want immediate satisfaction of their demands. As parents, we teach them to anticipate that we will meet their expectations at a future date if they can learn to wait. In this manner, they learn frustration tolerance. But if children are continually disappointed and their needs are never met, they learn that they must have what they want *now!* or they fear they will never have it. Abusive parents often expect an immediate response from their children. The resistance of a normal two-year-old would not be acceptable to these parents.

5. *Abusive parents have not learned that they are responsible for their own actions and not the actions of others.* "If I hadn't gotten pregnant with you, I would never have had to get married!" was the refrain that Rose often heard from her mother. In fact, everything seemed to be Rose's fault in her mother's eyes. When this became too overwhelming, Rose developed an imaginary friend she called Lily. It was always Lily's fault when anything went wrong. But as an adult, Lily was no longer of use to Rose. Instead, she began to blame everyone else in her life.

Abusive parents whose childhoods were spent defending themselves against guilt often fail to learn where the responsibility really lies when they become adults. Accepting responsibility for their own actions is too reminiscent of the guilt they felt as children.

In addition to never learning these important tasks, physically abusive parents often experience isolation, have moved frequently, are unemployed, or have left a trail of failed relationships. It is not uncommon for the abused child to have been the result of a pregnancy before or very shortly after marriage. Frequently, the mother has had a difficult pregnancy or labor with this child, or the child was born in the throes of the parents' marital discord. Many of these parents also see their children as extensions of themselves and place unusually high expectations on them, yet when the child fails to meet these unrealistic expectations, it reminds the parent that he or she feels like a failure and the anger becomes displaced onto the child.

Most physically abusive parents do not intend to harm their children. Based on the behavior of their own parents, many abusive parents believe that the severity of their own discipline is appropriate. "My parents used to beat me, and I turned out okay!" is the cry of these parents. This is often true in cultures that condone corporal punishment of children, but hitting children to the point of doing them physical harm is illegal in the United States, no matter what the parents' child-rearing practices.

There are a few — fortunately only a few — parents who, as part of their own pathology, actually intentionally hurt their children, for whatever distorted reason. These parents need psychological help, and their children need protection from them.

Many physically abusive parents do recognize that what they are doing to their children is wrong. What they need is support and aid in finding resources to teach them to cope with frustration. For example, those parents who refer back to their own abusive pasts as children with approval might be helped to understand that there are more effective disciplinary methods — ones that do not bring them to the attention of CPS.

## Parents Who Are Emotionally Abusive

I will spend only a moment on parents who are emotionally abusive — first, because the characteristics of these parents can be much the same as either physically abusive or neglectful parents, and second, because CPS is not as likely to be able to become involved with families where emotional abuse is present, because such abuse is not typically clear cut.

> *Bob remembers his military father as being quite strict. In keeping with the father's military training, Bob was to arise early in the morning, make his bed, and endure inspection by his father. His bed was to be made in military fashion with everything in his bedroom in its place. Hearing this father relate to his son would have reminded one of a drill sergeant with his troops, but the effects on a young boy were even more profound. Bob developed asthma when he was seven, a fact that intensified his father's criticism of him as a "wimp." Bob loved baseball and collected baseball cards. He had amassed quite a collection and had several that he suspected were quite valuable. He kept these away from his father as Bob instinctively knew that his parent would not approve. But a "special barracks check" uncovered the precious items. His father's response, as the boy suspected, was not positive. He berated his son for his "idle and wasteful pastime" and increased his chores. In addition, he burned the beloved cards in front of his son. It was a scene that Bob would never forget.*

The emotionally abusive parent often has a poor self-concept, which he attempts to compensate for by gaining power over others. Often unable to stand up to other adults, this parent chooses a handy target who is not likely to talk back, possibly until size and age give this child the courage to do so.

Despite how one may dislike the way in which they treat their children, these abusers are themselves also in need of support and encouragement to feel better about the positive aspects of themselves.

## The Family in Which There Is Domestic Violence

Domestic violence has long been recognized as a problem in families, but the recognition of its impact on children has been more recent. The batterer is usually the male parent who beats his female partner, often in front of the children. The children are sometimes intentionally beaten as well, or they may come between their battling parents. There is also often a correlation between the battering of the mother and an incestuous relationship with her female children.

Several theories prevail regarding spousal/partner abuse. Although they are not discussed at length here, we consider a few components. Some feel that domestic violence is a result of the social stressors that come from living in close proximity with one's spouse and often with the extra stress than children can generate. The use and abuse of power certainly come into the equation. The abuser (since this is usually the male, I refer to the abuser as "he" from now on) seeks to gain power over his wife as a way to compensate for his own inadequacies. The wife, in turn, is usually inordinately dependent upon him, whether emotionally, financially, or both. Sometimes alcohol abuse is also a factor.

The batterer typically exhibits the following characteristics: He is usually from a family in which he was exposed to some type of violence as a child. His sexual identity and self-concept have become defective, and he seeks to build himself up in his own eyes using his own distorted means. Deep down he believes that he is a "loser," but frantically guards against anyone else suspecting this. He is conservative or traditional, favoring male supremacy as a family model. Paradoxically, he has difficulty asserting himself and can only do so by becoming violent. He does not do well with relationships, has few if any friends, and has problems with authority and keeping regular employment. He can be moody and belligerent and often punches walls when he is not punching his family members.[9]

Why would a woman stay with a battering husband and allow herself to be assaulted again and again? Domestic violence usually follows a cycle, and during the "good times" the wife is often lulled into believing that her husband will not abuse her again.

The cycle of abuse is characterized by a tension-building stage during which the batterer makes demands and the victim tries to placate him and meet his demands. There may be some battering as the cycle progresses, but the woman often convinces herself that, had she been better at meeting his needs, he would not have hurt her. During this phase, everyone in the family feels as if they are walking on eggshells. Other family members may also join in the activity of trying to keep the abuser content. At some point there is an explosion, and the acute battering phase begins. This explosion may result from something very minor and, in fact, is more a product of the batterer's own internal cycle than dependent on any external stimulus. The severity of the beating may actually seem to take both participants in the relationship by surprise and is followed by a respite phase, in which the offender is extremely contrite and loving, and can seem like the model husband. He promises that he will never harm her again and may actually be sincere at that moment. This period of calm can last for days, weeks, months, or years, during which the wife wonders how she could ever have thought about leaving him. But at some point, the cycle will begin again.[10]

Several common myths surround domestic violence. One of the most common is that it is perpetrated mostly in families from Hispanic, African

American, and other minority cultures. This is not the case. Nor is family violence an urban problem alone.

Although we have spoken of the male partner as the abuser to this point, women are certainly capable of being abusive too. When working with women who are reported to be abusive, one must consider that statistically these women may be reacting in self-defense. When they have indeed been the initiators, the effects on the victim may be similar to when the abuser is a male. While men are more likely to use no weapon and may overpower based on superior strength, women are more likely to employ some type of weapon.

Working with the violent family is quite a challenge. The obvious first step if approached by a victim who feels that she or her children may be in danger is to refer her to a shelter where she (and her children) will be safe. Once the family becomes involved with the social service system, clergy can offer supports, which are discussed more fully in Chapter 7.

Next we discuss the dynamics of sexual abuse, which are somewhat different from those we considered in this chapter.

# Chapter 4

# The Sexual Abuser and the Family

## Why Do People Sexually Abuse Children?

The idea that a man or woman would be sexually attracted to a child is a foreign and even abhorrent concept to most of us. What motivates an individual to become sexually involved with a child? Some theorists contend that the sexual abuse of children is an addiction that follows an addictive cycle, similar to drug or alcohol addiction. Here, the addict develops delusional thinking, denies that he or she has a problem, and rationalizes that the child asked for the abuse. Eventually the abuser begins to believe that he or she is merely the victim of an urge that cannot be controlled. But the addiction theory does not fully address the complex nature of sexually offending against children, and it does not explain why these offenders are attracted to children as their victims.

One theory that has shed light on this question is the *precondition model,* which suggests that, in order for abuse to happen, four preconditions must be in place. The first of these preconditions involves the *motivation of the offender,* which is based upon three factors. First, those who are motivated to sexually abuse children feel an *emotional congruence* or an affinity toward them based on the offender's own arrested development or pathology. In addition, the offender becomes sexually attracted to children as a result of some past experience that has programmed the person toward this sexual arousal. Finally, when normal sexual outlets are blocked due to poor social skills or fear of adult partners, interest turns to children.[1]

The second precondition that must exist in order for abuse to take place is that the internal inhibitors — the little voice which lets us know that something is not okay to do — must be missing or fail to impede the offender's abusive behavior. This *lack of internal inhibitors* may be a result of drugs or alcohol or an experience in the offender's childhood that normalizes sexual contact between adults and children. Not feeling this inhibition, the offender rationalizes that what he or she is about to do to the child is acceptable. For some abusers this rationalization is fleeting, while for others it is an integral part of their lives.

In order to abuse a child, the offender must also find the opportunity to do so, which is often based upon a *lack of external inhibitors* or those people and circumstances that protect the child from the offender having access to him or her. For example, when a child is closely supervised or has close relationships with parents and other adults, the offender may have less opportunity to isolate the child for the purpose of abuse. Granted the offender might be one of those adults whom the child trusts, but the key to being able to abuse a child is isolation from others. When a child must be inordinately dependent upon just one adult, when there are unusual sleeping arrangements, or when others are not vigilant about the safety of children, a child may be at more risk for abuse.

Finally, in order to abuse a child, the perpetrator must *overcome the child's resistance*. Children who have poor self-esteem often become prime candidates for abuse. Because they do not feel positively about themselves and do not believe that they can question adult authority under any circumstances, they may be easily led to allow the perpetrator to abuse them. Children who have not been educated about their right to personal space and the dangers of sexual abuse may also be easier targets for abusers.[2]

One of the helpful aspects of this model of child sexual abuse is that it enables us to recognize that there are some areas in which prevention can lower the risk to children. While no short-range solutions exist to address the offender's own psychological makeup (preconditions one and two), we can bolster the external inhibitors that protect children by seeing that they are properly supervised and have adults with whom they can talk openly. We can also make efforts to educate children about personal safety as well as helping them to feel confident about themselves. These steps alone lower the risk for an individual child.

## Characteristics of Abusers

Much debate has surrounded the question of whether or not specific characteristics define sexual abusers. Some theorists would say that there are not. However, enough others have postulated that there are to make a discussion necessary.

Early theories characterized male offenders as those who became fixated at an early age and abused (usually boys) in order to redo or undo their own abuse. These abusers were more likely to be loners who did not find satisfaction with adult females and who rationalized that their abuse was justified.

Another type of offender is often one who has married, but who has become frustrated and conflicted and turns to children for comfort. This offender tends to abuse girls, elevating them in his mind to little women who are much less demanding than another adult. This individual is able to feel guilt and shame, and the prognosis for such abusers is better.[3]

*Bart Barjarian and his wife, Celeste, had been members of the church since they were both children. Bart was the youngest child in a family that had a relatively successful imported rug business. His two older brothers had both died within a year of each other, and now Bart was the sole owner of the business. He recognized that he did not have the business sense of his brothers, but the business was fairly well known and everyone assured him that he would do fine as the new proprietor. Furthermore, with a wife like Celeste, who wouldn't succeed? She was a forceful woman who reportedly forged quite a business deal. She had busied herself with a variety of other activities when Bart's two older brothers ran the business. But now Celeste felt that it was clear that she was needed and gave up her women's clubs and tennis to work at the store full-time. People began to feel that it was Celeste rather than Bart who ran the store.*

*Celeste and Bart had three daughters, all of whom seemed closer to their father than their mother. He clearly had been more of the nurturer than his ambitious wife since the girls were born. When Paulette, the oldest, was hit by a car while riding her bicycle, it was Bart who stayed at home with her during the ten-year-old's convalescence. After she had somewhat recovered, Bart volunteered to homeschool her so that she would not be taxed by a long school day. Father and daughter became inseparable, and it was not until one of the younger girls mentioned something to her teacher about "what Daddy and Pauli were doing" that anyone realized that the relationship had become one of sexual abuse. The shock reverberated throughout the community.*

Other characteristics that have been attributed to sexual abusers by various theorists are as follows:

- Inadequate child rearing, leaving them looking for nurturance in adult life
- Faulty bonding in childhood
- Poor ability to cope emotionally

- Poor self-regulation (the ability to nurture as well as control one's own activities)
- Low self-esteem
- Difficulty empathizing with others
- the ability to interpret reality in ways that justify their own actions (called cognitive distortions)

How these characteristics manifest themselves from offender to offender differs according to individual personalities.

## When Women Abuse

My references thus far have been to males as the abusers. The prominent typologies for many years focused mostly on men, for even though it was well known that women abused children, such abuse was also more difficult to detect or accept. Abuse by women is often hidden within typical mothering activities. Women are also taught by our culture to develop attitudes that make them less likely to become abusive. Traditionally women have been the primary nurturers of children. In this role, they saw the whole child, someone who was not to be victimized or sexualized.

For all that, a common misconception is that only a very few women abuse children. The incidence may be less frequent than men, but woman nevertheless abuse children sexually. The sexual acts committed by women run the same gamut as those perpetrated by men, despite the differences in anatomy. For example, the lack of a penis does not prevent women from using objects to penetrate their victims, in some instances injuring them severely.

Women tend to abuse in one of three ways: as part of caretaking activities, in cooperation with male abusers, and as solo offenders. Saradjian, in her study of female offenders, divides abusers into women who target young children, women who abuse adolescents, and women who are initially coerced by men into abusing children.[4] Like their male counterparts, women who target young children are often products of difficult childhoods themselves. They tend to be distant from their mothers, who they have sometimes idealized, and fear their fathers, who may have abused them. Sexual abuse in their own childhoods is quite probable, and they frequently assumed that others knew of their abuse and sanctioned it. As a result, women abusers may either resent the fact that they were not protected from the abuse while, at the same time, the abuse becomes normalized in their minds. As children, these women felt emotionally isolated, failing to develop healthy self-esteem. As adults, they tend to find themselves in abusive or unsatisfying intimate relationships, with few if any friends for support. This woman identifies with the children she abuses and gets pleasure from what she sees as mutual dependence. Her victims are usually so young that they may not perceive the relationship as sexually abusive.[5]

By contrast, the sexually abusive woman who targets adolescents acts toward them more as a peer than as a parent or adult, mirroring her relationship with her own mother. Her father played little role in her childhood, as he was either absent or uninvolved. Sexually abused herself, perhaps when she was an adolescent or preadolescent, she believed that others knew and did not intervene or even sanctioned the abuse. She, too, was emotionally abused or rejected and grew to think little of herself. In her adulthood she tends to have numerous relationships, maintaining these out of desperation even if they are abusive. Her dealings with peers are superficial, and she constantly feels stressed. She tends to groom her adolescent victims by cajoling them and manipulating them, only sometimes using coercion. She idealizes these children, seeing them as answers to her multitude of needs.[6]

Some women who abuse children do so because of their involvement with and possible coercion by the men in their lives. These women have usually idealized their fathers, no matter how dysfunctional they may have seemed to others. Some, but not all, were sexually abused as children. They were probably emotionally abused, but deny this fact, often remembering only the positive aspects of growing up. Although they may begin the abuse of children in conjunction with their male partners, they may also begin to abuse on their own.

*When Tara married Fred, he brought to their union his seven-year-old daughter, Charlotte. Charlotte was a withdrawn child who never really took to Tara. It bothered Tara at first, but the girl would mind her, so Tara figured that it didn't matter that Charlotte wasn't that friendly.*

*One night the three of them were home alone. Charlotte was in her bedroom, and Fred and Tara were having a few drinks in the living room. They had sprawled on the couch and were watching a movie that was the most graphic thing Tara had ever seen. When Charlotte wandered in to ask her father a question she was already in a skimpy nightgown.*

*"Come here, honey," Fred told her, and she lay on the oversized couch next to her father and Tara. Fred began to stroke her while they continued to watch the movie.*

*"Should she be seeing this?" asked Tara dubiously.*

*"No problem. She's seen them before," Fred chuckled and kissed Charlotte on the mouth. Tara began to realize that he was also stroking the girl between the legs.*

*"Fred . . . ," she started.*

*"Aw come on, Tara, honey. We'll have some fun, you'll see. You love me, baby, don't you? And you want me to love you." He twisted Tara's arm as he spoke, "Then shut up and just have fun."*

*Charlotte had obviously been taught from early childhood to let her father do what he liked with her. At first Fred stimulated both Tara and his child sexually, but then encouraged Tara to join in.*

*By the time the couple was finally found out, they had both been abusing Charlotte either together or individually for some time.*

Clinicians who work with female offenders such as Tara report that they have much greater pathology than their male counterparts. The boys who are abused by them tend to have difficulty with gender-identity issues. The woman who abuses a female child, especially if it is her daughter, is among the most pathological. This child will often end up with anger issues, gender-identity confusions, and enmeshment issues that make her unable to determine where her mother's identity leaves off and hers begins.

## How Offenders Sexually Abuse Children

One myth about sexual abuse is that there is force involved. Since this is usually not the case, how then does the offender ensnare his or her victim? This becomes apparent as we look at the phases of sexual abuse. These phases are not necessarily clear-cut and easily distinguished, but analysis of sexual abuse cases reveals a fairly predictable pattern.

### *Phases of Abuse*

Sexual abuse happens in phases during which the perpetrator gains access to the child and engages him or her in the abusive scenario. Since force is not a tool in most cases, the offender must have a more persuasive approach. We teach children that they are not equal to adults and therefore must listen to and comply with what adults tell them. Granted, some of this is necessary to guide children through life, but perpetrators find ways to use this teaching to serve their own abusive ends.

The first phase of abuse is *engagement,* in which the abuser begins to develop a relationship with the child to whom his future actions will be directed. There are basically four styles that a perpetrator might use in engaging the child. In each style there is an "or else" — that is, a consequence that the child believes will happen if he or she does not go along with what the abuser wants.

*Enticement* refers to an offender cajoling a child into a relationship through spending time with him or her, promising or giving the child gifts, or generally making the child feel special.

The second type of engagement strategy is *entrapment*, when the offender uses some type of leverage to ensure that the child will not resist. For example, Georgina's stepfather gave her anything the thirteen-year-old could want.

> *He treated her like his "special girl," calling her "my princess" and showering her with gifts. Her mother was pleased that her new husband and her daughter got along so well. She now worked the night shift at the hospital and was relieved that Georgina would have someone with her. During one cuddle session of watching TV, the stepfather began to fondle the girl. At first she resisted, until he said, "Come on, Georgie, after all I have done for you, this is the least you can do for me."*

Georgina had been placed in the difficult position in which many sexually abused children find themselves. Here was someone whom she felt she owed something to, and now he was asking for his price. Not to comply would seem ungrateful and would make her feel guilty. Thus, the offender uses the "or else" of guilt to enlist the child's cooperation.

Some offenders use *threats* to engage the child. The threats may be of harm to them or to someone whom they love. An offender might say, "Unless you do this for me, I will do it to your little sister instead," or "I will hurt you." The child complies out of fear of harm to herself or himself or to others.

Finally, a few perpetrators use *force* to complete their sexual assault. Fortunately, they are few — although those who do not force children also have a detrimental effect on them. Obviously, the children who are forced become victims because they are afraid of further harm.[7]

The abuser's engagement strategy is based on his or her initial approach to the child. Most offenders have a favorite style. If an abuser uses enticement, he may entrap later in the relationship, but initially he prefers to cajole and entice. Most offenders do not jump from the more benign styles like enticement and entrapment into threat and force. But, although unlikely, it is always possible for them to do so if they have been sufficiently thwarted.

Another part of the engagement phase is important to recognize: unless the abuser uses force, he or she must overcome the resistance of the victim. Although the offender can do so to some extent through engagement strategies, the child is also groomed by the abuser. *Grooming* is a term used to describe behaviors from the least intrusive to the most intrusive through which the abuser tests the child's readiness for the abuse. Another purpose of grooming is to desensitize the child to what is occurring to the point that the child may be the victim of abuse and yet be unaware of the abuse to some degree.

A familial offender may begin by *being nude* in the house in the child's view. One adult survivor recounted that her father would go from the shower to his bedroom with nothing on, commenting to his children that he had forgotten a towel. Since it happened on a regular basis they soon became used to it and thought nothing of it. An offender might *expose him or herself* or disrobe in front of the child and observe the child's reaction. Some perpetrators also have or make an opportunity to *observe the child* either nude or at such times as bathing or using the toilet. These relatively nonintrusive behaviors give the child the message that exposure and nudity are permissible.

The abuser may then become more intrusive. He may *kiss the child in a manner that would appear sexual* to an adult, may *fondle* the child or even *masturbate* him or her. If a child resists anywhere along the way, the offender will usually back off and renew his or her efforts when the child is comfortable once again. Eventually, the child will become desensitized and allow the offender to go on. The more the child does not resist the offender, the further he or she feels able to go.

Masturbation is often followed by *oral-genital contact* (termed fellatio when performed on a male and cunnilingus when performed on a female) and *digital penetration* of either the vagina or the rectum. *Penile penetration* may then follow. Some offenders may also rub themselves against the child to the point of ejaculation. This is referred to as *frottage* or dry intercourse.[8]

The engagement and grooming of the child merges into the second phase, which is the *sexual interaction* phase. It is difficult to determine where those two phases intersect, but one might say that it is when the interaction becomes blatantly sexual. Again merging into the sexual interaction phase is the *secrecy phase,* when the perpetrator compels the child to secrecy about their relationship. It is rare that an offender does not ask for, demand, and indeed coerce secrecy. After all, he or she would have a great deal to lose if the secret were disclosed, and secrecy allows the relationship to continue.

The abuser might have various ways of asking the child to keep the secret. He might suggest that their activities are a special secret that should be kept only between them. He might caution that they will be separated if anyone found out, or that the child will never be believed if he or she tells. Incestuous fathers sometimes tell victims that the incestuous relationship is preserving the abuser's marriage, and disclosure would be tantamount to destroying the parents' relationship. Some abusers resort to threats by suggesting that the child or someone the child loves might be hurt if the secret is told. Others use force, telling the child that if he or she tells, there will be more of the same or worse. Usually the child believes the abuser, and most children do not tell, at least initially.

The *disclosure phase* may or may not happen when the victim is a child, or it may never come out that the individual has been abused. If disclosure *does* happen in childhood there are two types of disclosures, accidental and purposeful, which are discussed in depth in Chapter 5.

The final phase of sexual abuse is the *suppression phase.* If there is disclosure, the victim's family and friends, no matter how well-meaning they are, may try to suppress publicity, information, and intervention. "We are protecting the child!" they say. They try to make the child forget as quickly as possible. But abuse is not that simple, and it is in the child's best interests to have an opportunity to work through the issues with support and guidance.[9]

Abusers clearly are often skilled at enlisting a child's "compliance" in their abuse. Through grooming, the offender mentally prepares the child to the point at which the child begins to feel that he or she is a willing participant in the activity or perhaps even initiated it. The offender then uses the child's feelings of guilt to keep him or her in the relationship, which explains not only why many children never disclose their abuse, but also why children have feelings of intense guilt and shame when the abuse becomes public knowledge.

Sexual abusers come from all walks of life. They may be family members, relatives, acquaintances, or friends. Research tells us that they may be any age, race, ethnic background, or profession. For the church, abuse by clergy becomes especially problematic, as addressed in Chapter 9.

## *Children Who Abuse Other Children*

It is not only adults who sexually abuse children; other children may also perpetrate abuse. The common misconception is that when a child acts out sexually against another child, he or she is an abuser and may be so for life. In fact, several types of children act out against others sexually. For some children, their own abuse has stimulated a reaction as they try to make sense of what happened to them. For others, sadly, it may the beginning of a career of abuse if there is no or insufficient intervention.

At one time, when a child touched another sexually, it was frequently swept under the rug. Adults have difficulty with seeing children as sexual beings, and for one child to sexually assault another child was out of the frame of reference of most adults. In other instances, adults assumed that it was all part of childhood exploration and should be discounted as the normal going a bit awry. If anyone did perceive that the sexual acting out was beyond "normal limits" (whatever those are), there was no agency from whom one could seek help. Thus, many children who needed help fell though the cracks. After a brief period of overreaction during which every child who was sexually aggressive became seen as an offender, researchers began to look more deeply into this complex issue. Now we have several helpful typologies that describe different groups of sexually acting-out children and the etiology of their behaviors.

Children may participate in *normal sexual exploration,* but these activities have specific characteristics. The children are similar in size, age and developmental level, and their activities are clearly for information gathering. These playmates usually have a positive relationship with one another, and the sexual play is agreeable to both. If they are caught, they may express embarrassment but not anger or resentment. In general, the sexual activity has a lighthearted experimental nature to it.

A second group of children, referred to as *sexually reactive,* express a sexuality that is "out of balance" with their ages and developmental levels, and their peers. They may have received this knowledge either by being overly sexually stimulated at home or by having been sexually abused. They usually act out with similarly aged children, and are not coercive. Their acts are usually impulsive, and the purpose is to reduce the anxiety they are feeling over their own sexual abuse or overstimulation. Their families most likely give them little emotional support and may be dysfunctional. If the children are caught participating in these sexual behaviors, they tend to become upset, fearful, and confused. These children are in need of help to understand their premature introduction into sexuality.

Another group of children become involved with *extensive mutual sexual behaviors* with other children. Their partners in the sexuality are usually peers, and they have agreed on either a conscious or unconscious level. This is demonstrated by the planning that goes into the encounters. These behaviors may be much more pervasive than simple exploration, including vaginal and oral intercourse. Their aim is to gain reassurance about themselves and provide another to whom they can feel attached. Their family life is dysfunctional with the possibility of abuse, substance abuse, extramarital affairs, and poor boundaries. They do not trust adults and are needy and unattached. Sexual relationships are the only way that they can feel connected to anyone. Both this group and the sexually reactive group are children who need help and, when given proper help, are not likely to continue to act out in this manner.

There are some *children who molest* others and whose pathology has already developed to a greater degree. Their sexual behaviors are pervasive in nature, including all types of adult sexuality. They tend to sexualize contacts with people and things and seem preoccupied with sex. They approach sexual acting out in a premeditated manner that is angry, and aggressive, yet confused. They use bribes, threats, and coercion to engage their victims who are often younger, or at least have less knowledge or resources than the abuser. These abusers are often problems at school with poor peer relationships, limited social skills, few outside interests, and faulty problem-solving abilities.[10]

The families of children who molest demonstrate violence, abuse, psychiatric disorders, and general dysfunction. Due to their own unmet needs, these parents are unable to meet the needs of their children and have inflicted upon them the ravages of abuse, violence, poor boundaries, and a myriad of other traumas. Therapy for these children is essential and often is undertaken in residential settings. The families also are in need of intervention.

If one were to encounter a sexually acting-out child in a Sunday school class, for example, it might be difficult to determine the group into which the child fits. However, any child who is sexually aggressive, as opposed to participating in normal sexual play, needs help and should be brought to the attention of someone who can provide that help.

## The Etiology of Sexually Offending against Children

The common question when one is faced with sexual offenders is "What made them that way?" This is a question to which many clinicians and theorists would love to have the answer, but there are few who believe that they have it.

Some offenders, but not all, were sexually abused themselves as children. Others had sexual experiences with adults or older children that they did not necessarily consider to be assaultive, but nevertheless affected how they see sexuality. For many, there were other types of abuse and neglect that left their minds, and sometimes their bodies, scarred. Their childhood experiences were not those that would have built healthy self-esteem or developed positive relationships with others. Many offenders did not experience the adequate attachment that helps children bond with their caretakers and which then provides the basis upon which future relationships are based.

Why, then, do some people who come from these backgrounds never go on to abuse others, while others become sexual offenders? Researcher Jane Gilgun outlines four factors that seem to be associated with explaining the risk of offending when one has been sexually abused. Her study with male subjects found that the male victims who went on to offend had the following: few or no confidant relationships that gave them opportunities to process feelings; families of origin that were filled with maltreatment or domestic violence; peer relationships that tended to center around antisocial activities where proving masculinity with sexual conquest were paramount; and they tended to begin masturbation prior to the age of twelve, using the activity for equilibrium and accompanying it by repetitive and coercive sexual fantasies. The men who did not become abusers did not experience these deficits.[11]

It is not clear what childhood experiences motivate women to abuse, except that these abusers tend to be the most needy and pathological, thus pointing to even more dysfunctional childhoods, usually punctuated by severe trauma.

## Families in Which There Is Sexual Abuse

Incest dates back to biblical times and probably earlier, yet it wasn't until recently that we began to look closely and from a psychological perspective at the families in which incest occurs.

### *Incestuous Fathers and Their Partners*

The incestuous father shares many of the same characteristics that nonfamilial abusers demonstrate — deep-seated feelings of inadequacy, vulnerability, and dependency. He often lacks social skills and feels — on some level — ill prepared for adult life. Some fathers are tyrannical, masking their fear of vulnerability with an obsessive need to control their wife and children. Other fathers seem to be meek and mild men who are often the primary nurturers of their children. Despite their different presentations, these offenders are in fact very similar. They feel isolated and separate from what they believe to be normalcy and competence in adulthood. Because other adults seem, in their eyes, to have things much more under control than they do, these abusers turn to their children, who they feel are able to accept them when adults cannot.

The father who abuses his daughter sees her as a nonconflicting female partner, someone who will accept him despite his faults. The dynamics of a father who abuses his son are quite different. This father is seeking power through the abuse of his son. He may see this son either as a rival or as an extension of himself. Despite their choice of a male victim, these fathers usually consider themselves to be heterosexual.

The partners of incestuous fathers who abuse daughters are often characterized in one of three ways: this mother may be cold and withdrawn, someone who is psychologically absent from the family and who pushes her daughter into what should be her own role within the family; she can be a mother who feels powerless and defeated, unable to protect herself, let alone her daughter; or she can be a mother who learns of the incest and seeks to protect her daughter. Before we judge this mother, we must remember that she may be dependent upon the father either financially or emotionally. She may also believe that it is sinful not to obey him or to seek divorce. The mother's own self-concept is usually shaky, and she may not know where to run or if she will be heard. In addition, her own childhood or culture may have taught her that she has few options for intervening in what is happening before her eyes.[12]

The mother in a family in which the son is abused by the father is often a silent partner. The father may actually have chosen her due to his own childhood experiences of an overbearing mother, or feelings of inadequacy. Brandon did not believe that his mother knew about his abuse.

> *My mother was the typical homemaker, but not a great one at that. She would do as Dad told her and not ask too many questions. When he wanted to take me off for days at a time, she didn't say a thing. When I was really young and we'd go off on these trips — Dad and me — and he'd abuse me, I used to think that Mom knew and just didn't care. But looking back, I don't think she did. Even if she had, I am not sure what she could have done about it.*

Like Brandon's mother, these women frequently are highly influenced by their spouses and may not even know that the abuse is taking place. Even if they do, such women often feel powerless to intervene.

### *Incestuous Mothers and Their Partners*

Women who abuse their children sexually are portrayed differently depending upon the victim. There was a time when mother-son incest was almost eroticized in literature and movies. In reality, there are not many reported cases of mother-son incest, but this may be because, as mentioned earlier, mothers are more likely to hide their abuse through caretaking, and boys are not as likely to report being abused.

When a mother does abuse her son, there is frequently no father in the picture, or if there is, he tends to be distant, inconsistent, emotionally unavailable, or overly busy outside the home. The boy then becomes a substitute that the mother turns to for her affectional and sexual needs. Sometimes the abuse is covert, involving bathing together and sleeping together beyond an age at which it might be deemed appropriate, or the abuse may involve more overt activities such as sexual intercourse. The boy gains acceptance and affection from the relationship and often does not see it as abusive. Instead he feels powerful, like the "man of the house." The mother plays the role of being needy and dependent upon him, flattering his ego. In some cultures (e.g., Hispanic, in which a mother's love is almost sacred), abuse by the mother creates even more conflicts, guilt, rage, and fear that become internalized.

Mothers who abuse their daughters are some of the most pathological offenders, and their abuse has a profound effect on the victim. But because this type of incest is underreported, there have been fewer opportunities to study it. Most of the abusive mothers experienced some type of abuse or trauma themselves as children. As mothers, they are unable to adequately distinguish their daughters from themselves, and thus the abuse takes on an almost masturbatory quality. The mother seeks nurturing from her daughter, who, often feeling that she is needed, becomes her mother's emotional caretaker. Because this mother is so needy, the daughter does not feel that she can resist, break away, or even hate her mother without reviling herself. Breaking the intensely symbiotic relationship would seem, for both mother and daughter, the ultimate in rejection.[13]

Where is the father in these mother-daughter incestuous families? He too is unavailable either physically or emotionally; in his absence, his needy partner turns to her daughter for nurturance.

### *Abuse between Siblings*

While some research has argued that incest between siblings leaves few scars, other theorists argue otherwise. More recent studies have shown that victims of abuse by older brothers or sisters resented the lack of their parents' protection and in later life experienced such effects as the inability to form healthy relationships, alienation from parents, promiscuity or conversely aversion to sex, and difficulty with self-esteem.

Why might siblings abuse younger siblings? Frequently, though not always, the climate in which this type of abuse flourishes is one of heightened sexuality. Parents may be more obviously sexually active either with one another or with other partners. There might already be incest in the family. In general, the children are often trying to make sense of the sexual stimulation by acting it out.

One type of child is curious and sees the younger, less powerful sibling as someone on whom he or she can experiment. The fact that the older sibling has more power and resources, and either coerces or forces the younger sibling into compliance, renders the behavior abusive rather than consensual. Another type of child is fraught with serious psychic conflict. Retribution, humiliation, or power and control may be the older child's motivators. These sexual attacks are a result of the perpetrator's own disturbance.[14]

Families in which there is abuse between siblings have a variety of reactions. Some admonish the perpetrator and forget about it, putting the victim at risk for further abuse. Conversely, families may also punish the perpetrator severely, placing upon him or her shame that is often internalized into rage. Other families recognize the need for better supervision, and some may get help for the perpetrator. The health of the family and the support that they are able to seek will certainly influence the outcome.

### *Abuse by Other Family Members*

It is not uncommon for children to be sexually abused by family members outside the immediate family circle, such as uncles, aunts, grandparents, and cousins. Grandfathers who abuse may have abused their own children, raising the question as to why these children, now parents themselves, do not limit the contact the grandfather has with their own children. The reasons are multifaceted. Some former victims have repressed the memory of their abuse, or perhaps they were not one of the children who were abused and their siblings never disclosed the history. Some parents who were abused believe that it will never happen again, perhaps because

Grandpa is now older. Still others, usually on an unconscious level, offer their children sacrificially to maintain the relationship with their parent.

Or a grandfather may never have abused his own children, but now that he feels less needed, less powerful and capable, he reaches out in this manner to his grandchildren as a salve for his own issues. The relationship may also make him feel more manly and assure him that he is still sexually capable.

When an uncle is the abuser, the abuse often occurs when the child is being cared for by surrogate parents, such as grandparents, or in the child's own home. Because the uncle is an accepted family member, the child begins to believe that the abuse is also known and accepted by those who care for him or her. This belief often results in difficulties in establishing and maintaining healthy relationships later in life.

## Why Does the Incest Stop?

Usually incest ends because there is no longer opportunity for it to occur or because the child finds a way to stop it. As children grow older they become more aware, more powerful, and often more assertive.

"I knew it was wrong, and I had had enough!" recounts one survivor who told her father she would tell everyone if he did not leave her alone. The threat worked. Some victims find release in incapacity. There is a high correlation, for example, between eating disorders and sexual abuse. The attention and treatment given to a child with an eating disorder may rob the offender of further opportunities to be alone with her. In some cases, others discover the abuse and intervene. Some victims find that the only way they can escape is to leave home. Early emancipation of sexually abused children is not unusual. Whatever the reason for the cessation of incest, victims and other family members will benefit during this time from caring support from clergy and church members.

When there is no intervention when children are young, the wound of incest may fester over the years. Adult survivors find that they are dealing not only with the initial effects, but also with the intensity that repression has imposed upon them. They too are much in need of support.

## Chapter 5

# The Dilemma of Reporting and How It Works

*Amanda and the youth minister both looked at me expectantly. Moments before, Sandy, the youth minister, who had developed such an excellent rapport with the children of the church, had asked if he could bring Amanda to talk with me. I was hardly prepared for what she had to say.*

*"My father's been messing with me," she told me hesitantly, her eyes downcast. She had felt comfortable telling Sandy, and Sandy felt that she should tell me as the pastor.*

*"You tell him the rest," whispered Amanda to Sandy. The story unfolded that, for over a year, Amanda's father had been sexually abusing her.*

*"I just want it to stop!" she blurted now, beginning to sob. "And I am worried about it happening to Terry!"*

*I looked at Sandy. "Terry is her younger sister," the youth minister explained.*

*I had been to training on how to respond to child abuse situations, but now I was feeling crippled by the ramifications of the story that had just unfolded in my small office. Nevertheless, I knew that it was time that I must act.*

What if you were in this pastor's shoes? How would you respond?

First, *above all, the child needs to know that you believe her and that whatever happened was not her fault*. Children often feel guilt about abuse that they have suffered, feeling that they somehow deserved it. You must help the child to understand that the responsibility for abuse rests solely on the shoulders of the abuser, not the child. Moreover, the abuser may well have told the child not to tell anyone, insisting that no one would believe the child anyway. Thus, a child needs to feel that he or she is believed.

Second, *do not act shocked or make derogatory comments about the abuser.* No matter what you think about someone who abuses a child, remember that the child may still care very much for the abuser and hearing negative comments might make her or him retreat back into silence.

Third, *tell the child that he or she needs help and that in order to get that help you must talk with another professional at an agency that works with children in similar situations.* If the child seems hesitant, reassure her that it is because you do not want to see her hurt that you are urging her to have this help. *Never tell the child that you can keep their information totally a secret.* You cannot. In terms the child can understand, explain about confidentiality. Say that, as you seek help for the child, you will not talk with anyone who does not need to know what is happening.

*Never assure a child that things will automatically and immediately get better.* Instead, let the child know that you are glad that he or she told. Say that things might be tough for awhile, but that going through all this is the only way that things will get better. Let the child know, too, that *now that the story has been told, he or she must stick to it.* People might ask the child to take the story back. Letting the child know about this possibility is important to prevent the perpetrator, in his or her panic after disclosure, from pressuring the child to retract the story.

*Determine how the child can be safe while you make the report.* It may not be wise for the child to go home immediately after telling you. However, *you cannot detain a child* for any amount of time. Amanda was able to return with the youth minister to her activities at vacation Bible school, while the pastor called the child protection agency. A social worker came out to speak to Amanda before the end of the day's program. Even if you are in a more difficult situation than this, never take a child to your home, because in many states this would actually be considered kidnapping. If there is no way to naturally keep a child until CPS can interview him or her, ask the child how he or she feels about going home. Does the child feel safe? When you call CPS, mention the location of the child and your assessment of the child's safety.

*Let the child know what will happen next.* Tell the child that usually a CPS worker will come and talk with him or her. The child's parents might also be interviewed. When you call CPS, ask the person with whom you speak exactly what will happen so that you can prepare the child.

*Arrange for or be a support to the child after he or she has disclosed.* The child may be frightened and anxious about what will happen. *Assure him or her that you will be available, or arrange for someone to be available as the child goes through the investigatory process.* Imagine if you had just disclosed something that you realize, on some level, will alter your whole world as you know it. This is how the child will be feeling, and it is vital that he or she has support.

## Some Tips for Validation and Reporting

Believe it or not, having a child disclose abuse or neglect to you is the easy way to discover it. There are other ways in which it might come to your attention. Once in a while, a parent may seek out your advice because he or she does not know how to respond to an abusive spouse. In this situation, the ideal would be that this parent reports the situation to CPS, possibly with your support. Otherwise the parent must be told that you are obligated morally and possibly legally to report to an agency that can provide them help.

A staff member or teacher within the church might report their suspicions that a child is being abused or neglected. You will naturally assess the credibility of that individual and how he or she might have gained this knowledge.

You might begin to suspect that a child has been maltreated from signs that you observe yourself. No matter how abuse or neglect is disclosed to you, *it is not up to you to investigate*. Investigations, however well intended, by those who are not well-schooled in maltreatment situations can actually do more harm than good.

You also need to know the protocol of your particular denomination. Some denominations require that a hierarchy be observed before a call is made to CPS. Hopefully the person to whom you must report on a denominational level is available. In some cases, there is a sense of immediacy in making a report. In general, the following situations should be attended to with some immediacy:

- When a child reports directly to someone and does not feel safe in returning home
- When a child has been battered by a parent and is afraid of further abuse upon returning home
- If a child is afraid to go home for any other reason related to abuse or neglect
- If a young child is found alone or abandoned
- Any hospitalization related to abuse or neglect (although medical facilities are mandated reporters and may report the case)

Other situations may not be emergencies but should be responded to in a timely manner. CPS sees cases on a priority basis. The child in the most immediate danger is seen first.

## Validation and Documentation

You only need a suspicion in order to report. In those cases where you suspect there might be abuse or neglect in a home and yet feel you have insufficient information to be sure, follow these suggestions:

*Gather together all the information that you have.* This may mean sitting down and thinking about what has given you this inkling about a child being maltreated. Or you may remember comments that others have made or that the child has made. *Compare these against the material you have on the recognition of abuse* (see the checklists in Chapter 2). Do any of your original observations take on new perspective when compared with the symptoms of abused or neglected children?

*Is there anyone with whom you can discuss your concerns without compromising the family's confidentiality?* It is vital that your suspicions not be voiced to too many people, and that those involved understand that the discussion is confidential.

*Document all you have discovered,* not in any official spot but in a confidential notebook or on note cards of your own. *Analyze the data.* Does it appear to be sufficient to make a report? If you still do not believe that your information constitutes a suspicion, keep these notes in a safe place where they cannot be read by others. *When something else gives you cause for concern, add this to your notes.* You may well find that compiling this data over time gives you more to go on.

When you have thoughts that there might be abuse or neglect, you might be inclined to question the child. This is not always the best course of action. If you lead a child in a discussion, you might actually be jeopardizing later attempts by CPS to get the accurate data. The child might repeat the story using your words and impressions, not his or her own. In addition, if a case is taken to court, as sexual abuse situations often are, the discovery that you have led a witness may result in a mistrial.

Some well-meaning professionals decide that the best recourse is to speak to the parents. Again, that is not always wise. Before doing so, assess the consequences of this action. Would speaking with the parents put the child in danger? For example, a physical abuser might take out his or her anger on the child if he or she felt that you were getting too close to the family's secret. Or a sexual abuser, afraid of discovery, might put more pressure on the child to never tell that he or she is being abused. Some neglectful families will actually move rather than risk intervention by CPS.

If still unsure, you might call the local CPS office and ask if there is someone with whom you can speak unofficially just to discuss the situation. Call it hypothetical if you wish. Most offices will help out in this manner. If you find the interchange helpful, you might ask if this person would be a resource person if you or your church staff have future questions.

Another option is available if your church has developed a safety response team, which is discussed more fully in Chapter 13. Such a team is made up of others within the church community specially chosen to offer support when problems of child maltreatment arise. Knowing that you can take a situation to a safety response team, rather than having to make a decision alone, can provide you with both comfort and insight.

Finally, some denominations require that you report suspected abuse to someone else within the denomination. Together you might be able to respond to the dilemma of feeling that there is perhaps insufficient information.

## Why Clergy May Not Report

Why must a report to CPS be made at all? Some clergy believe that they are much better able to work with the family toward healing than a social services person is. While the spiritual help that clergy can give is vital for many families, most clergy are not trained in how to handle child maltreatment. I have also heard people complain that child protection agencies make things worse rather than better because when a pattern of abuse or neglect is interrupted, a period of upheaval in the family often occurs. Even dysfunctional family balance is some kind of balance. Good functioning cannot begin until the family first becomes "unbalanced."

Some professionals complain that CPS workers do not care. As a former CPS worker myself and later someone who consulted with CPS agencies, I know that social workers on the frontlines sincerely care about those assigned to them. The social worker wants what is best for the children and will make every effort to help the family to provide for them.

Clergypeople often fear that if they report child maltreatment to a social service agency, they will lose the ability to minister to the family. We cannot prevent families from leaving the church after a report has been made. However, learning how to present the fact that you are trying to provide them with the help that they desperately need may preserve the relationship. Offering to stand by the family as they go through the CPS investigation and perhaps later treatment will also be a support for them.

Agencies such as CPS for generations have provided services to violent and neglectful families. Their methods have worked for many families. The ideal is to have the intervention of social service agencies combined with the cooperative efforts of those who are experts in the spiritual realm — clergy.

## Making the Report on Familial Abuse

You have collected any information that you might have to report, and you are ready to take another step. What is next? You must first ask yourself the following:

- *What do I know about my particular denomination's reporting protocol?* Am I required to contact someone on the denominational level before making a report to the local CPS agency? Chapter 13 has a chart outlining different types of polity. Churches with congregational polity tend to expect that the local church will take care of reporting. Churches with a hierarchical polity (e.g., Catholic, Episcopal, etc.) often require a report to the denomination. You'll want to find out this information before a report becomes necessary.
- *If you must notify someone at the diocesan (synod or conference) level, once that person has been contacted, who then makes the actual report?* If you are mandated by law in your state to report child maltreatment, there is also a penalty for not doing so. If you report to your superior and he or she decides not to make the report to CPS, you are still liable for not reporting. Thus, if you inform your superior and he or she tells you that no report will be made, you must determine what to do. Some states accept anonymous reports, but if you have not given your name, you could still be penalized for not reporting.
- *If the person at the denominational level is the one who makes the report, what else is expected of you?* Can you continue to support the family emotionally? If not, who will?

Let's say that either your denomination requires that reports be made only on a local level or that your denominational representative tells you to make the report to the local CPS agency. By now you will probably have investigated the child abuse law in your state, and have determined the agency to which child abuse and neglect must be reported. (Appendix 3 lists resources for your particular state.) Before you make the call, check and see if you have covered all the bases. The following list summarizes what you need in order to report a child abuse case.

### *A Clergy Checklist for Preparing a Report*

Have you . . .

1. documented and collected the data and organized the information in your mind?
2. analyzed all the information that you have, and are you able to answer the question: "Why do you believe that this child is being abused or neglected?"
3. had an opportunity to observe the child's interaction with the parent and gleaned any information from this?
4. spoken with other church staff or those who have had contact with the child in an official capacity? Do they have any comments?
5. familiarized yourself with the reporting policy of your particular denomination? Do you know to whom you must report within the denomination?
6. determined who makes the child abuse report to the local agency, you or a denominational representative?
7. collected all the information necessary to make the report? (You will need to keep this handy or pass it on to the denominational representative if he or she makes the report.)
8. talked with the denominational representative if he or she makes the report determining what will be expected of you when the report has been made, and what you can do with the family in the meantime?
9. obtained the phone number and address of the agency to which you will be making the report, if doing so is up to you?
10. discovered if a follow-up form is required after you make the call? If so, do you have a form readily available?
11. set up supports for yourself once you have made the report? (Whether to the agency or to your denominational representative who will then make the report, making a report may be emotional for you, especially if it is your first time. You may feel vulnerable and need someone to talk with about your feelings.)[1]

You then make a call to the CPS agency. Make sure that you have the following information easily accessible.

- Name of the child and the parents
- Address of the family
- Age and gender of the child in question
- Type and extent of the child's injuries or complaints
- Evidence of prior injuries
- Explanation of injuries given by the child (if you have that information)
- Your name and telephone number
- What actions you have taken (e.g., talking with the child, talking with the parents, etc.)
- Any other pertinent information

You may not have all this information, but this is what you will be asked; the more information that you have, the better. You may feel better asking if your name will be given to the family, but usually it will not be. The reality is that most families at some point figure out who made the report. It may be better that you explain to the family yourself that you made the report so that they might get the help that they so desperately need. Ask the CPS intake worker if or when you should talk to the family about having made the report.

While you are talking, the worker is taking notes, probably entering the data on a computer. In this manner, the agency can then determine if the family has ever come to their attention before and what has been done for them. The worker may also be comparing the information that you give against a risk matrix based on the assumption that some factors put children at more risk than others. The higher the overall risk, the more timely will be the CPS response. If CPS does not respond immediately, it is possible that they do not feel that the child is in imminent danger. CPS will probably ask your assessment of the child's safety as well and whether you know where the child is at that moment. The first priority of CPS is to see that the child is at as little risk as possible.

If you are a mandated reporter (designated by state law), most states are required to investigate the situation. If you are not a mandated reporter, the office will decide if the case warrants investigation. The more information you can provide to support your suspicions, the more likely the report is to be investigated.

Your phone call will begin the agency's initial screening process. In some states that is all that is required. In other states, mandated reporters are expected to file a follow-up form usually within forty-eight to seventy-two hours. Ask the CPS worker what else if required of you. If a form is necessary, one might be faxed to you. For future reference, ask the screener to send you some forms to be kept in the church office or easily at hand. You might also want to ask about the time frame in which the case will be screened. Are they able to let you know if it will be further investigated?

Once you have made your call, the case will be screened by the CPS intake unit. This process of screening may take several days unless the agency feels that the child is in immediate danger, in which case they will work much more quickly. An investigation, on the other hand, will take more time, usually weeks or sometimes months.

A note of appeal for busy social workers is in order. Having been on the frontlines as well as supervising many students and workers who are also, I can tell you that there are peak times when you are convinced that everyone is in the process of abusing their children. Holidays and school vacations as well as a string of snowy or rainy days bring in the abuse reports. Most of the social workers I have known are extremely conscientious, but there are times when high caseloads and a peak in reports mean that the waiting time for an investigation will be longer. It is especially important at these times that the intake worker know any concerns you have for the safety of the child. And after the report, you must have faith that the worker would not be in child protection unless her or his priority were to see children protected and to get on the case as soon as possible.

If you become concerned and want to know what is happening with the case, call the agency. A supervisor is often the best one to ask for as they are usually in the office while workers may be out in the field. Typically, professionals do not want to be questioned about whether or not they are doing their job, but you can develop a collegial relationship if you both show understanding that the case worker will get to the case as soon as possible, and be upfront about your own need to know how things are going. You might also offer to do what you can for the family and ask how you might help. Although the agency may not be able to give you much information, it might be reassuring to you to talk with someone at CPS.

If your church has decided to institute a safety response team, the process might be a bit different. See Chapter 13 for more information.

## Reporting Nonfamilial Abuse

Clergy may also be in the position of reporting abuse that is not perpetrated within the family. Since physical abuse and neglect are only defined as such in a familial context (physically harming a child outside the family is termed assault), nonfamily abuse will be sexual. States differ as to where one should report nonfamilial sexual abuse. Some states still require a report to CPS, while others designate the police as the first responders. Fortunately, most police departments now have child abuse or domestic units of officers trained to talk with children. Responding officers are usually in plain clothes and are women or men who are particularly sensitive to dealing with such situations. They will probably ask similar questions to those of the CPS and will want to interview the child. Whenever a child is interviewed, it is helpful for all concerned if you can provide a quiet, private place for the interview.

You might also be in a position to be of support to the parents of a child abused outside the home, as discussed later in this chapter. Likewise, abuse by fellow clergy is discussed in more depth in Chapters 9 and 10. Basically, this type of abuse is also reported to the police or the district attorney's office, and usually an investigation is done by the latter. Helping the victims of clergy abuse is discussed in Chapter 10. Whatever the type of abuse and neglect, clergy can play an important role in giving support to those who have been victimized.

## What Happens Once a Report Has Been Made?

A report about child abuse and neglect generates several questions for the investigating agency. The following questions are the most significant:

### *Will There Be Further Investigation?*

Whether or not there is further investigation depends upon the risk to the child of further abuse or neglect or if CPS has enough information to determine the disposition of the case, especially if it will go to court.

A worker then is assigned to investigate, beginning with an interview during which he or she will observe the reactions and interactions between parents and children. These parents may or may not choose to cooperate in the investigation. During the investigation, some parents know enough about the system to behave in a manner that would make anyone not skilled in this type of investigation assume that the report was erroneous, yet investigative social workers become well versed on exactly what to look for: how consistent is the injury with the explanation, was the injury intentionally inflicted, does the parent take responsibility, and are there other risk factors like substance abuse, a history of abuse reports, or other violence or police involvement? They look for indications of parental strengths such as maturity and stability, close extended family relationships, and support systems that the parents might have. They also assess the parents' willingness to cooperate with the agency.

If the parents are not willing to cooperate with the investigation, the social worker might initiate a petition in juvenile or family court that will legally mandate the parents to cooperate. If you are in the position of supporting parents who are being investigated, you might suggest to them that cooperation will be beneficial for them. If the court becomes involved, there will be a similar type of investigation that will result in a report for the court.

The decisions made as a result of investigations are not arbitrary and are usually made by several professionals as a team. Agencies want children to remain with their parents, but more important is the children's safety.

### *Is the Child Safe at Home?*

For several reasons, one hopes that the parents cooperate with the investigation and agree to accept help from CPS. They may sincerely want to help, or they may fear the legal consequences if they do not. Some parents just want the social workers out of their lives and see cooperation as a means to that end. Some cultures, taught to be respectful of authority figures, feel that they must at least appear to cooperate.

### *How Does an Investigation Proceed?*

When CPS investigates a suspected abuse or neglect situation, a worker interviews those who have knowledge of the family and the family members in order to determine what type of help the family may need. The goal of CPS is to ensure that the child is safe and to help the family to provide a healthy environment that enables the child to grow. The last resort, used only if the parents cannot protect the child, is to remove the child from the family.

While some parents will never be able to give their children what they so desperately need, other families have a better prognosis and, with sufficient support, will be able to care for their children adequately. In these situations, the CPS investigation often uncovers undeveloped strengths that can be built upon to help the parents perform their roles more effectively. Most CPS agencies identify these abilities in the investigatory process and then, with the family, develop a plan that outlines the services that will be provided and the expected outcomes of those services. Thus, the culmination of the investigation will be either a service plan for future service or closure of the case. The case is closed either when it is determined that there is no abuse or neglect (or there is not enough evidence to believe that there is) or CPS cannot provide services for the family. For example, it may be determined that the family's failure to provide for their children was due to homelessness or poverty and not a result of significant parental deficits. In such a case, the family would be referred to other agencies that could provide housing and financial assistance.

Once the investigation has been completed and it is deemed that the family needs services, the case is usually transferred to a social worker who acts as the ongoing case manager.

### *What Type of Services Are Needed?*

Most CPS agencies do not have the time or resources to provide treatment to abusive or neglectful families. Instead, an ongoing social worker will offer case management, connecting the family members with the various services that have contracts through CPS. For example, if a parent is neglecting her children because she is drug addicted, CPS might arrange placement of her children with a relative or in a foster home while the mother attends a detoxification program. Or families may need homemakers or parent aids to model for them the skills of keeping house and parenting. The range of services are outlined in the service plan, along with the period of time during which these services will be made available. Some services are tangible ones with measurable outcomes while others are more long term, like counseling or other mental health supports. Typical services needed by abusive and neglectful families might be concrete services like financial assistance, medical assistance, information about family planning or budgeting, advocacy services to help them obtain those resources for which they are eligible, culturally based services like a translator to help them understand what is expected of them, or mental health services.

Unfortunately there are not always sufficient services available to meet the needs of those who are the neediest. At such times informal supports in the community and the church are often the only recourse.

### *How Long Will Treatment Take?*

It is difficult to determine how long a family will need to receive services from CPS. While some families receive sufficient benefit from services over the course of a few months, others require years of help and support. Still others require more services than can be made available. Much depends on the family's willingness to cooperate and to change their dysfunctional patterns. Service or treatment plans are reviewed periodically by staff, sometimes with clients, to determine what progress is being made. Some states agree to service families for a specific period of time. If the family is unable to demonstrate an improvement in parenting skills by the end of the service plan, removal of the children may be an alternative.

Where is the child while the family receives services? If CPS considers that the child is safe at home and the parents are able to adequately care for him or her, the child remains at home. If this is not an option, the first alternative is usually placement with relatives (called *kinship care*) in order to preserve at least some part of the family structure. Relatives are often already aware of the abuse occurring in the family and want to help. Caring for the child is a concrete way for them to do so. The philosophy of CPS is to find the best permanent plan for the child that is possible.

The last alternative is placement of the child in an unrelated foster home. Although foster homes can be therapeutic, this option separates a child from all that he or she knows. Filling a bag or suitcase with your belongings and going to a place with people you have never met is an unsettling thought for anyone.

### What If the Case Goes to Court?

The prospect of having a family that you know be compelled to go to court can be disturbing. Even more distressing for those who are not used to the court scene is being called to court as a witness, but careful preparations and knowing what to expect make the latter task less daunting.

A protective case might become involved in the court system in several ways and in several types of courts. The first is involvement with family or juvenile court, which is a part of the civil court system. This is not criminal court and no one is being accused of anything. Instead, CPS uses family or juvenile court when the children need some type of intervention and protection. Some states may automatically involve juvenile court, but, more likely, appearance before this court is required only in situations when children have been abandoned or parents are unwilling to cooperate and a legal incentive is necessary. There may be other instances in which the child is perceived to be in severe and immediate danger, and action must be taken by CPS. In all of the above cases, CPS files a petition, and the police or another concerned agency states that the child needs the court's protection. Such a petition initiates a hearing to go over the facts of the case.

Courts that are exclusively for juvenile hearings aim to minimize the trauma to the children and may seem quite informal. Thus, the imposing judge's bench may be replaced by a desk or table, and the participants sit behind tables or in theater-style chairs. No matter what the appearance, the concept of court intimidates many people.

After filing a petition, there may be a pretrial hearing that could — if the situation can be handled without one — preclude a formal hearing. If there is to be a hearing, CPS may have gathered together witnesses who have knowledge of the case. These people, including clergy, may receive a subpoena. The hearing is held in a closed courtroom (meaning closed to the general public) with only a judge or magistrate, the family court officers, probation officers, lawyers, social service personnel, and witnesses. In some states, the children appear at this first hearing only to be identified but usually do not attend subsequent hearings.

The purpose of this first hearing is to present the case and to have the court determine what is necessary to protect the children. The witnesses may be called upon to offer information that enables the court to make a judgment on this case.

If you are asked to testify about your involvement with the children or family, these tips might be of help to you:

- Document what you intend to say in order to compose your thoughts. Even if you cannot take your notes to the stand, it will be helpful to have gathered your thoughts.
- Courts tend to be quite conservative, so appropriate dress is important.
- Discover from the social worker or attorneys if there is to be a briefing before the court date.
- When you testify, speak slowly and concisely, thinking out each response.
- Answer only what is directed to you. Remember that courts are dedicated to facts and not opinions, although it is always possible that you will be asked yours. But do not offer it unless asked.
- Do not be hesitant to say that you do not know an answer to a question if you don't.
- If heated cross-examination does occur (although this is not as likely as one is led to believe on television), do not let it bother you.

- Keep in mind that this is not about you. You are not the subject of the hearing. You are only there to help a child.
- Feel free to contact the social worker after the hearing to inquire about the outcome.

The decisions made at this hearing include the custody and residence of the children, the type of treatment the family is expected to undergo, and various other plans to determine if the family will be able to care for their children in the future. Usually, a "continuance" will be imposed for a period of weeks or months while these plans are carried out. Some families attend numerous hearings before either their case is closed or they lose custody of their children permanently.

Occasionally abuse and neglect cases reach probate court if the guardianship of the children is sought by someone other than the parents. Often, this is a relative, or in some cases, CPS will use this as a method of giving the children a more secure future.

Finally, sexual abuse cases and some more severe physical abuse cases (especially if a child has died) may end up in criminal proceedings. This can be stressful for all involved, but the most important concern remains the future protection of the children.

What might clergy do to help families who are required to go to court? If you have been called upon to testify about the family's abuse or neglect, it may be difficult for them to see you as a supportive figure. However, if you are in no way involved on this level, the family and/or the children may need a great deal of support. Some social workers try to play this role, but time and high case loads do not always allow it. However, many social workers would be glad to have supportive help for the family from another sector. You might talk with the social worker assigned to the case and let him or her know that you will be available to help.

In some situations, it is not the parents who are in most need of support, but the children. There are some excellent books for children about going to court; see if they are available through your local libraries or bookstore.[2] Reading such a book with a child and helping to answer his or her own questions can be particularly helpful.

### *How Might Clergy Be Involved?*

Clergy can be helpful in a variety of ways to families that are going through an investigation by CPS. The most important aspect of helping, however, is not to get between CPS and the family. No matter how you feel about intervention by this agency, the fact remains that they are trying to help.

Ask the social worker how you can be of the most help. CPS workers are used to having families surround themselves with other allies and professionals who the family expects to protect them from intervention by CPS. If you receive any hostility from a CPS worker it is probably because he or she assumes that you are trying to make the CPS job more difficult. A careful explanation on your part will hopefully alleviate this confusion.

Families or children may need anything from prayers to support through the process to tangible help like transportation. If you are willing and able to provide such concrete services, it will also give you an opportunity to provide a supportive presence. Though you cannot fix their problems, you can stand by them as they attempt the often painful steps toward becoming better parents.

## Supporting Families Whose Children Have Been Abused Outside the Home

Some children are abused by someone other than a parent. Such abuse tends to be sexual. The parents of these victims have a myriad of reactions and feelings. They may be feeling guilt that they have not recognized what was happening to their child. Parents have often given perpetrators access to a child as a result of trusting in them. This often translates for parents into self-blame for making the abuse possible. They must be helped to recognize that they would never have knowingly put their child in danger. Parents may also feel rage toward the perpetrator and be bent on retaliation, which would not benefit anyone.

Parents of children abused outside the home have often been victims themselves as children, raising all types of conflicts that are problematic for them. Dealing with the abuse of children can have a detrimental effect on the parents' own relationships, especially if there were already marital problems. This might be a time when you can help them to find support, sharing the burden rather than isolating themselves from one another.

In addition, parents may feel all kinds of emotions about the child, some of which they do not want to experience. They may feel embarrassed for both the child and themselves and not want to face anyone. They may feel anger toward the child, as irrational as that may seem, while still wanting to protect the child by isolating him or her from contact with anyone.

These parents are probably the least addressed of anyone who is victimized by perpetrators. They are expected to support their victimized child while trying to deal with their own conflicts. A clergyperson can assist greatly in this area. Several excellent books are available to acquaint you with the issues that parents face, and you might also recommend that parents read them.[3] Educating yourself in this area can be a significant benefit to all concerned.

One of the most difficult times for families, and a point at which they may seek the help of a priest or minister, is when the abuse is first discovered. The following are some recommendations that you might give to families when a child tells them that he or she has been abused outside the home:

- No matter how you feel, underreact. Listen calmly, not seeming to be angry with the child.
- Tell the child that you are very glad that he or she told you.
- Be careful that you do not blame the child for what happened, even if he or she was somewhere he or she should not have been.
- Stay close to the child right after the disclosure as he or she is probably frightened. Reassure the child that he or she is now physically safe and that you will protect him or her from further harm. If the child was threatened if he or she told, explain that these threats are the perpetrator's attempt to keep the child from telling anyone, and you will not allow that person to carry out the threats.
- Do not tell the child to forget all about it. Like adults, children need to process traumatic events by talking about them in order to make sense of them. Let the child know that it is okay to talk about it, while at the same time not processing the situation too much.
- Consult caring, sensitive professionals. If the police must be involved, make sure that they are trained in dealing with children.
- Recognize that the child might have positive as well as negative feelings about the perpetrator and the abuse. People who abuse children work hard to engage them, first gaining the child's trust and regard.
- Continue to show the child affection and attention, letting them know that you still love them. One feeling that children often have is of being tainted or damaged.
- As the crisis of getting help unfolds, remember that the child needs your attention and guidance and may need you to offer support as he or she interacts with various professionals who will intervene.

- Try not to restrict or isolate the child too much because of your own fears. Follow normal routines. There is safety for children in normalcy.[4]

In the stress of dealing with the emotions of a child having been abused, parents may not be able to remember all these suggestions. A supportive presence goes a long way toward enabling the parents and the child to cope with this trauma.

## From the Sidelines: Help for the Clergy Helper

It is natural for clergy to have their own conflicting emotions when they have been involved in making a report and in supporting the family along the way. What if you were the one who found it necessary to make the report to CPS? What do you think your feelings would be as you watched the events unfold?

Since we clergy are dedicated to change and healing, it is sometimes difficult to accept that we may not be able to make a significant difference in the lives of abusing families. But the fact remains that their patterns are often generational, and intervention to change those patterns is a complex and lengthy process. It may require more than caring support. It may necessitate the jolt of upsetting their balance in a manner that will allow them to search for new behaviors. Taking a family to court, removing the children, and other such interventions are last resorts when these wakeup calls are all that will get the family's attention and commitment to change. I have worked with many clergy who have suggested there might be a gentler method of dealing with such families, but experience tells us that the gentler approach does not always work.

If you are the concerned professional who has found it necessary to bring an abuse or neglect situation to the attention of CPS, you may feel that you have plunged the family into a mire that none of you expected. Some people, recognizing the family's pain, may try to go into the fray and save them from the disorientation they are feeling. This is not advisable. Dysfunctional families have many mechanisms by which they protect their dysfunction. The most common of these involves their attempt to get anyone and everyone to save them from the change that they so desperately need. The refrain goes something like this: "Do you know what that CPS worker did to me?" A family member may even know that you were the reporter and be returning to you with a well-directed "I told you so! Look what you have done!" The key is to remember that all you have done is be concerned enough to try to get them some help.

When members of abusive families come to you with such a complaint, the best course is to listen to their frustration and recognize how difficult it must be for them. Try not to get pulled into their emotional crisis by feeling as if you too are in crisis. Families who constantly live on the edge of crisis know well how to pull others into the morass with them. It is also advisable not to become the go-between for the family with CPS but rather to aid the family in working *with* the agency.

Some professionals who work closely with children feel anger toward the parents who have abused them. Your hostility will only throw the child into conflict. The best way to protect the child is to get the family the help that it needs to change. If the family members feel your hostility, they are very likely to take the child and "run," finding another church or even moving to another town.

If you take it upon yourself to support the family as they work through their issues, remember two things. First, your best help will be to stand by them as they work with CPS; second, the process of standing by such families can be exhausting. Later on in Chapter 7, we consider what it is like to be a "good shepherd" as you watch families attempt the difficult task of change with the help of the social service system. And Chapter 14 addresses clergy self-care.

## Chapter 6

# Responding When There Is Domestic Violence

*There had been rumors within the parish that the Harrises had a tumultuous marriage. Neighbors reported hearing screams well into the night, and the police knew the address well. Yet Janet Harris insisted that theirs was a good marriage and that Frank only "lost his temper" when he'd been drinking. She swore that he was now sober. She never ventured out after a major fight, and people suspected that she was hiding the bruises. People shook their heads and assured me that there would be a "next time." As the new assistant minister, I spoke to the senior minister about what the church had done.*

*"What can we do?" he responded. "Janet protects him and will not leave. We have all tried to help her and Frank, too. We can only pray for them."*

*I was sure that more could be done to help this troubled family, especially the three children who were captives in this war zone. It was ten-year-old Renee who made us all realize that something must be done. At Sunday school we were all used to Renee's frequent aches and pains and her angry outbursts. At other times, she would show little emotion at all. She had few friends and kept to herself much of the time.*

*"I think she's disturbed," remarked one teacher.*

*How could she not be if her home life was as turbulent as people said? Then one day when I was helping with a Sunday school class, I saw this sad little girl intentionally stab herself with the scissors. It was then that we all realized the toll that her parents' violence was having on this child.*

Despite the fact that domestic violence is a very old problem, only recently have we recognized that violence's impact on children. The inclusion of this type of child maltreatment as a responsibility of child protective services agencies is even newer. Now many agencies have units trained in and designated to deal with domestic violence.

Traditionally, domestic violence has been the domain of the police and agencies that are set up to respond to the needs of battered women. Due to the volatility of emotions, the probability of further violence, and the possibility that weapons may be involved, police officers consider domestic violence situations some of the most dangerous of those to which they are asked to respond. Recognizing this, *clergy must be especially cautious about how they intervene in these situations.*

Crisis centers or battered women's hotlines exist in most communities (see Appendix 4 for national listings). It behooves every pastor to identify these *before* there is a crisis. These agencies are skilled in handling the often delicate relations that characterize families in which there is domestic violence. Agency staff advocate for women and their children and are usually quite aware of the legal and psychological resources available to victims within the community. Some of these agencies, though not all, are receptive to providing resources for the batterer, but most will know where these services can be found.

Increasingly, child protection agencies are involved when the family violence affects children. The identity of the first responder (CPS, police, or crisis centers) usually depends on who reports the situation, the circumstances at the time of reporting, and who is being addressed as the primary victim. In other words, if there is a violent fight in progress, it is more likely that the police will be called. If a child reports the violence, the case may be referred to CPS. Mothers, even children, sometimes seek out the help of crisis lines. One hopes that all of these agencies will work together no matter who is the first to be called.

The intent of this book is not to deal with domestic violence per se. Rather, we are considering the needs of the children who witness domestic violence. However, one cannot fully respond to such situations without also looking somewhat at the total family situation.

## A Mother's Plight and How the Children Are Affected

The mother is most often the parent who is battered; for this reason so far I have identified her as the victim. Though sometimes fathers become victims (as I discuss at the end of the chapter), it is so rare that I have chosen to focus on the typical situation.

In earlier chapters, we discussed the cycle of violence and the effects that children might suffer as a result of their parents being involved in this type of conflict. Remember that the batterer has exerted control over the mother in several significant areas:

- isolating her from a support system
- controlling the household finances
- controlling who she sees
- often controlling what she does, what she wears, and her activities in general
- affecting her image of herself, including her ability to parent
- influencing how her children see her[1]

But the children too have been subjected to these controls even if they have not actually been hit. In addition to experiencing the father's domineering control, children see the actual incidents; hear the terrifying sounds of slapping, beating, screaming, and sobbing; and often are called upon to deal with the aftermath when the victim is left bruised and bleeding. As one man explained:

> *The worst part of growing up for me was trying to help Mom after Dad had beaten her. I remember still how helpless I felt. I'd want to hug her, but she was too sore.*
>
> *"Just help me to the bathroom to clean up," she'd say when I knew that she needed a doctor. Those memories haunt me just as much as watching Dad beat her.*

Children from violent homes know what it is like to live in constant fear, to walk on eggshells, never knowing when the battering will happen again. Because of this, intervention from the outside may seem like it promises relief, but the child, like the adult victim, is often fearful of the consequences.

## How Might the Children's Plight Come to the Attention of Clergy?

Much like any other type of abuse, the situation may be uncovered in a variety of ways, some intentional and some more accidental.

Sometimes children will tell someone about the violence in their homes in the hope that another adult will be able to make it stop. Even though the children have had the courage to come forward, they are still fearful and anxious. What will happen to them or to their parents if they tell someone, they wonder. They may also feel embarrassment. They know on some level that their family is different. The isolation that may have been imposed on them makes children feel ashamed of what is going on at home. Children wonder about what others will think if they disclose what is happening in their family. They may also have very contradictory feelings about both the batterer and the victim. They may be fearful that they too will be attacked. The child who tells an adult thus needs a great deal of support.

A child who seeks to tell his or her story needs the opportunity to do so without an adult interjecting. Even premature reassurance can cut off some children in midstream. *Listen to and believe the child.* Children do not usually describe extreme violence in their families without some realistic provocation. *Your first concern after hearing the story should be for the child's safety* and for the safety of the victim. What type of plan can be put in place to ensure the child's safety?

> *Anna flew into my church office in a frenzy.*
>
> *"Pastor Jane, you've got to help me!" she sobbed. After calming her a bit, I listened to her tearful story about how her mother's boyfriend had beaten his partner and left her bleeding in their apartment a block from the house. Anna said that the boyfriend was gone and that she had run to get help. Although my first inclination was to rush over to the house to assist Anna's battered mother, I also recognized that the abuser might well return and put all of us in danger. I was also aware that I did not want to re-expose this child to whatever awaited us at the apartment. I explained to Anna that I needed to call the police to come and help her mom. I knew that she had an aunt who lived nearby, and I said that I'd like to call her. Anna agreed, and after I had called the police and alerted them to the situation, I called Anna's aunt and made arrangements for the child to stay with her at her home. I promised Anna that I would let her know about her mother's condition as soon as I knew something.*

This pastor's concern about the child's safety and her own was appropriate. When the police arrived at the apartment, the boyfriend had indeed returned and was beating Anna's mother once again. The police subdued and arrested him, and took the bleeding victim to the hospital. The pastor was able to return to the aunt's home to assure a weeping Anna that her mother would be fine after some medical treatment.

Oftentimes it is not safe for women and children who have been abused to return to their own homes and risk repeat attacks. Far better for them to go temporarily to a shelter for battered women and their children, whose location is known only to shelter staff and a few other professionals, in order to protect victims from retaliation by their abusers. Shelters are residences where women and their children can live in safety while they begin to heal from their trauma. These shelters have different regulations regarding the length of time clients are allowed to stay. During the family's time there, staff from the women's crisis center work with women to help them to plan for the future, including finding housing and employment, and coping with the responsibilities of single parenthood, all services to strengthen the woman and empower her to gain some independence. Therapy or support groups for both mothers and children are often part of the program.

Shelters and police may recognize the importance of clergy in the lives of families and offer resources or include them in the services to victims of domestic violence and their children. You might also be asked to be a sounding board, and to offer comfort and support in domestic violence situations. Victims commonly feel that they are betraying God by separating from their husbands, even though they are abusive. Although what many clergy often feel obligated to do is to encourage the woman to work out the differences between herself and her partner, statistics show that without significant professional help, violent abusers are quite likely to abuse again.[2] In addition, the severity of abuse usually increases over time, putting the woman in more and more danger.

Some victims and clergy argue that the Bible demands obedience on the part of wives to their husbands. Others would point out that the Bible was written in a time when patriarchy allowed for the use of women in any way that men chose. A closer reading of the passages that are invoked by abusers to justify their actions actually tells husbands and wives that they should care for and respect one another (Eph. 5:21–33).

Today, we are more apt to consider relationships as covenants that value equal respect and care for one another. Those looking for a biblical basis to condemn domestic violence need not look far. Numerous scriptures speak of the wrong of those who are violent to others, especially their intimates.[3] Most of us today would suggest that if the choice is between a life or a marital union, the victim should be protected and the union dissolved. The future of the marriage as well as the victims' safety may also depend upon the batterer's ability to admit his problem and seek help.

As a clergyperson or church leader, you may also be called upon to minister to children. Mothers who are being beaten by their husbands are often trying to attend to the safety of their children as well as themselves, and make choices that will provide for that safety. Even though they desire to do so, many such women are in so much conflict themselves, or else have so little psychological energy, that they cannot hear or respond appropriately to their children's pressing needs.

Children of any age need to hear that they did not cause their parents to fight or to separate. They need assurance that they are now safe from harm. Certainly, these are issues that shelter staff members address, but sometimes children see clergy as God's representatives and need assurance from this source.

## Responding to a Report or Disclosure

When you receive a report of violence from a victim or child there are some important considerations: First, *it is important to believe what you are told about the violence the victim is experiencing.* In reality, most victims underplay what is happening, and the severity might be much worse than you are being told. Women or children who muster the courage to reach out for help when there is domestic violence have usually endured it for some time already. Statistics show that things will get worse without intervention.

Second, the *victims need to be reassured that the abuse was not the fault of either the mother or her children.* Most victims assume that they have somehow brought the abuse upon themselves. Some victims of domestic violence may be confused about their relationship with God and their faith, and wonder whether the abuse is God's punishment for their not being a good enough wife. An important role for clergy is *to help the victim to realize that God is benevolent and to give her and her children strength and courage for the days ahead.* The victim might need to pray with you and to feel the acceptance and love that will sustain her. She might need you to assure her that leaving an abusive mate is not breaking the marriage covenant; rather, the covenant was broken by his ill treatment of her. It is vital that you *not blame her for the violence that she has suffered.* She is already blaming herself. It is also vital that you reach out to her. I have talked with battered women and the children of violent homes who report that their priest or pastor told them to "forgive him, go home, and sort things out." In fact this advice might be tantamount to signing the victim's death warrant.

*Provide referral numbers* for the mother, and be available if she needs help accessing them. Many a victim will opt to return home, assuring you and herself that it will not happen again or that she can prevent further violence. In fact, most women report having left an abusive relationship between three and seven times before they take steps to extricate themselves permanently.

Although you must *respect her choices,* plans can be made if the victim chooses to take her children and return to her home. The first is to *help the victim to establish a plan of safety.* If she does contact a hotline or agency, they will also take this step, but it is best for her to start thinking about this as soon as she tells the first person. If that person is you, it is important that you help her with this safety plan. You might suggest that she think about the following questions:

- Where can she go if she needs to leave her home immediately?
- Has she thought about where she will go if she is attacked again?
- To whom can she turn?
- Does she have the number of the local crisis hotline?
- Is there a place where she can safely keep money that is easily accessible if she needs to leave in a hurry?
- Is there a place where she can keep a change of clothes in case she—and possibly her children—needs to leave in a hurry?

We have been discussing steps that one might take in dealing with the mother. Although this book is designed primarily to address the needs of the children, in this type of violence, the needs of the mother and those of her children usually go hand in hand. But it is also important to discuss specifically with the mother how she might minimize the danger to her children.

Do the children know whom to contact in an emergency? Can they dial 911? Where might they go for their own safety? One mother, for example, arranged with a neighbor a plan to protect her children. If the mother was subjected to beating by her spouse and she feared for the children, the children were instructed to run to the neighbor's house for safety. This neighbor would call the police and shelter the children until the police arrived. The plan was kept secret from the batterer for the neighbor's protection. He never learned where the children had gone when they disappeared from the house. Although this exact plan may not be the best one, there may be others that provide for the protection of the children.

It is often helpful for you to walk through a variety of scenarios for the mother who plans to return home. What if she is battered and needs to leave and the children are at school? What if the children are asleep? Being prepared for any eventuality will help the victim regain some control over her own life and perhaps offer a bit of protection for her in the future.[4]

Part of ministering to the mother is to help her be assured that her children are also of the utmost concern. Children need to be encouraged to talk about how they feel. Their inner worlds are probably wracked with as much conflict as their outer ones. They are struggling with a variety of immediate feelings. They may be angry with Dad for his selfishness and cruelty, but also be in awe of his power. He may also exert some charm with the children. They may resent him for having hurt Mom, but also feel shame about the times that they joined with him in laughing at her or being cruel to her themselves. On one hand, they may fantasize about overpowering Dad and driving him out of their lives. On the other, they may worry about him or even want to join with him in his power. Children may also have conflicted feelings toward their mom. They may resent her inattention to them and her emotional unavailability as she battles for her own survival. They may be ashamed of her because she seems so unable to protect herself and angry that they do not feel her protection. Many children of battered mothers act out behaviorally in their desire to both punish and get attention. Yet when there are moments that she turns to them, they may devour her affection and attention, thereby further draining her emotional resources. Children may also want to protect their mother and save her from violence. Not being able to do so makes them feel guilty without recognizing the fact that they do not have the strength or resources to render that protection. Helping these children to recognize that any of these feelings are normal will go a long way toward beginning their own healing.

Not everyone feels comfortable or skilled in working with children, especially children who are suffering the effects of a battering relationship. Even if you do not feel able to do any initial counseling of these small victims, it is important that you recognize how they feel, reassure them, and advocate for them to get some help so that the children's well-being is not overlooked.

## Addressing the Needs of the Batterer

Clergy may also be called upon to minister to a man who batters his wife and possibly his children. This is typically not easy to do, especially if you have witnessed how he has damaged his family. But beware: some abusers can be totally charming and have the helper convinced that the problem is his wife's rather than his own.

> *Duncan came into my office and promptly began to cry. He told me that he had accidentally pushed Marjorie down and she had "gotten bruised." She had just returned from the doctor's office and was resting. He said that he was really concerned about her and whether she was capable of caring for their children. He seemed so contrite and concerned that he had me convinced that his wife needed help. The family was new to my parish, having moved from another state several months before, and I knew little about them. But I promised this man I would try to help.*
>
> *When I called on Marjorie the next day, I was stunned by her appearance. Her right eye was badly swollen and she had huge bruises on her arms and neck. Shocked, I stupidly said something about her trip to the doctor. She looked at me blankly, and I realized that she had not sought medical attention.*
>
> *"Did Duncan do this?" I finally managed. She nodded mutely and then, sobbing, poured out the story of his intermittent abuse since their marriage ten years earlier. She said that she was concerned about their children, as the oldest had almost been injured during this last episode. Had I not made that visit, I would never have suspected the real problem.*

Batterers like Duncan will actually seek help but often present the problem as someone else's, usually the victim's. Pushing this violent man into admitting that the problem is his can put you in jeopardy, so instead, make a referral at the outset. Do not try to work alone with a man who can be or has been violent.

Where might one seek help for a man who comes forward to admit that he has abused his wife or partner? An increasing number of agencies are dedicated to helping batterers, among them *Emerge.* Many crisis centers also have the names of other agencies to which a batterer might be referred. Above all, it is crucial that a violent abuser receive counseling, without which prognosis is poor.

Though at times an abuser or his victim will present himself or herself to you, some clergy suspect abuse during the course of couples counseling. This instance requires a referral as well. Most clinicians believe that *family* counseling in situations in which there is domestic violence is not advisable. The first priority is the safety of the victims. In addition, the abuser is often an expert at manipulating, distorting, and outsmarting others while the victim often lacks these negative abilities. Thus, a counselor who is not skilled in working with domestic violence situations may actually be drawn into the batterer's web of deception at the victim's expense.

Yet the batterer also has a right to being ministered to and is in as much need of it as the victim. People who feel good about themselves do not abuse others. This man may feel most vulnerable and worthless and is often crying out for acceptance and liberation from his abusive behavior. Some men want to confess their transgressions and seek divine forgiveness. Feeling accepted by God despite their behavior can actually begin to lead to a transformation. But it is vital that the batterer become involved in intensive treatment as well as counseling to help him to begin to forge a relationship with God.

The abuser should be helped to understand the impact that his behavior has had on the children. The children should not be used as weapons by one parent against the other, and helpers need to be cautious that the abuser does not deliberately come between his partner and his children, such as manipulating his children to report on their mother. A batterer may find it difficult to repair his relationship with his children, but it is usually beneficial for all if this does occur.

## Getting Help for the Family

In a domestic violence situation, the type of help that a family will receive also depends somewhat on the agencies that intervene. When police intervene in a battering event, they will often call the battered women's agency in the area. More recently, some police departments have been trained to involve CPS immediately if there are children in the home. Battered women's agencies are also more likely to involve CPS than in years gone by. Either of these agencies will strive to develop a plan for the safety of the victims, but CPS tends to see the children as their primary client while the women's shelters see the mother as theirs.

In the past, children were sometimes removed from homes where there was domestic violence until it was recognized that this further punished the victim/mother who was already overly stressed. Now more of an attempt is made to keep the mother and her children together. In addition, more emphasis is now placed on insisting that the batterer receive counseling.

## What If the Victim Is the Father?

I have only encountered one situation in which the father was the victim of his wife's abuse, but I have been told by other professionals that this is being seen more and more. The following is an example:

> *Glorianna and Barton married when they were quite young. She was a very large woman who always impressed me as quite self-absorbed. Barton, on the other hand, was small, quiet, and retiring. They were not enjoyable to be around due to Glorianna's frequent jokes at her husband's expense. He said little when she criticized him or made him the brunt of her humor.*
>
> *The couple had had four children when I first met them, and I marveled that Glorianna had taken enough time away from her various interests to have them. It was clear that Barton was the caretaker, but the arrangement seemed to please both of them. The children were quiet and well-behaved, and their father brought them to church regularly.*
>
> *I was taken aback when I received a call late one night from the sheriff. He said that he was at the emergency room with Barton and the children.*
>
> *"The Mrs. really beat him up bad," the law officer explained. "The kids are really scared. Could you come down and talk to them, Pastor?"*
>
> *I later learned that this was not the first time this mother had beaten her spouse when he displeased her. The children had stories of numerous nights when they were locked out in the barn while their mother raged at their father in the house.*

Most agencies that serve battered women are unlikely to intervene when the victim is the father, so law enforcement or CPS are typically the agencies that become involved in these rare cases.

The feelings of the victim are much the same except that there is an additional stigma that is created because of how society sees men and women. The children also suffer from this stigma, but otherwise suffer many of the same effects as other victims of domestic violence.

## Chapter 7

# Being the Good Shepherd While the System Does Its Work

Once an investigation has been completed and CPS decides that the family needs services, the work of real change begins. Families often find it quite difficult to change their styles of parenting, and they may need support as they undertake this difficult work. Like the shepherd who tends not only the members of the flock that are in pain but is also mindful of the well-being of all of the flock, you as pastor can play an important role during a maltreating family's involvement in services. To be a good shepherd to them, it is essential to know the social services process and how you and the congregation can help.

### The Nature of Treatment

To undergo treatment from a medical perspective is to undergo a series of technical procedures (surgeries, tests, or prescribed drugs) to correct the problem. Psychiatric patients must participate in treatment aimed at helping them to change attitudes or behaviors. But for families or individuals who are abusive or neglectful, the problem may be their values, attitudes, and lifestyles. There is usually no easy treatment. Further, although medical treatment may consist of a professional administering technology to the patient, treatment in maltreatment situations requires the recognition by the client that treatment — or, rather, behavioral change — is necessary and demands the client's full cooperation. When families refuse to cooperate, removal of the children may be CPS's last alternative. Even if a family does agree to treatment, there may be impediments to their receiving help.

### Impediments to Treatment

One of the most disturbing impediments to treatment is the lack of resources that often exists. Because treating families in which there is maltreatment is time consuming, lengthy, and expensive, few programs have the time or resources necessary to treat such families. The role of CPS is to find such services and see that families make use of them until these parents are no longer abusive or neglectful. The best-case scenario is that some agency will have a grant to do more intensive work with families. But these grants are the first to be cut during financial crisis.

## Providing Help

Given these challenges, where do these families get help? Ironically, it often falls back on the community to provide ongoing support. You may be asking, why even report these situations to CPS? The answer is simple. CPS has the expertise in case management and the coordination of services for these families. It then becomes the task of the community — churches included — and CPS to work together on behalf of abusive and neglectful families. Let me suggest an example:

> *The Cartier family was brought to the attention of CPS by eight-year-old Hannah's teacher and the pastor of their parish almost simultaneously. Both had noticed severe bruises on Hannah's arms and legs, which the family had attempted to hide by dressing the child in long sleeves and tights despite the May temperatures. An investigation by CPS uncovered an overworked and overtired mother, Amy, who was pregnant with another baby. Besides Hannah, there were four-year-old Nathan and two-year-old Jacob. David Cartier, the father, was known to have a severe drinking problem, and at the time that CPS first investigated, he had been on a binge.*
>
> *Once the case was screened in by CPS, Mr. Cartier agreed to go to a detox center. At the same time, it became clear that Mrs. Cartier was having difficulty managing her children and maintaining her house. No funds were currently available through CPS for either a homemaker or child care. The CPS worker assigned to the case after the assessment approached the pastor, asking how the church might be of help. The pastor and a group of the women from the women's guild organized a support network that joined together to help Mrs. Cartier with such tasks as shopping, cleaning, cooking, and some child care. These women also modeled effective parenting for her. The daughter of one of the women also ran a child care center, and she arranged for the two preschool Cartier children to attend child care several days a week to give this mother some respite. The fees for this were provided as the daughter's donation to the church. When the new baby*

*was born, volunteers from the church went into the home on a regular basis to help the new mother manage. In addition, the woman's group had long sewed canvas bags which they filled with baby supplies and donated to the local maternity unit of the hospital. One such bag was given to Mrs. Cartier.*

*The church happened to be the site of meetings of Alcoholics Anonymous, and, following his release from detox, Mr. Cartier began to attend there. A church member who had himself been a longtime member of AA agreed to become Mr. Cartier's sponsor. Together, they worked to combat Mr. Cartier's drinking problem.*

*While these supports were in place for the Cartiers, the CPS social worker was able to refer them to a program that did intensive casework with abusive parents. It was discovered during the investigation that it was actually Mrs. Cartier, in her distressed and overwrought state, who had beaten Hannah. She received counseling to help her to problem solve and prioritize, reducing the stress that she felt. Had the church not offered the supports that they did, none of the family members would have had the emotional energy or stability to benefit from the treatment that they received.*

Through the cooperation of public agencies like CPS and community groups like churches, families feel true support and are inspired to change.

In addition to offering supports that make treatment possible, churches and communities can help families to use treatment services. Knowing more about what might be available helps to frame the help that can be given.

## Resistance to Treatment

Many people believe that they do not need outside intervention and can handle difficult situations themselves. How many of us have neglected to go to a doctor, trying to treat an ailment on our own, until the pain became unmanageable? Despite their involvement with CPS, for a variety of reasons many family members insist that they can handle their problems.

Added to this "I can do it alone" ethic is the fear of losing control. To recognize that they need help from the outside makes many people feel that they have lost control. Some people fear agencies or bureaucracy, believing that they might somehow be swallowed up by the unknown. One help that you might give to families facing treatment at the hands of social agencies is to normalize the need to look to others for help. Perhaps sharing a time when you sought help might be of comfort. In addition, some family members benefit from knowing that they have rights when dealing with social agencies, and these rights can give them some protection from feeling totally out of control.

Some individuals are afraid of social agencies due to their misconceptions about them. For example, I once worked at a child guidance clinic that happened to be at the foot of a hill on which sat the county psychiatric hospital. Often, I spent the first part of the first session explaining to a frightened parent that just because we were situated in the shadow of that hospital did not mean that anyone believed that the parent or his or her child was "crazy" (their word, not mine). If a parishioner is referred to a particular agency, it might be especially helpful to explore the individual's perceptions of that facility, and explain what the agency does, dispelling any fears that might be present.

Some people are concerned about what they perceive as the stigma attached to receiving certain kinds of help. We believe that everyone is born with the right to parent. To suggest that someone is not an adequate parent is taken by some as the most grievous insult, along the lines of "Are you telling me that I don't know how to raise my kids?" Helping the parent to recognize that every parent needs help sometimes may ease the shame.

Finally, change is difficult. People who are referred for treatment know that it is about change, which may be difficult for them to hear. Sometimes they must be helped to see the benefits of change before they can accept it. Helping them to recognize what will be accomplished with this change and how their lives might be more rewarding can often help an otherwise resistant client to be more compliant.

## Types of Treatment

Each type of abuse or neglect has some variations in the type of treatment goals and the techniques suggested. The following gives a broad overview of each.

### *Treating Neglectful Families*

Neglect is the most difficult type of maltreatment to address partly because it is so much a part of the family's values, attitudes, and heritage, following families down through generation after generation until someone is able to interrupt the pattern. Depression and antisocial behavior often go along with neglect, and these sap the energy needed to change. Neglectful families are also difficult to engage in treatment. What was good enough for Mom and Dad is certainly okay with them.

The goals for a neglectful family are to begin to meet their children's needs while offering an adequate environment that provides some structure, consistency, and stimulation. This is not an easy task, however. Neglectful families practice concrete thinking, and because the goal is not that concrete, treatment requires a great deal of step-by-step training. One of the old adages in protective work with neglectful families was "Parent the parents so that they can parent their children." So deprived are most neglecting parents that their primary concern is meeting their own needs rather than their children's. It falls to those who intervene with neglectful families to discern exactly where the parents' deficits lie and try to compensate for them. At the same time, these parents need to be nurtured. By engaging the parent through meeting some of his or her needs, the helper can strengthen that parent's ability to care for the child.

Neglectful parents have many needs that CPS alone cannot address. Many of these individuals have never felt accepted or loved, and the experience of feeling rejected hampers their ability to use CPS services. The church's expertise is in projecting love and acceptance. Church members are in an excellent position to extend the hand of friendship, model effective parenting, and help neglectful parents to believe that the world is not an unfriendly place.

Sometimes CPS will refer a neglectful family to an agency that provides intensive family-centered services (IFCS). The IFCS worker assigned to a family takes over the case management and attempts to involve the family in a combination of intensive services over a short period of time. Such services might include values clarification, parenting training, problem-solving training, and such concrete services as medical care, transportation, employment training, and day care. Intensive family-centered services may also make use of community supports, one of which might be the family's church. The hope of such services is to bring about effective parenting by barraging the parents with services and support. For many families, this works well.

Not every family is capable of improving behavior just by support. Some neglectful families resist treatment with such ferocity that CPS finds it necessary to use alternative methods. Such a family is protecting its dysfunctional balance, and sometimes the only way to compel change is to throw the family into disequilibrium. This may be done by filing a court petition on behalf of the children or even removing the children for their own protection, which may be enough for families who are motivated to cooperate with the efforts of the helping agency.

When a family loses its children or is taken to court on behalf of their children, the reaction of by-standers is sometimes to assume that this is one more instance of the "child-snatchers" taking away children. For many reasons, placement of children is the very last resort. First, separation, no matter how dysfunctional the family appears to be, is detrimental to children, robbing them of their security and safety and profoundly affecting them emotionally. It is only necessary when remaining in the home is *more* detrimental to them. Second, there are not always an abundance of foster homes available to take children. In order to remove children from their own families, CPS must ensure that they have something better, at least temporarily, to offer them.

The removal of children does not motivate all families to positive action. There are some cultural implications to using this model. Some cultures, like Native American and African American, protest by withdrawal and silence. As a result, when their children are placed in foster care, these parents may not contact the agency and may resist CPS's attempt to reach them to discuss the situation. The family is protesting what they perceive as an injustice, while the social worker unfamiliar with their cultural values may assume that these parents do not care. In such a situation, the culturally aware pastor might well be in a position to advocate for the family.

Although disequilibrium techniques are sometimes used, CPS would certainly prefer that the children remain at home while the social worker tries to strengthen the parents' ability to parent. The pastor and church members can be invaluable in providing support while these services are rendered to the neglectful family. Some families surprise us in what they are able to accomplish with such help.

> *Leda was the single mother of four children. She became involved with CPS when she was forced to call 911 when one of her children stopped breathing. He was rushed to the hospital, where it was determined that he was malnourished. The hospital reported the case to the attention of CPS. The investigating CPS social worker found that Leda's home was filthy, and there was little food in the house. CPS opened the case and attempted to help this young woman to become the parent that she had never had.*
>
> *"I got so depressed about the whole thing, having these people come into my home and all," explained Leda, "that I walked into a church down the street to see if I could figure out why the Lord was*

*doin' this to me. I met the preacher and he started talkin' to me. He told me that God wasn't against me like I figured he was, and right there he told me that we should pray and talk to God. So we did. I felt like someone finally heard how tough it was to be me with the kids and no man and all. I started goin' down there every chance I got."*

The alliance that Leda found with that church in her neighborhood helped her to comply with CPS's requests and turn her life around. She cleaned up her house, got a job while the children were in daycare and school, and worked with a local parent support agency to learn how to be a better parent. The pastor and his congregation gave her support and encouragement as she undertook what were, for her, monumental steps. Later observing the work that Leda had done with the support of the church, the pastor commented with a chuckle, "And it all began with a prayer!"

The enormous needs of neglectful parents result in the people working with them expending a great deal of energy. For this reason, a pastor and congregation must know what they are able to do and what they cannot do. Advocacy, support, help with child care, or whatever else is offered must not fall to just one or two people, as the task will soon be overwhelming. Remember too that neglectful families have most likely experienced one rejection after another. To begin helping them without some time frame and definite boundaries is to invite one more instance when they will exhaust the helper, who retreats leaving the family feeling abandoned once again. Clear boundaries and a timeframe at the outset actually provide some therapeutic work for families who need structure in their lives. Helping neglectful families can be a tall order, but reaching out to such families is in the very nature of what we are taught to do in the name of God's love and grace.

### *Treating Physically Abusive Families*

The major goal for physically abusive families is to stop hurting their children. But battering is a very small, albeit a destructive symptom of a much larger set of problems. Parents who abuse children do not feel good about themselves; thus, another goal might be to improve the parents' own self-concept. These parents may also have learned that the only way to get their needs met was through violence. They may not know how to problem solve or cope with stress. Many feel isolated. All of these issues need to be addressed if they are to interrupt their abusive behavior.

Although it is clear that neglect affects the whole family system, this may not be as obvious when one child in a family is physically abused. Although a family may target one child for abuse, it is a family system issue profoundly affecting the other children as well. It may only be one parent who is the batterer, but the other parent is involved either by his or her lack of action to prevent the abuse, or by complicity. Some parents actually perform the battering that the other parent would like to do (either consciously or unconsciously). The pattern is a complex one, and the treatment must address the entire family.

Abusive families too may be candidates for the intensive family-centered services mentioned above. However, funds are not always available to include every family, and the particular area in which the family resides may not offer IFCS. If the family is not eligible or able to receive intensive services, CPS will strive to improve the functioning of the parents in three specific areas: parenting, self-esteem/coping, and any other areas of pathology (e.g., substance abuse, mental illness, etc.). The social worker will strive to match the family members with services that meet their needs.

In addressing parenting, many abusive parents have never had positive models themselves and have little knowledge about what it takes to be an effective parent. Parenting skills programs or parent aids might be an appropriate resource for them. They may also need to learn about child development to normalize for them some of the behaviors their children are exhibiting. For example, a two-year-old child who constantly says "no" may infuriate the parent who is trying to gain his compliance. But if the parent learns that this is age-appropriate behavior and is schooled in ways to handle it, the outcome of their interactions will be much more positive for both parent and child.

Abusive parents may not know that there are methods to discipline other than hitting. They may have to be taught to communicate their wishes more effectively to the child and then explore other methods of discipline. Parents from some cultures, frequently those who have immigrated, use corporal punishment as a form of discipline. In these cases, CPS workers will endeavor to explain what is acceptable in the new country.

Abusive families may need as much nurturing as their children. Many of these parents do not know how to make their needs known, and have gone through life feeling rejected because others did not know their needs. Their frustration is often turned inward or on their children. At the same time that CPS helps these parents find treatment programs, those in the community, like church members, can provide valuable support and encouragement. Isolation is a major issue for abusive parents. Being drawn out of this isolation by concerned people and encouraged to become involved in a variety of activities helps these parents to change.

### *Treatment for Families, Victims, and Sexual Abusers*

CPS tries to find services for sexually abusive families similar to those for families who are physically abusive or neglectful. The issues of poor self-esteem and poor parenting may be similar for these parents as well. In addition, sexually abusive families need to establish appropriate generational boundaries between children and parents. The goals for these families are that the sexual abuse stop and the family learn new ways of functioning that include adequate communication and the realignment of family roles.

When sexually abusive families initially come to the attention of CPS, they tend to deny any abuse vehemently. Because sexual abuse is usually much less obvious than physical abuse, the denial often seems credible. CPS tries to help the family give up their denial and recognize the sexual abuse that has occurred. This step is much easier if those around them do not collude in the family's secret. Once the fact is established that the abuse has occurred, the pastor must be comfortable in discussing sexual matters with the family if the issue arises.

Once the family agrees that sexual abuse has occurred, there often follows a period of blaming. The offender may say, "If my wife hadn't gone to work, I wouldn't have turned to my daughter!" The mother may blame her daughter for being too seductive. The daughter may blame her mother for working at night and so on, in a cycle that is not at all productive. It is important not to fall into this blaming with the family. The abuse is the offender's responsibility, but everyone may have had some contribution to the family dysfunction.

After accepting the fact of the abuse and that the problem lies within the fabric of the family structure, some families are then able to pick up the pieces of their lives and begin to structure them differently. Members must look at how they function as a family, determine what there is that is worth saving, and how this can be accomplished. Each family member will have specific tasks that he or she must accomplish. For example, the mother in an incestuous family needs to take back her authority, the abusive father needs to seek his own offender-specific treatment, and the children need to learn that they cannot take the parents' roles. The entire family will need a great deal of support. For some families this task of change is too great, and CPS may be forced to seek placement for the children.

Of all the family members, the child victims of sexual abuse often do not receive treatment. Instead the focus is often on treating the offender and helping the nonabusive parent to be available emotionally for the children. Yet children also need treatment and may require a concerned advocate—perhaps the pastor—to suggest that they receive some type of counseling.

Offenders often receive treatment outside the family unit initially. They may also be incarcerated. The latter, although it may seem to have some advantages, may put an extra level of stigma and stress on the remaining family members. Some offenders are refused contact with their victims while others are allowed supervised visits. Helping to supervise visits is one task that a church community may usefully take on. Search out agencies that will train you to effectively supervise visits between abusive parents and their children.

### *Treatment in Domestic Violence Situations*

Families where there is domestic violence have many of the same needs as the abusive and neglectful families mentioned above. In domestic violence situations, treatment often does not begin until a woman flees with her children to a shelter or until someone in the family is seriously harmed. CPS might also be notified by those who observe or suspect that children are witnessing the abuse. Treatment may be initiated either through an agency geared to handle domestic violence situations or through CPS. Eventually, many cases where children are present do come to the attention of CPS, no matter how the report was initiated.

Today, most CPS workers who are trained in domestic violence recognize that they must strengthen the mother's coping and protective abilities and support her as she begins the arduous process of rebuilding her and her children's lives free from abuse. Not every woman is ready to do this immediately. In her excellent book *When Dad Hurts Mom: Helping Your Children Heal the Wounds of Witnessing Abuse*, Lundy Bancroft suggests to battered mothers that they should expect from social workers the following:

- That they join with the mother as a team
- That they give her the time she needs, not bullying her to press charges or leave the abuser
- That they are trained in and recognize the impact of domestic violence on families
- That they assess the severity of the effects that the abuse has had on the mother and children

- That they are aware of and assess the efforts that the mother has made to protect her children
- That they take into account the impact that the battering has had on the mother's parenting
- That they keep mothers and children together as much as possible
- That they provide resources to protect the mother and help her to protect her children
- That they place focus on the man as the abuser[1]

In domestic violence situations, family members are often separated for treatment. The abuser undergoes a program that teaches him how to handle his anger effectively, which can be a long and difficult road for many offenders. He will need a great deal of support in addition to his therapy, perhaps as much as if not more than his family. It is easy to have empathy toward the abused and little for the abuser, yet feeling accepted and cared about is essential for his successful treatment. It may fall to you as the pastor to help the congregation to recognize that this man too is in need of God's grace through their love.

In the meantime, the abused mother and her children are attempting to cope with living without the abuser and to heal from the years of abuse. There may be a myriad of logistical issues, like securing and furnishing housing, tasks with which churches are well equipped to help. One church hosted a "shower" for a battered mother and her children who were embarking on a new life. Those who attended brought items specified on a previously compiled list of the family's needs.

Children of violent households are especially in need of understanding. They may have developed survival techniques that do not serve them well outside the fight for survival that typified their home life. They may have used lies to cover up what was occurring at home, have acted out aggressively by mirroring what they saw, have isolated themselves or have become overly attached or aggressive to one parent or the other, usually the victim. It is important for the people in these children's lives to understand that they need compassion and guidance as well as safety and structure.

Some families are reunited after the offender receives treatment. The hope is that this is not done prematurely, allowing the battering to begin again. When reunification is a reality, it is important to accept the entire family and help them to avoid the isolation that might have covered the abuse in the past.

## Interface with the Social Service System

Although CPS may provide treatment for families, the most effective healing comes through a united effort of both formal and informal helping systems. Pastors and church members are in an excellent position to provide informal assistance while still working as a team with CPS. Some CPS workers may be initially weary of community intervention, even though they know that they themselves cannot provide all that families need. It might be helpful to set up a meeting with CPS and the family to discuss what the church can do to help. Such modeling can present to the family a picture of how respect, communication, and cooperation can accomplish a great deal.

## Counseling Families and Victims: Who Does It?

Counseling abuse victims, families, and offenders requires specialized training, without which the counselor can do the client a grave injustice. It is recommended that abuse issues be referred to specialized counselors.

Pastors and counselees sometimes express the concern that the individuals or families need a spiritual component to their therapy. Some argue that many social workers, psychologists, and psychiatrists fail to address the spiritual needs of the individual. However, in the last few years, there has been a recognition of the importance of treating the *whole* person—mind, body, *and spirit*. Some secular therapists have chosen to address this by enhancing their own training, while others have joined together with clergy to provide the client with the best of both worlds.

In their book *Shared Grace: Therapists and Clergy Working Together*, authors Marion Bilich, Susan Bonfiglio, and Steven Carlson discuss the collaboration that they worked out to address both the psychological and spiritual needs of a woman who had suffered severe child abuse. Jewish psychologist Marion Bilich enlisted the help of Christian minister Stephen Carlson in the treatment of Teresa, a survivor suffering from multiple personality disorder as a result of her abuse. Carlson and his senior pastor brought in a support group of church members including Susan Bonfiglio, a social worker who works with mental health patients. Together, the three professionals crafted a sensitive and creative treatment program that did much to meet the needs of Teresa. The book is well worth reading as a model of collaboration.[2]

An effective proactive policy is to discover the therapists in your area to whom you could refer parishioners with abuse issues, noting those who are willing to work with you and your church members as part of the healing. Lists of therapists may be available at your local CPS agency. Finding out which ones are interested in working with the "whole person" — body, mind, *and spirit* — may require a bit of work on your part but would be well worth it.

## Case Closing

In order for CPS to close a case, the worker will want to see positive outcomes. In addition to no longer abusing the child, the parent should be taking responsibility for past abuse or neglect while responding to the child, appropriately disciplining, and generally enjoying child care responsibilities. In addition, the parent is expected to be cooperating with the agency, have developed a healthier support system, feel better about himself or herself, and be interested in self-growth.

Not all cases are closed because these goals are reached. Sometimes families are not able to improve their child-rearing abilities or to refrain from abuse, and removing the children is the consequence. Funding also impacts the ability of CPS to provide services. When resources are not available to help families, CPS may be forced to close the case, unless the CPS worker feels that the child is in immediate danger of further abuse. Increasingly states are also developing criteria that impose time limits upon the amount of time that a case can be open. When that time limit is reached, CPS must make a decision about the safety of the children and close the case. If the children are deemed safe in the home, the home is left intact. If the children appear to be in danger of further abuse or neglect, the CPS worker will probably initiate proceedings to remove the children from the home.

Even after CPS officially closes a case, a family may be in need of support. This can often be done informally through community groups like the church.

*The Cortez family had immigrated several months before they joined the church. Once they joined, Maria and Juan Cortez and their four children attended regularly. After the service one Sunday, Maria, who was still struggling with her English, tried to explain to Father Paul that someone had come to their home and she felt that they were threatening to take her children away from her. After asking Maria's permission to engage the help of a Spanish-speaking church member, Father Paul was able to determine that CPS has been called when one of the Cortez children came to school with bruises inflicted upon her by her father.*

*"It is as it was in my country," the interpreter translated. "My daughter was not respecting her father's authority and must be punished."*

*Father Paul secured permission from Maria to go with her when she met the CPS worker again. He also suggested that Maria request an interpreter or ask that she might bring her own, as the Spanish-speaking church member was more than willing to help.*

*The meeting with CPS went well, and Father Paul discovered that the worker was willing to work with this mother to help her with the family's transition to a culture that did not allow the same disciplinary practices that Maria's native country had. The family also enlisted the support of the church member who had acted as interpreter. Although CPS did have interpreters available, Maria felt more comfortable with her friend, and CPS agreed to the arrangement.*

*After involvement with CPS for eight months, the social worker, recognizing the family's sincere love of their children and desire to fit into their new culture, closed the case. During the time that CPS had been seeing the Cortez family, Maria had enrolled in ESL (English as a second language) classes and had taken parenting classes that were offered through the YMCA. Juan agreed to go to a group at the local neighborhood center that specializes in working with Hispanic men who have newly immigrated. In addition, the church formed a Care Group to help the Cortez family with a variety of needs. The greatest benefit of this group, however, was to support Maria and help her to understand what was expected of her in this culture.*

*After CPS closed the case, the Care Group continued to function. By this time it had become more informal, and several of the members had become close to Maria. Today, Maria would say that she has no idea what she would have done without her church friends at that difficult time in her life.*

The pastor and the church might take many roles in the lives of families deemed abusive and neglectful. In the next chapter, we discuss in more detail how congregations, too, can be involved in helping families who often believe that no one cares.

## Issues for Clergy

As a clergy member helping an abusive or neglectful family, you will face some conflicts and frustrations. Being aware of them will help you to address them effectively. The following are some of the most frequent issues that you might encounter.

### *The Desire to Save the Family*

We would not be in helping professions if we did not have the desire to help people, yet not everyone is interested in or able to use our ministrations. Some families would prefer to keep their dirty laundry at home and resist even the best-intentioned efforts to reach out to them. "Leave us alone, Father," one young mother told her priest. "I'd rather not have God see my bad side." Because you represent God, in the eyes of many people, some parents feel exposed by having your involvement.

Conversely, other families will come to you for some type of miraculous divine intervention. You cannot change whatever has happened, nor can you banish CPS from their lives. The task of change will be up to them. You can only work with them in the future and, through prayer, resources, and hope, help them to change. As one mother put it, "My pastor let me know that she could not perform miracles, but that she would pray with me and help me to find the help that I needed to become a better person . . . someone that could stand proudly in God's presence."

With some families you wish that you could make the hurt go away and feel powerless to do so. Yet families need to learn to cope with their own hard times and make the changes that are necessary by themselves. Support and empowerment can help, but you cannot save them from doing the work that they need to do.

One of the most frustrating things that I found in working with dysfunctional families was the difficulty that many of them had in changing. Some were never able to change. Time and again, I would watch people miss appointments, get drunk again, or hook up with an abusive partner, and I wanted to cry out in frustration and anger. But we all fashion our own lives by the choices that we make. When family members make one poor choice after another, all we can do is help them to pick themselves up and start over.

When we try to "save" families, we forget that they learn little when they do not take the baby steps themselves. The old adage that "you can give a man a fish and he will eat for a day, while if you teach him to fish, he will have fish for a lifetime" is so appropriate here. It is important to find the right mix of support and empowerment as we work with abusive and neglectful families. If we can help them to feel empowered, then they will have the impetus to change. To do things *for* them is only to replicate what is often a long pattern of neediness and taking.

Not only can we not save the family from themselves, but we cannot save them from involvement in the system. No matter what some people believe, the CPS system is designed to *help* families. Social workers choose their work because they want to see families and children enjoy better lives. Being a CPS worker with all its setbacks and frustrations is one of the toughest jobs that I know. These workers have an investment in doing what seems best for children and their families. Thus, when a family becomes involved with CPS, the best course is to encourage them to cooperate and to not get in the way of CPS as they try to do their job.

It is human nature to believe that the way we go about things is the best. When we, as seasoned pastors perhaps, watch young and seemingly inexperienced social workers bring anxiety to the family with whom we may have a personal relationship, it is sometimes difficult not to want to intervene. But many dysfunctional families actually protect their dysfunction by pitting helpers against one another. It might be better to stand back, observe the situation, and offer your assistance to CPS rather than siding with the family that believes that CPS is a threat to themselves and their children. By working with the system instead of helping the family to resist it and by modeling communication with another professional, you might well be teaching the family a valuable lesson.

### *Countertransference Issues*

Countertransference refers to the helper's reactions to the client/counselee (feelings, thoughts, behaviors, and attitudes) that are based on the helper's own life experiences. For example, let us say that a helper has an abusive father who blustered and battered him or her, terrifying the helper as a child. Now, as an adult this same helper is faced with a client/counselee or parishioner who is blustery. The helper begins to feel small and helpless, aware that he or she is perspiring, that the whole body seems geared up for fight or flight. This individual before the helper, who may never have laid a hand on anyone, brings up the reactions that the helper once had to his or her abusive father. These reactions could become problematic to the relationship between the helper and this current individual unless they are recognized, processed, and checked.

Countertransference is common among clinicians, but they have also been trained to recognize and deal with it, often through supervision, so that it does not impede their work. Clergy, too, may grapple with such reactions, but are not necessarily trained to recognize or interrupt them. Dysfunctional family members bring up all the ghosts of our pasts, and we must face them in order to be of maximum help.

Sometimes the depth at which emotional material can be buried necessitates that someone else — possibly a professional therapist — help us to recognize the strange feelings that are invading us in the face of particular people in our current lives. At other times, it is enough to acknowledge that an individual makes you feel uncomfortable and try to determine the exact symptoms you are feeling. Then imagine, "Who does this person remind me of?" This may be enough to bring the memory to the surface. "Ah, yes, he reminds me of Uncle Joe, who was always at our house and who traumatized me when I was a child." Once you remember, try to figure out all the differences between Uncle Joe and the person with whom you are interacting today.

Clergy too may have been abused when they were children. Interactions with abusers and families as well as victims may well bring this material to the surface. This is the time to seek help in resolving any issues with which you may be encumbered as the result of the abuse.

### *Setting Personal Boundaries and Burnout*

One of the valuable lessons that you can teach needy families is how to set boundaries. Unless you set your own, you will burn out quickly. Not only is it problematic if you begin to feel overwhelmed by the family's need for attention, but your tendency then will be to pull back or remove yourself from such a situation. When you abruptly cease to give them the attention that you had been giving, it reconfirms for them that everyone will abandon and reject them . . . even a servant of God. How then can God be there for them?

The most caring way to support a maltreating family is to set your boundaries early and empower them to do their work themselves. This may require guidance, but not doing it for them. For example, one neglectful mother complained to a pastor that CPS was threatening to remove her children if she did not clean her house. The pastor did not stop to think that there might be more to it than just a dirty house. So she and a group of church women went into the home and cleaned it up for the mother. The pastor was quite disturbed when several months later the children were removed from the home. When the concerned cleric went to visit the distraught mother, she discovered a house that was worse than it had been before the church women cleaned it. The pastor came away feeling disillusioned and somehow betrayed.

It might have been better to recognize that a dirty house was not the mother's only problem, but just a small part of what needed to be changed in her life. The pastor might have asked to be present when CPS visited or talked with the CPS worker about how the church might help. Together CPS and the pastor might have empowered this mother to make a difference in her own life.

In working with abusive and neglectful families, we must know our own limits. This too is essential modeling for those who have never learned to set their own boundaries. In addition to limits on your time and what you can do for them, consider limits or boundaries on space. There are places that are our own and that must be respected.

There should be places that we can call our own. Perhaps a church office or a parsonage study may be used to see people, but a closed door should be a message that no one is invited in without at least a knock and an invitation. People who have never encountered such limits may have to be taught with care.

Some clergy prefer to be contacted at the office and not called at home unless in an emergency. But some people think nothing of showing up on the doorstep at all hours of the day or night. Even in the community, limits may have to be set. One pastor recounts the story of taking his family to the movies. Well into the film, a parishioner sat next to him and proceeded to tell him in loud but conversational whispers about her husband's latest drinking bout, how he abused her and that the police had to be called. It had been a week before and recounting it then constituted no emergency. The pastor was forced to leave his family and the movie just to explain that this was not an appropriate place for the interchange. He suggested that he meet the woman in his office the next day.

Helping abusive and neglectful families cope with their lives and with the intervention of the social service system can be a challenge both personally and professionally. However, with well-thought-out parameters, this work can be a rewarding piece of extending God's grace to others.

# Chapter 8

# Helping the Congregation Be a Supportive "Family"

> *I first heard through the church grapevine that Leanne Kirby was being abused by her stepfather. Some people confessed that they were trying not to repeat the story, ostensibly to protect all involved, but I soon learned that Burt Kirby's arrest had made the papers. I suspected that the church members' well-intentioned attempts at secrecy would make Leanne and her family members feel even more isolated and alone. Ours was a strong congregation, and I decided that, given the appropriate information and proper training or guidance, the members could become an integral part of the healing for the entire family.*

As a result of some wise handling by this minister, a situation that could have become a chain of gossip was instead transformed by a congregation becoming a supportive faith family.

## The Makings of a Healthy Christian Family

As Christians, we hope to share and practice the message that Christ taught us, that of love for one another and our God. While the pastor's role is to minister in God's name, members of the congregation are as much a part of this ministry as their spiritual leader. In a world that often rejects, stigmatizes, victimizes, and misunderstands, the church community's environment of mutual responsibility and sharing becomes a refuge for those in need.

"But I have no training," your parishioners might say. What training does one need to show compassion? Our training lies more in our faith than in any psychological principles. It is rewarding for a pastor to see his or her congregation minister to one another. This may require guidance on your part, however. The pastor can play a part in helping congregants to prepare to reach out by helping them to value and fine-tune these qualities in themselves. In particular, members may need help in developing "sacred silence"[1] or confidentiality. Families touched by abuse have the right to have their confidences respected and kept confidential. This is not always easy for the beginning helper. And there are also instances when confidences cannot be kept when someone reports wanting to hurt himself or herself, wanting to harm someone else, or when he or she is abusing a child. Congregants offering to help a family in crisis must learn when confidentiality is essential and when it cannot be kept.

## Creating a Congregation That Heals

For healing to begin, families affected by abuse and violence also need restorative relationships that foster trust, are consistent, and promote optimism. Churches must be able to provide healing environments that foster these relationships. This necessitates the church being healthy.

A healthy congregation is one that provides a safe and emotionally and spiritually satisfying environment for its parishioners as well as its pastor. Such a congregation is aware of its own mission, is able to handle anxiety and conflict, welcomes new members, respects one another's boundaries, provides open communication, and still looks to the future. This congregation values its history and welcomes growth in individual members and the congregation as a whole. In such a community, it would be unlikely for abuse by the pastor to occur, and families where there is abuse or neglect would be addressed in a caring, responsible manner.

A congregation is a delicately balanced group of subsystems. The unique interrelationships, values, and attitudes, and a variety of other factors, create the whole system. A change in just one of those variables can unbalance the system and create a change in the outward "personality" of that congregation—not only for ill but also for good.

To become a healing congregation, let us recognize that our strength and ability to heal come from God through Christ. The community that works to put God and Christ at the center of its mission is the group that will find success. Members will regard one another as made in God's image and thus worthy of love, grace, and respect. When congregants are respectful of one another, then they are ready to minister to families.

Another factor in creating a healthy and supportive congregation is found in its leadership. As a pastor it will be important for you to arm yourself with the skills that enable you to guide your congregation in working with maltreating families.

As part of my work in training social workers to treat sexually abusive families, I discovered five factors that made one worker successful while another was not. The first two — comfort in discussing sexuality and comfort with one's own sexuality — are only helpful as the pastor is engaged in addressing issues of sexual abuse. Integral for the maintenance of a healthy congregational atmosphere are three further factors: comfort with differentiation, a sense of your own autonomy, and comfort with your own vulnerability.

*Differentiation* is a term that family therapist Murray Bowen offered to describe an individual's ability to forge a healthy, independent relationship from the family that raised him or her. Friedman further defines this term in Bowenian terms by explaining that differentiation means "the capacity of a family member to define his or her own life's goals and values apart from surrounding togetherness pressures, to say 'I' when others are demanding 'you' and 'we.' It includes the capacity to maintain a (relatively) non-anxious presence in the midst of anxious systems, to take maximum responsibility for one's own destiny and emotional being. It can be measured somewhat by the breadth of responses when one is confronted with crisis."[2]

Differentiation from one's own family system allows the pastor to maintain the slight distance he or she needs in parish work. When conflicts occur within a congregation, this trait enables the pastor to step back, observe the dynamics of the situation, and empower the congregation to do its work in resolving them. The differentiated pastor is also one who does not take unrest personally. By the same token she or he can look at her or his own behaviors and assess whether these are in any way contributing to the problems at hand. Although the pastor remains an integral part of the system, he or she can, when needed, become the pivotal gear that, by knowing how to adjust slightly, enables the system to again find homeostasis.

A well-differentiated pastor creates a congregation that is also well differentiated — that is, a community where individuals can work together but are less dependent upon one another to function. Yet there still remains a healthy connectedness within the group. When anxiety does arise in a congregant, others are not contaminated by it and are more able to help the individual cope or problem solve. Church members have learned to take responsibility for their own actions, without impinging on the welfare of others. The congregational atmosphere is one that fosters mature, responsible, and caring adults who are also capable of nurturing and protecting their children.

*Autonomy,* and the ability to exercise it, is very similar to differentiation. By recognizing his or her own need for autonomy, the pastor is able to step out of the system and act in a manner that the system might not like.

Exercising autonomy in certain situations is not a popular decision, but one that might have to be made for the good of all involved. At the same time, it gives permission to church members to assess situations in more depth, and when necessary not to be afraid to exercise their own autonomy.

In addition, the pastor must recognize her or his own *vulnerability.* We all make mistakes. One pastor related an incident that happened when he was conducting a Bible study with a group of teens. This particular day the only ones in attendance were five girls from fourteen to sixteen. His co-leader was also ill, and the group was meeting in his office with his secretary in the next room. The biblical discussion was on Genesis and specifically the children of Jacob. When Genesis 34:1 was read, a recounting of the rape of Jacob's daughter Dinah, one of the girls began talking about how she had been raped by a peer. Three of the other girls then disclosed that they had also been victims of date rape, recounting in some detail what they had experienced. It seemed clear that all of the incidents had been addressed at the time, so there was no reason for the pastor to feel a need to report these incidents to anyone. Nonetheless, he was uncomfortable with the discussion. Mindful of his secretary in the next room, who might hear bits and pieces of the discussion, the pastor became concerned that she might wonder what this male pastor could possibly be discussing with these young girls. As a result, he was anxious to get them off the subject. He abruptly suggested that they go on in their reading and was met with silence. Most of the girls looked down at their Bibles, but no one volunteered to read. After several minutes, he saw by the clock that the time for their study had elapsed, and he dismissed the girls.

Upset by the girls' frank discussions of their rapes, the pastor mentioned the incident to his wife that evening, expecting her sympathetic response to what seemed to him as having been a difficult position for him to be in. Instead, she said, "How could you do that to those girls! They were talking about something that was probably very difficult for them, and you cut them off!" At first he felt defensive, but after continuing to discuss it, he had to recognize that his spouse was right. In his concern over his reaction to a topic that gave *him* discomfort, he had neglected an opportunity that might have been healing for these young girls. But what should he do about it? He had several options. He could forget the incident and go on with the Bible study group as before, he could tell his co-leader and perhaps have her talk to the girls, or he could openly admit that he had made a mistake and see where that took them.

By the next meeting, the pastor's co-leader had returned. Before the meeting, the pastor filled her in on what had transpired at the last meeting and shared with her his plans for this one. He began the meeting by saying that he owed the girls an apology. He suggested that what they had discussed about teens raping other teens was a topic that he did not like to consider, although he knew that it was an important one. He also thanked the girls for sharing with him and suggested that they help him to understand their feelings. The meeting became a meaningful one for all involved. Not only were the girls able to discuss a topic that was obviously one with which they were still dealing, but the pastor had modeled an adult in authority who was able to confront his own vulnerability, deal with it, and share this struggle with them. It was an important lesson for all, and it sent a message that we are all vulnerable and only by facing that quality in ourselves can we hope to learn or grow.

The effective leader is one who is not caught up in the power of his or her position. Recognizing that her or his "power" comes through Christ and the Holy Spirit through ordination, this must be a leader who is ready to share that power for the good of the congregation. Differentiation, the acceptance of autonomy, and the recognition of vulnerability speak of an individual who possesses a power that comes from within — a God-given gift that is meant to promote growth and a deepening of faith. That power comes *through* the pastor so that the congregation can be helped to grow.

An effective leader then fosters a congregation that works well together and can heal others. Healthy congregations foster communication and share control. In Romans 12:4–5, Paul describes the church as analogous to parts in the Body of Christ. We know that one part — one member — is usually not able to function effectively without the help of another. Communication within congregations cannot be overly emphasized as it is lack of it that allows abuse to flourish.

There are two keys to sharing control and promoting communication. The first of these is to recognize and identify the gifts of congregants, and the second to promote an "other-directed" style of being in community.

When control is centralized in one person or one group, it is usually assumed that these individuals have the authority or the skills to warrant this endowment of power. Authority in congregational communities is most effective when some aspects of it are shared with the congregation. How and what to share may well be decided after looking at the gifts that are present within the community. Everyone has God-given gifts, some of which have not been discovered or recognized.

Much has been written about gifts within congregations, how to recognize them and how to equip laity to do God's essential work. Congregants may have a variety of gifts that enable them to help families in trouble.

Through tapping into the skills that are present within the congregation, a pastor not only lessens his or her own load but also complements the skills that he or she brings to the church. Congregants feel more appreciated and more committed to the church, and recognize that they can return some of the grace that was given to them through ministering to others. For some members, recognition of their own ability to contribute to the church community deepens their faith.

Understanding some of the dynamics of a healing congregation, let us consider how to minister to various types of families and abusers.

## Congregational Ministry to Families

Ministering to abusive and neglectful families necessitates that we first recognize their pain. Can you imagine the pain that a young person feels when he or she does not feel loved, appreciated, or protected from harm? And what if the harm comes at the hands of one's parents? Might you not feel shame, guilt, and anger? Through trying to understand these individuals on a deeper psychic level, congregants can be helped to reach out more effectively.

What are some ways that you might help the congregation to gain this insight? One way might be to invite a speaker who has either experienced abuse as a child or who was abusive. Groups like Parents Helping Parents (or Parents Anonymous) might offer some insight or suggest speakers. Alcoholics Anonymous might also have speakers who are parents recovering from substance abuse who might talk about their struggles. The congregation could be asked to read a book by or about a survivor or parent. Any bookstore will feature a collection of such books (also see Appendix 2 for suggested reading). Alternatively you could study the dynamics of abuse and neglect using a resource such as the author's *Understanding Child Abuse and Neglect.*

Experience provides another teaching moment. Everyone has experienced something painful. Even if we do not fully understand abuse and neglect, we can recognize what we needed or wanted when we were in pain. Helping church members tap into their own pain may help them to understand the needs of families involved with maltreatment. Once one begins to understand pain, it is important to look at what that pain does to individuals — how they might react when they are hurt. When a family member cannot respond appropriately, the church members can understand the origin of this response.

### *Families Where There Is Domestic Violence*

*Loretta and Bob Cooper were regular members of the church community. Bob could sometimes be somewhat opinionated and controlling, and was well known as someone who should not be nominated to any committees unless the members were prepared for a great deal of dispute. But beyond this, he was fairly well liked within the community. Loretta tended to her three children (ages five, seven, and nine) and was more retiring, yet she too could be argumentative. She had few friends in the church and rarely took part in church groups, other than attending church suppers with her husband. Both attended Sunday services, bringing the children to Sunday school at the same time. Then Bob was transferred to the third shift at his job, and Loretta was forced to bring the children alone. One particular morning, she arrived with a black eye. When fellow parishioners expressed concern, she assured them that she had fallen and it was nothing. The next Sunday, the children came to church alone, saying that their mother was sick. It was five-year-old Annie who disclosed the truth. During a Sunday school lesson she fell asleep and, when awakened, told her teacher that she had had little sleep the night before. She further explained that she was worried about Mommy, who screamed and cried most of the night until Daddy stormed out of the house. The teacher, a young woman with limited experience, sought out the counsel of an older teacher who was also an aid at the local elementary school. The senior teacher admitted that the children had spoken of such things in the past and that she had seen other bruises on Loretta. She also knew that Bob was extremely jealous of his wife's time, and seemed to control almost every aspect of her life. The young teacher suggested that the minister should be told. Concerned, the minister decided to make a pastoral call after church. Here he discovered a badly beaten Loretta being ministered to by her frightened children, while Bob slept off a night of drunken rage, during which he had beaten his wife while the children looked on in terrified silence.*

The fear, confusion, and anger felt by the Cooper children mentioned above certainly manifested in their lives in the church community. Nine-year-old Robbie Cooper had come to the attention of the Sunday school superintendent numerous times after he punched or hit another child. Once it became obvious that Robbie's pugnacious behavior was a mirror of what he had seen at home, the explanation for the behavior became clear. Seven-year-old Gary and five-year-old Annie were quieter children who were handling their upset through withdrawal.

In situations like the Coopers', the church school staff can often meet together to devise a plan. Anyone in contact with the children should be given some idea of what to expect when children witness violence (see the chart on p. 44). Workshops for Sunday school staff or for the whole congregation might be set up to educate them about the effects of domestic violence on children. If this is a churchwide educational plan, it should probably occur before the fact rather than after a family has been identified within the community. Or the church may sponsor a community-wide educational session and enlist the support of the local battered women's center or CPS agency as speakers.

In the Coopers' church, the young teacher who had originally listened to Annie's report of her family's violence took it upon herself to volunteer at the local battered women's agency. She learned as much as she could about the effects of violence on children and brought this information back to the pastor. Together they helped the church school to structure church and Sunday school activities that would help any child who had witnessed violence. Classrooms were set up to ensure safety, emphasize mediation rather than conflict, and reflect the message of love that Christ taught. Biblical lessons were considered to determine the messages they gave the children. When a lesson featured a great deal of violence, it was either deleted for the time being or, more often, discussed in the light of the times and the alternatives to violent actions. Finally, a segment was added to the teen program on negotiation and the prevention of dating violence. In this way, those concerned about the Cooper children hoped to prevent future generations of parents who would subject their children to violence.

### *Providing Support for Abusive or Neglectful Families*

Families involved in abuse or neglect situations are often convinced that this very fact brands them and that no one will be interested in associating with them. Sexual abuse especially feels like a huge stigma. The most significant thing that the congregation can do is to show empathy and respect for the family members and their situation. The pastor may well be approached by one or more members for pastoral counseling or a referral. Families may also seek out their peers to talk about the abuse, complain about the treatment that they have had from CPS, or ask for advice. Parishioners must be prepared to listen when appropriate but also to set boundaries and refer to the pastor or another professional when appropriate.

## Providing Community for Returning Offenders

Sexual offenders are some of the most difficult people for congregants to consider helping. "I'd like to see him in prison and throw away the key!" is an oft expressed sentiment. But no matter what they have done, these abusers are still God's children. Who is more in need of a church community than someone who has committed an offense against a child?

It is natural for parents to have concerns about safety when an offender is part of the church community, but with some thoughtful pre-planning and an effective protocol (see Chapter 13), children's safety can be protected.

Offenders have usually been involved with some aspect of the criminal justice system, often prison, before they return to the church community. Smarto provides some concrete suggestions regarding returning offenders. He suggests that the church can play a vital role in helping such individuals readjust to life and grow spiritually. To do so the church must

- understand what the ex-offender is facing in trying to readjust to society and thus provide practical, balanced help;
- cultivate the ex-offender's sense of accountability for personal sin and guide him toward accepting responsibility for personal behaviors;
- detect and guard against ex-offenders' manipulations and game playing for the protection of both church members and the ex-offender; and
- assist the ex-offender in being an authentic disciple of Christ.[3]

Sexual offenders who have been incarcerated for their abuse have their own special needs. They may feel disoriented by the freedom of the community compared to prison life and may need structure and guidance. They may have idealized their home life and now find that it is not as problem free as they had imagined that it would be. Families rebalance without the offender and may feel resentment toward him at his return. Then the church family becomes even more important to him.

Prison for a sexual offender is a lesson in survival. In the eyes of other offenders, the lowest inmate in a prison setting is the rapist, and even below the rapist is the child molester. A child molester in prison has one of two choices; he can serve his sentence in protective custody away from the rest of the population or be subject to sodomy, beating, ridicule, and abuse by other inmates. Incarceration has taught the offender not only self-protection but also how to manipulate others to get what he needs. Now this individual is expected to return to the community, one that may not be sure what to expect of him, and is also expected to approach his new life with openness and trust.

Offenders need an opportunity to model not only their behaviors, but often their appearance. Contact with concerned church members enables them to experience how others live in this time and this community. The newly released offender is not unlike a child whose development is halted at a particular place. He may look like a fully functioning adult, but he needs opportunities for both healthy social and spiritual development.

Offenders also come to the church community with emotional damage not only from imprisonment or the effects of their crime but from dysfunctional childhood as well. What are some specific scars carried by offenders, and how might a congregation respond? Listed below are some of the most obvious issues that arise:

- issues around anger
- trust and relationship issues
- blame and responsibility
- feelings of powerlessness
- scars from childhood
- other mental health issues

Anger may stem from frustration, hurt, loss, feelings of helplessness, or a myriad of other emotions. We often express this anger in hurtful words or emotional explosions that do not serve our purpose. Offenders are no different. They have had a lifetime of the kind of experiences that would engender anger in any of us. Lenny was a good example:

*Lenny was the product of his mother's indiscretion at a party, and he was never allowed to forget it. When she later married and had other children, Lenny got used to being the one who was always left out. He hated his stepfather, and Lenny, at nine, could not hide his relief when the man deserted the family. Now, he believed that he could be the "man of the family" and win his mother's affection by helping her with his siblings. But the stepfather was quickly replaced by a succession of other men. When his mother finally remarried, it was to a quiet man who finally paid some attention to the love-starved boy. But Lenny soon found himself being required to provide sexual favors to his stepfather and his friends in exchange for money and some inclusion in their activities. People began to see a change in Lenny. He became an angry, sullen boy who was belligerent and mouthy. He had difficulty in school and skipped whenever he could.*

*Disillusioned by this turn of events, Lenny sought comfort in peers like himself. He and his cohorts, all boys as filled with anger as Lenny himself, began terrorizing the neighborhood, coming to the attention of the police. After several years in and out of detention centers, Lenny was placed in a foster home. Here he found attention and affection and managed to finish trade school. The family also went to church, and Lenny found solace in his time as an acolyte and in youth group. Just before graduation, he met Mindy, a girl whose life filled with abuse and disappointment was much like his own. Mindy already had a three-year-old daughter, Tammie, who had been born when her mother was fourteen.*

*Lenny continued to date Mindy after school and enjoyed the company of Tammie. He had found work in a garage and had hopes for a life better than his childhood had been. When Mindy told him that she was pregnant, Lenny insisted that they marry. He determined that he would give his new wife and children everything that had been denied him. But soon after the ceremony, Mindy admitted that the child was not his. Lenny felt betrayed, and his anger surfaced. He and Mindy fought constantly, often frightening Tammie with their angry words. Lenny tried to calm the little girl while Mindy spent less and less time at home. Lenny found it difficult to remember when his relationship with Tammie became one of sexual molestation. When Mindy learned of this and reported it to the police, Lenny was tried and convicted. His incarceration robbed him of all that he felt was dear to him. His anger became his worst enemy, until he was referred to an anger management program in prison. He also began to attend chapel and found some of the peace that he had had in his foster home. Fortunately, his foster mother had kept in contact and, when he was released, she invited Lenny into their church community.*

Having known Lenny when he was younger, this church community was willing to take him back and help him to reclaim his life. One of Lenny's greatest lessons was how to recognize his anger and determine whether it was based on the scars of his childhood or something more immediate. He was able to use some of the skills he had been taught in his prison anger management classes. Through the church, Lenny was also paired up with a spiritual mentor, a calm older man who was known for his ability to problem solve and find equitable solutions. Through understanding his anger and modeling, Lenny made considerable progress in getting control of his life.

If a spiritual mentor is not available, offenders may benefit from membership in groups in which negotiation is handled without anger or rancor. When offenders find themselves accepted in a community where they do not have to defend themselves, their anger may well diminish.

Offenders will also need to work on trust issues. The offender must first know that others accept him and that these ongoing relationships must be consistent. Helping someone who has difficulty trusting involves many of the same rules used in raising children. If you make a promise, keep it. If you absolutely cannot keep it for some unavoidable reason, help the child or the healing adult to understand why. Yet, like children, offenders who are learning to trust will test those in relationships with them, which can lead to misunderstandings. For example, you may have helped your parishioners understand that they must keep their promises to the offender, and then he begins to stand them up when they have set aside time to be with him. Here the congregation needs support in understanding that those lacking trust may sabotage the efforts of others to be trustworthy. At the same time, the offender must be helped to recognize his own actions and helped to accept the congregation's efforts.

Many offenders have or have had problems with authority figures. If you were raised by someone whose authority over you became abusive, for example, you may never learn what constitutes appropriate authority. Offenders frequently buck the system, challenging the authority figures in their lives. Then the criminal justice system with its issues around authority often intensifies the situation. Offenders must be helped to see the purpose of authority and feel authority in a positive way. In addition, they must be held accountable for responding to authority appropriately. As they learn to feel less powerless themselves, offenders are able to accept the healthy use of authority.

Some offenders have mental health issues that go far beyond what a congregation or even a pastor feels competent to handle. In these instances, it is important to have contacts in the wider community to make appropriate referrals. Offenders must understand that you and the congregation will be there for them, but they must take some responsibility for managing their own illness. The failure to do so leaves everyone in a difficult position. Helpful in dealing with such issues is *The Pastor's Guide to Psychological Disorders and Treatments*.[4]

## Mobilizing the Congregation to Help

How does a pastor call upon the congregation to be a helping spiritual family in situations of abuse? When church members learn of an abusive family within the church community or an offender wants to become part of the church membership, they may seek the pastor's help in responding. But it is also helpful to begin the education process even before such an event occurs. One of the most effective ways to bring abuse issues to the attention of the congregation is through sermons. McClure and Ramsay's book *Telling the Truth: Preaching about Sexual and Domestic Violence*[5] offers some excellent examples. In addition to teaching from the pulpit, clergy have found community agencies that are most interested in providing training that might be church sponsored. Beyond outside training, study groups within the church to discuss such topics as mediation, healthy relationships, and healing childhood trauma provide opportunities to raise the consciousness of the church members. There are also opportunities to talk about child safety in response to news reports about child abuse or agencies' efforts to advocate for children. Names of and contact information for agencies that might be helpful in learning more about abuse issues and incentives toward prevention are available in the Appendixes 4 and 5.

Along with opening the discussion about child abuse, develop a protocol and prevention plan in your church (see Chapter 13). These give the congregation guidelines for future behavior and confidence in their ability to respond to abuse situations in an effective manner.

Many clergy have discovered that church members are eager to provide support and caring to families and offenders if they are given guidance in how to proceed. Together the pastor and the congregation can be a powerful force in mirroring Christ's love through becoming agents of hope and healing for those in need.

# PART TWO

# Abuse by Clergy

# Chapter 9

# When the Shepherd Strays

## The Unlikely Perpetrator?

I began my life as the daughter of an Episcopal priest. It was a time when moral codes were more clearly delineated, and clergy were trusted, respected, and seen as individuals of high moral character. Most people did not imagine that such a revered person would be guilty of what we now recognize was occurring in many churches — the sexual abuse of children. I recall my parents speaking in hushed tones of a fellow clergyman who had "fallen from grace." What I could gather at the time was that someone had done "something bad" to a child, and my father and mother were shocked and deeply disturbed by it.

The abuse of children by clergy is hardly a new phenomenon, but in the past such clergy misconduct was typically handled secretively. Often the clergyperson was transferred to another parish or setting — and the abuse began again. In his *Sex, Priests and Power,* A. W. Richard Sipe traces sexual abuse back to the earliest church Councils in the year 309, when the sexual abuse of boys was specifically mentioned in the Canons.[1] Later, in the Council of Trent (1545–63), sexual behaviors were again mentioned and reform was called for. This was especially interesting as Pope Julius III, who presided over these proceedings, was known to have had a sexual relationship with a fifteen-year-old boy whom he later made a cardinal.[2]

In the late 1970s, as sexual abuse became more widely discussed, those abused by clergy began to speak out. By the 1990s the publication of Jason Berry's *Lead Us Not into Temptation*[3] and Burkett and Bruni's *Gospel of Shame,*[4] both chronicling histories of the sexual abuse of children within the Roman Catholic Church, shocked a public now alerted to the magnitude of the problem.

A new wave of clergy sexual abuse cases had emerged during the late 1980s and early 1990s. From New Orleans to Massachusetts, Chicago, New York, and even Canada, the scandal rocked the Catholic Church. And although cases in Catholic churches remained the most publicized, Protestant denominations did not escape their own sexual crises, with the most publicized of these being misconduct between clergy and their adult female congregants.

Presbyterian minister Lloyd Rediger suggests that we have learned several lessons through these scandals. We have learned that sexuality will not go away and that we must endeavor to talk about it more openly, including the importance of boundaries and limits. We have learned that clergy are human but have felt the sting of disillusionment when that humanness is manifested in sexual deviance. We have realized that, even though an offender may say that he or she is sorry and the church agrees to accept that apology, civil authorities still need to be involved. We cannot protect individuals and institutions while we sacrifice victims. Since pastoring is based on relationships, we must train clergy to recognize the difference between healthy and unhealthy relationships.[5]

That Catholic priests are the most frequently cited abusers Jenkins attributes to two main realities: First, the number of Catholic priests who are active in ministry in the United States today numbers about fifty thousand, and as a body, this number outweighs other individual denominational groups. Second, Catholic clerics are part of a hierarchical structure with a chain of supervision. At any level of this hierarchy, a cleric's secret might be covered up. In other types of polity — such as congregational, for example — there may not be this supervision above the local or regional level. In addition, records are kept of priestly activities, including complaints, at the diocesan level.[6] Critics have argued that this very system of checks and balances makes the crisis in the Catholic Church so difficult to comprehend.

## What Puts Clergy at Risk of Becoming Abusers?

The causes of the sexual abuse of children by clergy appear to originate from an interweaving of two sources: first, the current role of the pastor/priest and the stresses inherent in that role, and second, the individual's own makeup or pathology.

### *The Stresses of the Pastoral Role*

The role of pastors and priests in today's world is not what it was decades ago. Once clergy were knowledgeable about the role they were expected to play; today their function has changed somewhat, causing confusion, stress, and anxiety over the loss of traditional reference points. Now a pastor is expected to be tantamount to the CEO of an organization, but typically with no clear-cut job description. Even if there is a job description on paper, the expectations of the role go far beyond the duties listed. In the public's eyes, as well as in his or her own, the pastor is called by God to serve a community by providing spiritual leadership. Each individual and each community interprets that mandate differently, and the difference between those interpretations can cause considerable stress.

Ministry is based on relationships, and the success of the professional cleric is his or her ability to forge these "successfully." But success can be subjective. The needy parishioner who is constantly at the pastor's doorstep may have one picture of the success of a relationship while the exhausted pastor who has concluded that for his sake, as well as the parishioner's, some limits must be set, has yet another reading on success. Being constantly attentive to multiple relationships can be draining.

In addition, the life of a minister is often at the mercy of nature's rhythm. Illness and death do not cease just because you have a busy week. The best intentions of self-care may have to take a back seat to visitation or a funeral.

Part of the stress of relationships is influenced by how the pastor is viewed by others. A clergyperson is typically considered to have a close connection with God, and some extrapolate that this closeness equals perfection. Clergy are often discouraged from forming close friendships with congregants, and when they do, it is well to carefully guard confidences and guard against favoritism. Lack of close friends often leads to feelings of isolation and loneliness.

Leading a congregation, dealing constantly with the highs and lows of people's lives, can cause exaggerated emotional ups and downs. Moreover, while it is natural to want to be liked, clergy can be the most unpopular of people if there is conflict. Thus, the clergy role is one that can be subject to unpredictable fluctuations in public sentiment, which emphasizes the need for a strong sense of self, good boundaries, and emotionally healthy relationships beyond one's own congregation.

The role of a cleric can be not only rewarding but also difficult. The individual who brings expectations to this profession that cannot be met may be in for disillusionment and depression. Those who have studied clergy abuse warn that at these times of vulnerability clergy are most at risk for misconduct.

### *Background, Training, and Needs*

Individuals who become abusive clergy tend to have three indicators, the first being the individual's own background. Childhood experiences frame who we become; our later life is typically either a repetition of these patterns that we have observed as children or a conscious or unconscious attempt to avoid repeating them. Since the pastoral role consists primarily of relationships and how these are conducted, it is important to consider the development of attachment in the pastor's own childhood.

Attachment refers to the bond that develops between a child and his or her caretaker in the first few years of life. This reciprocal relationship affects every part of functioning — mind, body, emotions, relationships, and values — throughout life. Through touch, eye contact, and the fulfillment of needs and attention given to us in these early years, we learn trust, the ability to self-regulate, the ability to feel empathy and compassion, our self-esteem, and the resilience that arms us against stress and trauma.

For most of us, this monumental developmental experience happens naturally. Parents care about us, we form a bond with them, and our lives progress from there. But failure to adequately attach can also happen, whether as a result of neglect, abandonment, abuse, substance abuse by parents, or a myriad of other limiting factors. When it does, the result may be an adult who has difficulty trusting, trouble forming relationships, low self-esteem, difficulty managing impulses, few coping skills, and poor self-control. These characteristics are seen disproportionately in sexual offenders.

A potential cleric who has not had healthy developmental years may choose a career in ministry to seek acceptance. For many, training for the ministry does not occur until they are well into adulthood, by which time they may have had an opportunity to try out another career. But there may be a variation to this process in the Catholic priesthood.

Traditionally, boys became destined for the Catholic priesthood at a young age. Still in the prime of their desire for sexual experimentation, a natural developmental task for all humans, they anticipate a life of structure, repressed sexuality, and celibacy. Celibacy, in its ideal state, is much more than the denial of sexual activity. Sipe characterizes celibacy as "a freely chosen, dynamic state that usually results from a vow that is followed by an honest attempt to live without sexual gratification."[7] The basis of celibacy is a spiritual one, characterized by complete devotion to God, the devotion to divine love, and anticipated service to humanity. But to a young man, at the height of his sexuality, the requirement of celibacy inherent in entering the priesthood is an interruption in his developmental process. Developmentally, what is interrupted fails to mature. Sipe further comments that "the celibate/sexual system and the education of priests institutionalize and reward an adolescent level of adjustment."[8]

Looking at this fixation in the stage of adolescence in relation to the fact that many of the victims of abuse by priests were not prepubescent or very young boys — the targets of most pedophiles — but teens or post-pubescent boys, puzzled some theorists. In fact the term "ephebophilia" has been coined to describe this type of attraction to older boys and to distinguish it from classic pedophilia. Over the years, priests have had unusual access to teenage boys, who were often a part of youth groups or took the role of altar boys. Until recently when the scandals broke, parents were honored when their son was singled out to accompany Father to a ball game or do some special task for the priest. Some suggest that what is operating here is more a type of homosexuality in individuals of similar emotional developmental levels than an actual paraphilia. The problem with this is that the victims are nonetheless underage, the perpetrator chronologically an adult, and the acts therefore considered to be child abuse.

To assume that all priests are emotionally arrested would be doing a grave injustice to many and is totally untrue. However, this refuge for arrested emotional development explains why some individuals find this a vocation that meets their needs.

Even among Protestant clergy, training may have some significant gaps. Perhaps one of the most significant is the failure of many seminaries to require training in healthy sexuality; as future clergy the graduates will be expected not only to have exemplary moral standards themselves, but may also be called upon to counsel others with sexual issues. Only recently has there been any emphasis on such interpersonal skills as the delineation of and adherence to boundaries. Finally, seminary training has not put much emphasis on understanding, recognizing, and preventing child abuse, other than an occasional brief mention within another course.

The helping professions often attract people with problems of their own. Several times in my classes, students have come to me fearful that they might repeat the abuse that they suffered as children. It was the awareness of the dynamic of child maltreatment that enabled them to recognize their own problems and deal with them before there were unhealthy consequences.

The background and training of clergy may produce an individual who faces a career as a clergyperson with certain needs. Interestingly enough, the needs of many sexual offenders dovetail neatly with the offerings of clerical life in any denomination.

If we look at what a life in ministry offers, it becomes clear that this list overlaps with the needs of those who tend to offend against children.

The following are some of the benefits of life as a cleric.

- Community acceptance and sanction
- Freedom and opportunities to intermingle with parishioners of various age groups, including children
- Respect, a "special-ness"
- Head of a congregation
- Assumed close connection with God that provides a separateness (earlier this was framed as negative, but it can also be a positive)
- Unquestioned actions (which differs depending upon the denomination; the more fundamentalist the denomination, the more latitude clergy may have)
- Taken care of by a community (remember the casseroles)
- Protected by the "Mother" church (again dependent upon the denomination, but most provide room and board and backup in times of difficulty)
- A "family of God" in which people are expected to love one another[9]

The Catholic Church also requires celibacy (the benefit of which I discuss later).

Although I explain the characteristics of sexually offending clergy in more depth later in this chapter, it is sufficient to generalize here to make a point. People who may have the inclination to be abusive to children are attracted, either consciously or unconsciously, to the above benefits in the following manner.

Community acceptance and opportunity to have unquestioned access to children would be a pedophile's dream. These are frequently individuals with underdeveloped social skills, but if the expectation of acceptance comes with the job, who needs well-developed social skills? Respect and feeling special are things that the sex offender has sought all of his or her life. Frequently from a background where he or she was made to feel inferior, the sexual offender seeks acceptance from others continually. Since control is a major issue for offenders, the role that puts him or her at the head of the congregation gives a feeling of control. Having people assume that he or she has a connection with God, which often leads to unquestioned actions, sweetens the pot even further. This is also an individual who seeks to belong in a way he or she has never felt was possible. Being protected by an all-loving mother (church) compensates for the mother who probably was not there in childhood, and now this individual can also have a "family" that takes care of him or her.

Where does the celibacy come in? The classic pedophile is not interested in relationships, or at least not in sexual ones, with age mates. Celibacy offers an excuse to shun those relationships, and because keeping this vow is considered a holy obligation, he feels elevated to a position of honor.

Although at first glance this superimposing of needs and benefits may cause some discomfort and disbelief, the proof can be seen when one analyzes the life and motivations of individual perpetrators. It may not be so much that numerous clergy have been found to be abusive, but that the benefits of clergy lives are attractive to those who might have the inclination to abuse children.

A summary of some of the factors that put clergy at risk for abusing children are:

- Poor attachment and/or abusive childhoods, or otherwise unmet childhood needs that produce low self-esteem or feelings of failure
- Espousal of traditional/conservative values
- Sense of entitlement
- Like to see themselves as superior to others (narcissism)
- Difficulty with healthy intimacy
- Unrealistic expectation of life (e.g., all their needs will be met, always expect to be loved)
- Feeling isolated, lonely, "other"

As you look over this list, you may feel that you know someone who fits it nicely. That does not mean that he or she will sexually abuse children. It does mean that this clergyperson is in need of help.

## Clergy Who Are Abusive

In Chapter 4, we discussed the characteristics of sexual offenders who abuse children. Clergy offenders against children also fit into these categories, as we discuss further here.

### *Reviewing and Reframing the Typologies*

Male clergy who are sexually abusive to children may fit the two categories mentioned in Chapter 4. One type of individual would be seen as the classic pedophile — a man who abuses prepubescent boys. Some authors have added the category of ephebophile to describe men who target adolescents.

The ephebophile has probably had similar traumatic experiences in childhood, but perhaps not of the same type. The Investigative Staff of the *Boston Globe* reported on the background of John Geoghan, a Boston-area priest who became one of the best-known examples of the abusers that led to the scandal in the Catholic Church. Geoghan is said to have lost his father when he was five years old, a fact that had a significant impact on him, causing him to wet the bed for two years after the death. He described his mother as a "saintly woman" who tried to keep the family together. He was also taken under the wing of his mother's brother, who is described as "autocratic, old-school domineering, and — some would say mean."[10] This mentor is said to have "run interference" for the young Geoghan when he deemed it necessary.

Geoghan's early life was punctuated by a series of events that spoke of inconsistency, entitlement, and what was described as a "nervous condition." His life in seminary was "torturous," possibly because of his sexual dysfunction, depression, and immaturity. Although he reported an interest in females during adolescence, he explained that he repressed his interest in women due to his required celibacy. He rationalized that he instead sought satisfaction for his sexual desires with boys, to whom he was allowed greater access.[11] Geoghan was particularly attentive to altar boys, especially those from poorer families or those who may have been receptive to the attention of an older man, especially a priest. He is reported to have commented: "The children were just so affectionate, I got caught up in their acts of affection."[12]

We do not know the full story of Geoghan's background, only what he had shared. We do know the result — a man who was described as particularly immature, entitled, and one who rationalized and denied the harm he had done to children. His acts were apparently planned and certainly compulsive. His chosen victims were males; unlike some molesting priests who favor only postpubescent victims, Geoghan's victims ranged from ten through the teens.

Another type of offender profile among clergy is the situational abuser, a person like Bill. Although Bill had a relatively normal upbringing there were a few childhood traumas, like the death of his mother and possible abuse by a sitter. His father was dictatorial and demanding, making the boy and later the man always feel inferior. He had some interest in age mates and he married, although his sexual interest was not of paramount importance. His peer relationships were underdeveloped and based on the temporary intimacy that was mentioned earlier. Like many incestuous fathers, Bill was his daughter's primary nurturer, developing with her almost a substitute wifely relationship. His abuse of her was impulsive, perpetrated at a time when he was overwhelmed by life and seeking refuge. He remembers, on some level, the idealized woman from whom he received refuge in the past — his mother — and, seeing his wife as critical and unavailable, he tried to replicate this comfort with his daughter. Alcohol may also have played a part, not as the cause of the abuse but as a factor that may have lowered his inhibitions.

In this latter type of offender, it might be more difficult to detect abuse until after it has happened. However, the superficiality in relationships as well as difficulty mobilizing coping skills under pressure were red flags, but these tendencies may be present in many individuals and not just abusers.

### Female Clergy Who Abuse

Very little has been written on abuse by women clergy. Are there women clergy who are abusive? Probably, but they are not as prevalent as men. Wendy was one such case.

> *Wendy was the middle child of three. Her older sister, Greta, became a model at a young age and pursued this career into adulthood. Their mother was very involved in Greta's career, and everything seemed to take a back seat to this. When the mother was home, she insisted that both Wendy and Greta sleep with her. On one occasion, Wendy remembers waking up to discover that her mother was rubbing Wendy between her legs. It actually felt kind of pleasurable, but uncomfortable as well. Greta did not seem to mind when it was done to her, but Wendy soon found that she was looking for excuses not to go into her mother's bed.*
>
> *Eddie, Wendy's younger brother, seemed to be the forgotten child, and Wendy took care of him. She didn't mind. Eddie was loveable, and their relationship was close. Wendy's father was a salesman and was usually on the road. Once Wendy reached the age of twelve, she found herself alone with Eddie a great deal.*
>
> *When Wendy was fourteen, she was awakened in the middle of the night by the smell of smoke. Her parents and sister were not at home, and Wendy knew that she was in charge. Quickly she looked for the source of the smoke and discovered that the whole house was aflame. The fire seemed to have originated in Eddie's room. Hearing his screams, she tried frantically to get to him. By this time the fire department had been alerted by a neighbor, and they pulled Wendy*

*from the burning house. Hysterically, she told them that her brother was inside, but they were unable to rescue him.*

*Eddie's death and the loss of their home along with Wendy's belief that her parents blamed her for the fire was too much for the girl to handle. She was hospitalized and spent several weeks on an inpatient psychiatric unit. Following her release, she received regular therapy at a treatment center for teens. By eighteen, Wendy was able to accept that the fire started as a result of an electrical problem, was not her fault, and that she had done all that she could to save Eddie's life. She also knew that she needed to go on with her life and begged her parents to send her to college. She was successful as a student and began to rebuild her life. She became involved in the local church and found some solace in her activities there.*

*After graduation, Wendy worked for several years in the admissions office, where she became friendly with the college chaplain who told her that she should go to seminary. Three years later, Wendy had completed seminary and became the assistant minister of a large parish. She preferred to be the assistant. Her evaluations in field education had indicated that she needed to develop more assertiveness, and she guessed that she would have to work on this before she took a parish of her own.*

*Wendy's supervising pastor was a large, controlling woman who expected perfection. She intimidated Wendy, but Wendy told herself that she had to "get over it." For several years, Wendy performed her duties as assistant pastor, never quite feeling that she was doing things to her supervisor's satisfaction.*

*Gabe was a fourteen-year-old who helped his father do janitorial work around the church. He would often find Wendy working during off hours, and they began to develop a close relationship. He reminded her of Eddie, and she ached to be close to him. Stunted emotionally by her own childhood trauma, Wendy quickly fell into a romantic relationship with the young boy. Gabe, flattered by the attentions of a woman almost fifteen years his senior, appeared to be an eager participant. But when he began to spend an inordinate amount of time at the church, often skipping school to be there, his parents began to question, and the story came out. The church members were shocked, but her supervisor was not surprised.*

*"I always knew there was something strange about that woman!" she remarked. The resulting investigation sent Wendy back into hospitalization.*

Because this type of abuser is more pathological than her male counterpart, she might come to the attention of someone who could intervene a lot more quickly. When women violate boundaries, it is much more probable that it will be with adult men rather than children.

### *Clergy and Cybersex*

Over the last few decades, cybersex, a new form of deviance affecting children, has become a part of the American scene through the ability to access and experience sex through explicit pornography displayed over the Internet. New Hampshire police detective Jim McLaughlin calls this type of sexual deviance "technophilia." In a three-year investigation as part of a grant funded by the Justice Department Office for Juvenile Justice and Delinquency Prevention, McLaughlin and his colleagues uncovered over two hundred perpetrators of sexual solicitation and abuse through the Internet in forty states and twelve foreign countries.[13] These individuals came from a variety of professions, including clergy. Some of the overall group of perpetrators were collectors of pornography, some were interested in engaging children for abuse through pornography, some were manufacturers of pornography, and others intended to chat with children about sex with the possibility of meeting them.[14] Even those who do not intend to make contact with children may develop a compulsion for accessing pornographic sites via the Internet. This compulsion then becomes addictive behavior, and the technophile is in need of help.

How might an adult become involved in this network of pornography on the Internet? What makes viewing pornography on the Internet so appealing to people? The most obvious factors are that it is available to anyone with a computer and the ability to get online. Hooking up to a server is relatively inexpensive, and once one is online, accessing pornography is usually free. One can also access pornographic sites anonymously, making it appealing to anyone whose reputation might be damaged by such an activity. Currently everyone seems to be on the Internet and initially the perpetrator may feel that "everyone is doing it," so why not just have a peek at a pornographic site? One individual later arrested for his involvement in the production of pornographic sites recounted:

> *My wife had just left me. My life was a mess. I used to come home from work, and the computer seemed like my only friend. I'd go online for hours. I was curious about the obviously pornographic sites that were constantly in my Inbox. I used to read a lot of porno*

> *books when I was a teen. I loved the really young girls. So, I figured, what the heck, no one will know. I started accessing the sites and then got into some chat rooms. It opened a new world to me. I met a teenage girl online, and she and I would talk about all the sexual stuff we wanted to do with each other. She really seemed to know about some stuff that I wouldn't have thought a kid her age would. It was a real turn-on. After awhile, I'd rush home just to get online for sexual stimulation.*

Looking at pornographic pictures may be part of the experience of some clergy. Some find this a blemish on the clergyperson's character, while others do not. Nonetheless, for some individuals the compulsive accessing of pornography through the Internet can become an addiction. In addition, a pornographic presentation of sexuality desecrates what can be a beautiful and spiritual aspect of God's gift to human beings — their sexuality.

An addiction to cybersex might be problematic for a cleric for several reasons. Many clergy spend a good deal of time online, between creating bulletins, newsletters, and sermons — and an extra side trip to pornographic sites would be easy, free, and anonymous. He (offenders of this type are usually male) need not suffer the shame or embarrassment of the exposure of his interests. Nor, he may rationalize, does it go against any ethical standard that he agreed to in his ordination. The isolation that many clergy feel makes him susceptible to the adventure and excitement of a taboo activity. Also, the stress of negotiating relationships, some of which are problematic, makes him yearn for virtual relationships that can be less stressful and terminated without repercussions by simply exiting the site. As one recovered clergyman explained, "I kept hearing that we all need to practice self-care. Looking at pornography online was something I did just for me! It was my way of rationalizing that it was okay."

On a continuum, accessing pornographic sites might not seem as problematic as sexually molesting children. But when we consider the offender who frequents sites featuring children, this generates more concern. Add to this the statistical fact that many sexual offenders against children began their abusive careers by looking at pornography, and the problem takes on a new perspective. Cybersex can replace healthy relationships and can hamper the clergyman's ability to perform his role. In the worst-case scenario, such activities may spark an already underlying interest in the sexual abuse of children.

## Recognizing Offender Behavior

Because it is so far out of our frames of reference, most of us may not recognize the signs that our colleagues are abusive to children. Therefore, it is worth summarizing the clues that should make one suspicious. McGlone et al. suggest the following signs of a sexual predator:

- Insists on hugging, touching, kissing, tickling, wrestling with, or holding a child even when the child does not want affection
- Is overly interested in the sexuality of a particular child or teen (e.g., talks repeatedly about a child's developing body or interferes with normal teen dating)
- Manages to get time alone or insists on time alone with a child with no interruptions, such as weekend sleepovers, vacations, or camping trips
- Spends most of his spare time with children or teens and has little interest in spending time with someone his or her own age
- Regularly offers to babysit or take children on outings alone
- Buys children and teens expensive gifts or gives them money for no apparent reason
- Frequently walks in on children or teens alone in the bathroom
- Allows children or teens to consistently get away with inappropriate behaviors[15]

Sperry outlines the characteristics of abusive priests for which one should be watchful:

- Is confused about his (or her) sexual orientation and does not appear to have close ties to either gender as partners
- Appears to lack peer relationships in general
- Has a history of child sexual abuse or other type of childhood abuse which he (she) talks about
- Uses humor that seems especially immature or based on sexual themes
- Is particularly compulsive or seems especially narcissistic[16]

In pastoral counseling situations, clergy must be aware of the need for proper boundaries. The following characteristics might indicate the need for concern about fellow clergy counselors:

- Insists upon interviewing children alone in secluded areas
- Prefers to counsel children during off hours when few people are around
- Seems to see an inordinate number of children
- Is not receptive to suggestions that children be referred elsewhere for counseling

There may be mitigating circumstances in the above, but it is important that clergy use discretion and be aware of the need for being accountable, especially in the area of boundaries. This new climate of sexual abuse forces us all to be cautious and discerning. Careful attention to the safety of children should be our paramount concern.

## The Clergy Abuser and the Congregation

When we hear of clergy sexual abuse in a church, the tendency is to feel badly for the betrayed congregation. They too have been victims of the abuse. Yet, sometimes unknowingly, congregations can provide an atmosphere in which clergy abuse is more likely to flourish.

In a call process, needy congregations often attract pastors who have similar issues. The past sexual scandal in churches demonstrated that authority figures sometimes placed clergy about whom they had questions in congregations that tended to be made up of those who might not question—like poor or disenfranchised groups. Yet it is not only these groups that may unknowingly support abuse by clergy.

A congregation can be seen as a system not unlike a family. When something is amiss in one part of a system, it impacts another. To illustrate how a congregation may feed into abusive behavior on the part of clergy, it is helpful to distinguish between the two types of offenders mentioned earlier. There may be multiple danger signals with a fixated offender that a congregation either fails to recognize or does not respond to, possibly due to the congregants' own needs. For example, a priest or pastor's inordinate interest in the children, especially the boys, of the parish might not seem problematic to a congregation hoping to revitalize their youth or acolyte program or one populated by single mothers who are thrilled for the attention the cleric is giving their children. In addition, the pastor's immaturity and seeming developmental level not far above his charges may be dismissed. A discerning parent might recognize that the quality of play between children and the pastor seems particularly childlike, but may do little about it.

Many congregations see their clergy as having the ultimate power — a connection with God — and so they do not question the clergyperson's actions. The cleric's seeming assumption that he is entitled not to be questioned reinforces this. The crisis in the Catholic Church demonstrated that some offenders used their parishioner's unquestioning faith to exert their power in abusive ways. These congregations rarely held their clergy accountable for anything, and when they began to abuse, it was easy to hide from the unquestioning congregation. Church members need to remember that power and control are the best allies of the pedophile. On the other hand, a little healthy questioning and the requirement of some accountability on the part of the pastor may protect the church's children.

Despite the fact that a church can take over a clergyperson's whole life, it should not. For one type of offender, the church and its children *are* his life. The congregation that does not recognize this situation and become somewhat wary of it is asking for problems or, at the least, clergy burnout. For Catholic priests, the church potentially becomes their whole world — particularly as they are typically without wives and children. Most of the healthy priests I have known have parents, siblings, relatives, and friends (even if no wife or children) outside the church with whom they enjoy spending time.

Another type of offender may not be abusive when he enters the church community, but stress contributes to his downfall. The congregation that requires his undivided attention to the exclusion of his own family may set him up to fail. Once he has become all things to all people in a congregation to the detriment of his own life, some congregations are still not fulfilled. They may turn on him and by scapegoating rob him of his already shaky feeling of worth. In such circumstances, someone with the predisposition to become an offender might turn to children for comfort.

Some congregants suspect that their pastors are being inappropriate with children, but, not wanting to make waves or not trusting their own suspicion, they say little to anyone. Instead of checking out their feelings with appropriate church members, they continue to enable what is or may become abusive behavior on the part of the clergyperson. Like the alcoholic family system that tiptoes around the subject of Dad or Mom's drinking problem until it becomes more destructive to everyone, the church with an abusive pastor or priest may go on for years deliberately ignoring what is right in front of them.

Finally, churches are becoming more and more aware of the need to develop policies to respond to abusive behavior *before* it occurs and to adhere to those policies when it does. The church that fails to recognize the need for such protocol and to act upon that recognition is contributing to the risk of its children. Chapter 13 suggests how to begin to develop protocol in congregations.

Some congregations may be disturbed upon reading this section. They feel totally victimized when a pastor is found to be abusive and are not willing to consider their own contribution to the situation. Congregations do not *cause* sexual abuse on the part of their clergy. The responsibility is that of the offender. But like the incestuous family, they may contribute to an atmosphere that allows abuse to occur and fails to stop it in a timely manner. Congregations must learn to be aware of the signs of abuse and intervene when they are present. The next chapter explains what to do if *you* suspect that a colleague is abusive.

## Chapter 10

# Responding to Abuse by Clergy

> In the winter of 2002, when the initial reports about how the Catholic Church had handled priests who sexually abused children surfaced in the *Boston Globe*, the stories seemed almost too horrible to be true.... The extent of the betrayal — of children's innocence, of parents' trust, of priestly vows, of bishops' responsibilities, of the Church's basic tenets — was unnerving. Most shocking to everyday Catholics, and most dangerous to the Church, was the incontrovertible evidence that Cardinal Law and other leaders of his archdioceses had engaged in such a massive cover-up. Rather than protect the most vulnerable members, the Church had been putting them in harm's way.[1]

The words of the Boston Globe Investigative Staff cause outrage that so much abuse could be covered up for so long. Until recently, most clergy and church members knew little about the signs of such child sexual abuse. Even when they did, how many clergy were ready to point a finger at a colleague without the assurance that that colleague was indeed abusing children?

For a moment, assume that you are the pastor in a small parish. Try to put yourself in this situation.

> *There are four churches in this small town, three Protestant and one Roman Catholic. You and the three other clergy meet together for lunch on a regular basis to discuss various church matters and lend each other general support. One pastor, Pastor Jones, has been in the ministry for over thirty years, considerably longer than you and your other colleagues. Pastor Jones is a large imposing man who, despite his years in ministry, seems to require a great deal of reassurance. He enjoys giving his younger peers advice and seems to you to have some old-school views of being a pastor. He expects his congregation to give*

*him unquestioned authority, but nonetheless seems to be well-liked by them. His devoted members hold regular Bible study and prayer meetings. He often speaks of his excellent youth program, including support groups for children from divorced families and families in which there is alcoholism. His parish sponsors a Boy Scout Troop. He also does pastoral counseling at the church and appears to do especially well with the children. Pastor Jones has been in town for many years and enjoys the respect of the community. You and your colleagues feel you could learn a great deal from Pastor Jones. You have often picked his brain in your attempts to revitalize your own church's flagging Sunday school.*

*One Sunday, a young mother, Sally Cane, and her two sons come to your church. After the service, she asks if she might discuss with you her desire to join the church. At this meeting, you assess Mrs. Cane as a competent young woman who will be an asset to your congregation. Recently divorced, she had been attending Pastor Jones's church, where her ex-husband and his current girlfriend still attend. You assume that she had left because he has remained and comment that it must have been difficult. She says that she had intended to leave anyway as she did not "trust Pastor Jones with her boys." This is puzzling to you, given what the pastor has told you about his youth work. Mrs. Cane finally tearfully tells you that she believes that the pastor was sexually inappropriate with at least one of her boys. She tells you that her son, Jonathan, was an acolyte and used to spend long hours at the church. She had thought that it was good for him to be so involved in the church. When her younger son, Joshua, expressed interest in becoming an acolyte, Jonathan was adamant that he should not be. At first, Mrs. Cane admonished her older son for being selfish in not allowing his younger brother to enjoy something that he had enjoyed, but Jonathan argued that she did not know the pastor and wouldn't like it if she did. He suggested that the pastor may have done some "dirty things" to him but refused to elaborate further.*

*Mrs. Cane then told her husband, sure that he would be concerned. An active member of the church, the husband berated her for having an overactive imagination and refused to acknowledge her concerns.*

*"I just want my children out of there and away from that man!" she insists with finality. She refuses to take Jonathan to a counselor as you suggest.*

*Unsure of how to proceed, you ask one of your other clergy colleagues if she had ever heard anything about Pastor Jones. She had heard rumblings that he had left an earlier parish because of something that happened with a child, but that is all she knows. She doubts that it could be true because everyone here seems to love him.*

What are you feeling at this point? Confused? Helpless? Unsure of how to proceed? On one hand here is a pastor whom you respect and admire. On the other is the report of a mother who appears to you to be stable and to have the best interests of her children at heart. To make accusations against Pastor Jones would be to sully his reputation and perhaps ruin his career. Not to respond, if there was truth to Jonathan's allegation, would be to enable a sexual offender to continue to abuse children. Had you been trained in the recognition of child abuse, you might also have listened for some of the other clues as the pastor and his church members talked about the youth programs. Pastor Jones also appears to demonstrate the following:

- He is a loner, unmarried, and appears to have few peer relationships.
- His relationship with all of you is superficial at best and based upon your admiring him and his accomplishments.
- He can seem quite childish, and you have often thought that his jokes were somewhat immature and laced with unnecessary sexual content.
- He talks openly about having come from an abusive background in which he was beaten by his father and alluded to being sexually abused by an older boy.
- He has impressed you as narcissistic and entitled, expecting the congregation to cater to his needs.
- He enjoys talking about the sexual development of kids and how some of "his kids" are obviously growing up.
- He is often described as inconsistent with the children, very stern with some and a "softie" with his favorites.
- He takes his special kids a great many places. Most of these kids are from poor families or have single mothers.
- When he takes groups on field trips he is often the only adult.
- Mrs. Cane stated that her sons objected to him walking in when they were using the bathroom and commenting on their penis size.

Despite all these incriminating facts, it may not be enough to bring Pastor Jones to the attention of any agency investigating child abuse.

In this situation, some clergy would do nothing, feeling that they did not have enough information to proceed. But let us look for a moment at the consequences of cover-up.

## Consequences of Cover-Up

Adults abused as children speak about the loss of their trust in their faith — and even in God — as a result of abuse. Churches are communities of faith that are supposed to strengthen people and to help them recognize their God-given potential, their gifts, and their responsibility to others. Children abused by clergy are not only convinced that they are not worthy, but they often cannot accept the help of the congregation. Instead, they assume that the congregation must somehow know about and is complicit in the abuse. A common belief in church life is that "we are all children of God" and therefore benefit from the riches that God bestows upon us. Who would want to be the child of a God who betrays and abuses you?

In addition to the theological implications of loss of faith and trust in the clergy, the church, and God, children who are sexually abused by clergy experience all the effects of sexual abuse that other children experience, including the following:

- Difficulty with trust and therefore relationships with others
- Feeling like they are damaged, worthless
- Low self-esteem
- Difficulties in learning
- Anger or rage

Children often do not know how to speak out about their abuse, suspecting that no one would believe them if they did, especially when the perpetrator is someone as well respected as a clergyperson.

Given the implications for children when abuse is not responded to, it is vital that their interests be protected.

## Learning of Abuse by Other Clergy

You may learn of abuse by other clergy several ways. First, *a victim might tell you directly.* Second, *you might learn from a victim's parent or friend,* as in the case of Jonathan and Pastor Jones. Third, *you may observe an incident* that appears abusive. Given a variety of factors, *you may begin to suspect* that abuse is occurring.

If the report comes from a victim, the most important act is to *listen without asking leading questions.* If the abuse is later substantiated and your questions have contaminated the victim's testimony, the case could be thrown out of criminal court. *Believe the victim,* no matter what you might feel about his or her story. Children usually do not make up sexual abuse allegations. Sometimes a teen will report erroneously, but can usually be found out when he or she does not have sufficient tactile details or consistent facts. But younger children have probably not been exposed to sexuality unless something is done to them.

*A parent or friend should be encouraged to come forward* herself or himself and report the abuse. You might offer to support the parent or friend in this. *An observed situation that is clearly sexual should be addressed immediately. Suspicion may also require a report,* depending upon the situation.

## When Action Is Required

As a clergyperson, you naturally may feel hesitant when it seems necessary to intervene in abusive situations involving other clergy, perhaps assuming that you do not know enough. If this is the case, *first, consider carefully what you do know, using the guidelines and information that you have gleaned from your training. Are there others with whom you can consult without jeopardizing the reputation of the alleged abuser if the allegations are untrue?* In child abuse situations, you cannot afford to be 100 percent sure that the abuse is occurring; you need only suspicion to report a child abuse case. It is up to the appropriate authorities to then investigate.

In the earlier case of Pastor Jones, the clergywoman realized that several other families had transferred from Pastor Jones's church. She visited them, ostensibly on a routine clergy call, and chatted with them about their lives before they came to the church. Several of the families admitted their concerns about Pastor Jones, and the clergywoman felt that she had enough information to bring her suspicions to the attention of the local police chief. Fortunately, the police took her seriously and did investigate. What followed was the eventual arrest of a man who had been abusing boys for some years and had never been apprehended.

Having decided that the situation should be brought to the attention of a professional with more expertise in child abuse, what is the next step?

Presumably you have already explored the reporting protocol for your particular denomination and the following types of questions:

- Where, within your denomination, do you report a suspected case of clergy abuse (diocese, area, synod)?
- What individual is responsible for responding to your report?
- How are civil authorities alerted and by whom?

Any investigation is the responsibility of the civil authorities and not the pastor, the church, or the denomination. Many denominations have a simultaneous investigatory process, mainly to determine the church's response to the abuser or the victim's need for restitution, but the appropriate civil authorities must perform the initial investigation. Not to allow civil authorities to do the legal investigating is not only against the law in some states (where clergy are mandated reporters), but compromises any case that might be necessary in a court of law.

Before you consider confronting an abuser, be aware of the dictates of your particular denomination. Some denominations require that situations in which abuse is suspected be reported to a higher authority (e.g., bishop) and that this person interview the alleged abuser.

If it does fall to you to talk with the abuser, consider: *What access will the alleged offender have to the victim after you confront him or her?* Offenders frequently cajole, frighten, and harass victims into taking back their stories once the abuser knows he or she is found out. If the child recants the allegations of abuse, the whole affair might be covered up once more.

*Is the child physically safe from the alleged abuser?* Although unusual, it is always possible that the accused might physically harm the child in an attempt to ensure his or her secrecy.

*Will the alleged abuser be able to convince you that the abuse never happened?* Do you have an open mind, or do you really not want to believe that it happened?

If you are the one expected to talk to the alleged abuser, and he or she will not have access to the child, you still need to have a back-up plan. Some clergy report to the proper civil authority first and then talk with the individual. A suspected abuser may have a variety of reactions, some of which may be dangerous for the person who confronts and others dangerous to him or herself. Suicide attempts immediately after disclosure are a serious risk. It might also be wise to talk with the abuser with another individual in attendance.

Those who abuse children usually deny, manipulate, or rationalize what they have done. They may accuse you of having a dirty mind or fall back on old relationships to make you feel guilty. They may plead for you to understand the stress they are under. Other offenders will admit what they have done and beg your forgiveness. Confronting an abuser may take as much of a toll on you as on the abuser. Confrontation is often better done by someone who is not emotionally involved.

Once you have made a report to the civil authorities and possibly your denomination, try to determine what else will be required of you. You may be asked to give a deposition and required to testify in court if the case reaches that point. You will need to have emotional support, because reporting a case of child abuse is hard, especially when the possible perpetrator is a clergy colleague.

Consider ahead of time the possible reactions of both the offender and his or her family. Knowing these reactions may help you to handle any feelings of guilt, but remember that your intervention is the only way that he or she could have received needed help.

## Reactions of the Accused

The reactions of the abusive clergy member will differ depending upon his or her personality. The majority of accused offenders initially deny their abuse or rationalize that they had some understandable motive or that the victim asked for the abuse. Some project the blame elsewhere: "If my wife had been home more . . . ," or "The victim was seductive." Some offenders become angry that they have been apprehended and focus their anger on those who reported them. They rarely exhibit shame or guilt, arguing that the children were not hurt and actually liked the sexual interaction.

An offender may also initially deny, rationalize, and blame others, but finally admit the offense, agreeing that it was wrong. The guilt and shame felt put the offender at the highest risk for suicide. He may break down and play upon the emotions of anyone who will listen, pleading that he is sorry, and promising that he will never do anything like that again. Without help, he is unlikely to keep his promises regardless of his good intentions.

Though statistically rare, female clergy offenders who abuse are more likely than men to admit their offenses, but also tend to exhibit more serious pathology that must be addressed.

No matter the identity of the offender, as a member of the clergy he or she has lost his or her reputation, profession, and credibility, and with them, financial stability, a network, and a sense of personal accomplishment. Family members may not stand by him or her, causing further isolation, guilt, and depression. Though their theology preaches forgiveness, the abuser may either despair that it will never happen or feel unworthy of it. The future may seem very bleak to the abuser who acknowledges wrongdoing.[2]

## Partners and Family Members

The family of an abuser also loses its livelihood and reputation, and church members are often not quite sure how to relate to the family. Parishioners may feel pity, but this can be replaced by suspicion or even anger. What contribution, wonder the congregants, did the family have to the pastor's downfall? Were they not "there" for him or her? Did they put too much pressure on the pastor? The family, as a result, soon feels that they have lost their place in the church community as well, which might cause resentment. Why should they be ostracized when they were not the abuser?[3]

If you are in a position to support the partner or family, this is certainly needed. Before you even begin, however, you must assess your own feelings about her or his role. She or he needs to know that at least someone believes that the blame does not rest with the partner. You might give the following helps to an abuser's nonabusive partner:

*Help the partner to recognize that she/he is not the perpetrator, but has also been victimized.* The partner is certainly entitled to feeling like a victim for a time, but then needs to be empowered to regain the energy to make some difficult decisions and accomplish some weighty tasks. Help the person to recognize that he or she has borne the brunt of the fallout but need not be crushed by it.

*The responsibility rests on the shoulders of the actual abuser.* When one is married and a part of the couple strays sexually, the inclination is for the general public to believe that, had the abuser been content at home, he or she would never have looked outside for satisfaction. Although both parties are usually somehow responsible for a failing marriage, each partner has the choice of what to do about it. Child abuse is never an acceptable choice. This act was something chosen by the perpetrator, not the partner.[4]

*The abuser's partner needs to have help looking at the situation and discovering her or his options.* Choices must be made. Will she or he stand by the abuser? In what manner? Where will financial support come from? How will she or he get through the difficult months of legal and logistical issues ahead? What are the plans for the future? The best recommendation is for the partner to find professional therapeutic support. Support groups for partners of abusers may also be available in your area. She or he may also need a colleague's shoulder to lean on. Be careful just to listen and not to condemn the abuser. Deep down, that may not be what the partner really wants to hear, and you may compromise the help that you can give by doing so.

*Above all, the partner needs an opportunity to grieve.* She or he has lost a great deal — self-esteem, possibly a spouse and a marriage, an income, a lifestyle, a support system (in the church), perhaps a home, her or his own ministry as it pertained to the partner's, and so much more. If children are involved, the partner has also lost the ability to give them happy and conflict-free childhoods. She or he needs time to recognize these losses and grieve them.[5] Your help may be invaluable alongside that of a professional therapist.

## Helping the Abuser's Children through the Crisis

The children of an abusive pastor are perhaps the most forgotten of victims. Mental health professionals and adult victims alike tell us that children must process traumatic events to make sense of them.

*The children in such circumstances need to find some security.* They may find it if the nonabusive parent is able to be emotionally present for them or if another adult can assure them that the abuse is not their fault.[6] Children must feel that there is someplace where they can go to feel safe. That "place" need not be a location but may be a relationship.

*Ideally children should be provided with a counselor or therapist.* The issues with which they must cope are far-reaching. They need to have explained what will be happening to their abusive parent. They need to learn to trust again as they may feel betrayed by one or both parents — the abuser for what he or she has done and the other parent for not being able to intervene or protect the child from the feelings that the facts of the abuse have caused.

Children may also need someone to help them spiritually. The young children of clergy often have an idea that their clergy parent is closely tied or even synonymous with God. To be betrayed by that parent may feel like betrayal by God. Children thus need someone to help them interpret what has happened and separate it from issues of faith.

## The Aftermath of Disclosure

It is difficult to conclusively predict what will happen to a clergyperson who abuses children. For this discussion there are actually two areas in which help is needed. The first is legal/logistical and the area in which most of the work with clergy is directed. The second is spiritual and the area that is often neglected.

### *The Legal and Logistical Framework*

The disclosure has been made. The appropriate offices within the denomination have been notified. The police or district attorney have become involved. The abuser has probably been arrested. At the very least he or she has been denied further access to the victims.

What happens to a perpetrator from a civil perspective depends on the state in which he or she lives and the nature of the crime. At one time, individuals in positions such as the ministry would have been ordered by the court to receive treatment and the case continued until they had an opportunity to do so. More recently, with the increase of reported clergy cases and the public outcry about the impact of this type of abuse, courts are not as lenient. Many offenders are required to serve time in correctional facilities or in treatment programs.

Prior to the decision about the outcome, there will be an investigation — usually done by the district attorney's office — to uncover all the details. During this investigation, perpetrators are either held in corrections or, more likely if the judge feels that they can be trusted, allowed to live in the community, but ordered to have no contact with the victims. Whether a clergy perpetrator will return to the parsonage or rectory depends upon whether there are children there, upon whether or not his partner allows it, or upon the goodwill of the church or denomination. Typically the non-abusive spouse will often be allowed to stay in the church-owned property rather than the abuser.

After the initial investigation, a determination is made if there is enough information to go to trial in criminal court. As this step becomes imminent, the lawyers for the defense and for the prosecution will often be negotiating to see if the expense of a trial can be avoided. If the abuser and his attorney decide to accept a plea bargain, a trial is avoided. The offender may then be incarcerated, put on probation, or required to receive psychological treatment. Treatment and probation may follow.

At the same time, most denominations will conduct their own study of the implications for the church, the abuser, and the future of the abuser's affiliation with the denomination. Some of the concerns of denominations are as follows:

- Are the accusations accurate?
- Has this occurred in earlier parishes?
- How can the church be protected from legal and financial consequences?
- How can the scandal be minimized?
- Was there a reporting protocol, and was it followed?
- What will the victims need immediately? What will they need to begin the process of healing? Is restitution required?
- What will the offending minister need?
- What are the needs of the minister's family? How can those be met?
- What are the needs of the church community for healing?
- How can such situations be avoided in the future?
- What will be the disposition of the offender?[7]

It is vital that the church or denomination cooperate with the local civil agencies. Gone are the days when an incident of clergy abuse could be quietly handled by the denomination and kept out of the courts.

Should an abusive cleric be required to leave the ministry? Most would question whether an abusive individual can serve God after what he or she has done. Our faith tells us that forgiveness is possible for anyone. Yet what does forgiveness mean? Does forgiveness bring with it a reinstatement to God's service as a cleric, or do we remove the cloak of office before we can forgive?

Once taken out of a leadership role, can we invite him or her into the church community? One would hope that the church would be a welcoming place, but many defrocked clergy do not feel comfortable returning to a church community.

Another consideration is that the recidivism level for child sexual abusers is high. During the crisis in the Catholic Church, the solution that was often tried was to retain an offender as a priest, but be sure that he had an administrative appointment and therefore no access to children. But an untreated offender who is also not motivated to change will find a way to have access to his victims, which was the case in numerous situations in various archdioceses.

When a cleric is relieved of his or her standing in the interest of protecting future victims, he or she fades into secular life — but does not necessarily cease abusing. Such was the case of James Porter, a Massachusetts priest who left the priesthood, married, had children, and continued to molest. By the time he was arrested in 1992, Porter had claimed more than one hundred victims. Removing a cleric from priestly service makes it more difficult to keep track of his or her actions and more likely to put other children at risk.[8] The debate continues.

### *Ministering to Clergy Abusers*

You may find yourself in the position of ministering to a clergy colleague who has been abusive. This might be during the time when he is soul searching and deciding to come forward. Suggestions for such situations are as follows:

- *Listen to your own gut-level reactions.*
- *Ask the difficult questions.* Sometimes the facts are obvious, but we do not want to acknowledge them with the right questions.
- *Accept what you must do morally and, possibly, legally* (as a mandated reporter).
- *Never promise total confidentiality.* Letting counselees and colleagues know up front that you cannot keep confidences involving their harming themselves or others or abusing children gives them the responsibility of choosing what they will tell you. If they disclose one of those three facts, you cannot protect their confidentiality and must take the information to the appropriate authorities.
- *Tell the person what must happen, but give him or her a choice in how it is accomplished.* Knowing that abuse must be reported, the abuser should then have a choice as to who does the reporting. It would be better if the abuser turned himself or herself in. Indicate that you would be glad to accompany him or her, but if the abuser refuses to do this, you will be obligated to do so. Give the abuser as many choices as are possible on how this will be done. For example, ask: Shall I make a call to the police while you are here? Shall I tell someone else first so that you will have support? Shall I make a call and then we can have an opportunity to pray together while we wait?

- *Once the abuser knows that the situation will be reported, do not let him or her go off alone.* The likelihood that he or she will attempt suicide is great.
- *Help the abuser to recognize that the only way to overcome his or her problem is to get help.*
- *Be aware of and tell the abuser what will happen after a report has been made.*
- *Ask if he or she would like to notify his or her family or have you do it.*
- *Help the abuser to recognize that he or she has done the right thing by coming forward.* The abuse must not continue, and he or she needs help.
- *Offer to pray with the abuser* for strength through the ordeal to follow and for hope for the future.
- *Be aware of what this report will mean to his or her life.* No matter how negative you feel about what the abuser has done, he or she is a child of God and is in need of compassion, especially after coming this far.
- *Assure the abuser that you will stand by him or her once the report has been made.* It will not get any easier, and he or she will need support.
- *After you have done what you need to do, seek your own support with loved ones and in prayer.*

You may also be called upon to minister to an abuser at a point when he or she has already experienced some type of consequences and is trying to come to spiritual terms with what has happened. An offender needs to be reminded that:

- Our humanness keeps us from perfection.
- We are children of God and as such can be recipients of God's love and grace.
- In that grace can be transformation.
- What we need to do is acknowledge our wrongdoings, take responsibility for them, and strive to live out God's word.

Be aware of your own limitations. Most clergy are not trained to counsel offenders related to their sexual abuse. Healing and rehabilitation require more than just prayer or the recognition of God's role in our lives. Some in-depth psychological reparation is also necessary, and it is wise to refer to in-depth counseling with an abuse practitioner.

Often clergy are called upon to provide spiritual comfort while the offender is also seeing a secular counselor. Confer regularly with the counselor so that the help you are both giving the offender will not be contradictory. Counseling offenders is never easy, but it can be rewarding when one sees an offender begin to reclaim his or her life in a positive manner.

## Stepping Off the Path: A Word to At-Risk Clergy

It is always possible for someone to pick up a book such as this because of concerns about becoming or being an abuser. If such is your concern, this section is addressed to you.

The following are some issues that might put you at risk:

- Did you have a childhood during which there was sexual abuse or severe physical abuse, or were you made to feel worthless? If so, have you failed to deal with it?
- Was there a great deal of sexuality in your home growing up? Was there sexual material available to the children like pornographic movies or magazines? Were any of your siblings sexually abused at home?
- Do you prefer the company of children to adults? Do adults make you feel incompetent and unworthy?
- Have you become involved in some form of substance abuse that you do not seem to be able to conquer?
- Do you enjoy pornographic materials — especially depictions of children — and look forward to viewing them whenever possible?
- Do you spend a great deal of time looking at pornography — especially child pornography — on the Internet?
- Have you had numerous different jobs and can't seem to find a fit?
- Do you feel like people — especially adults — just do not understand or appreciate you?
- Have you been told that you would benefit from therapy, but you do not feel that you need to go?

- Do you feel that rules are stupid and not designed for you?
- Do you find yourself sexually aroused by children? Do you have sexual fantasies about children?
- Do you prefer to be alone with children with no other adults in attendance? Do you prefer taking children on outings, camping, and field trips where you are the only adult? Do you tend to enjoy counseling children in your home or secluded areas of the building?
- Do you find that your life is consumed with church activities, leaving little time for yourself or your family?
- Does your family complain that you are never available for them?
- Do you have few friends and prefer to be alone?
- Does your life seem particularly stressful and you wish you could just return to childhood?

If you discover that you are answering quite a few of these questions in the affirmative, you will want to seek some help to sort out your feelings. If you recognize that you have already been abusive, you need help now.

Having considered the clergy response to abuse by other clergy, let us look at the congregational response and the hope for healing within the church community.

## Chapter 11

# Helping the Church after Clergy Abuse

*We were all stunned when Father Nick was arrested for molesting some of the boys in our congregation. This kind, gentle minister who seemed so good with the youth? Who could have made such outrageous accusations? But one night my son told me that it was all true as Father Nick had approached him as well. The congregation went into a state of shock; the bishop became involved. Instead of going to trial, Father Nick plea bargained and was incarcerated. Some of us visited him, but after what my son, Josh, had told me, I couldn't bring myself to do it. I was disillusioned, my faith was shaken, and I wondered if God abandoned our congregation. Why had we not recognized what was happening?*

Members who learn that their pastor is abusive are shocked and shaken, not only emotionally, but spiritually. How can such an environment heal? The very vulnerability that members feel in the aftermath of such an event is an opportunity for the congregants to deepen their faith, to care for one another, and to use the energy of their consternation and indignation to develop strategies that will prevent such events from happening again.

## Phases of Congregational Response to Abuse by Clergy

The work of a congregation affected by abuse requires numerous steps. As in individual or family therapy around trauma, the actual healing is one of the last pieces of the process. The congregation goes through three phases: Recognition, Response–Re-visioning, and Reconstruction-Healing.[1]

### *Recognition Phase*

Church families responding to a clergy abuser often feel disequilibrium and panic. Some blame the victim, the individual who bought the abuse to their attention, or themselves for not recognizing what was happening. Many members deny the reality of the abuse, finding mechanisms to blur the facts, obscure communication, and focus on trivial activities that ignore the magnitude of the issue. Church bodies also find ways to protect the secret by a kind of selective amnesia, remembering past events — like an earlier time in the church or a former pastor — in a way that overidealizes them. They may discredit those who have left the church because of the conflict, or circulate inaccurate stories about why the offending pastor left the congregation. Any admission that events were not as they would like to present them meets with anger or shame.[2]

For many, the fall of the clergyperson erodes their confidence in the church and in their own beliefs. Parents chastise themselves for entrusting their children with such confidence to others in the church, including to the pastor. One father commented, "The church is one place where you consider that everyone's intent is honorable. You hardly know the people who teach Sunday school or lead the youth group and yet you, as a parent, think nothing of dropping your kids off for a couple of hours with a virtual stranger."

Parents often become hypervigilant right after a disclosure. People within the congregation may isolate themselves from one another or form camps of support to help them cope with a situation that may previously have been out of their frame of reference. At the same time that they may be criticizing one another within the church community, congregants often feel shame on behalf of their church. The congregation will often be unsure of how to respond to not only the abuser, but his or her family members as well.

There is a seemingly universal desire among church members for a quick solution. Some handle this need by becoming overly involved in the running of the church, convincing themselves that a better-functioning organization can somehow cover up and even forget the problems that it is facing. But clergy abuse usually attracts media attention, and the reality of the situation is difficult to totally ignore. In addition, the civil authorities as well as the ecclesiastical body to which the church belongs may be engaged in addressing the clergy offender's crime, involving church members in the investigation.

The church is often split by conflict. Some members will remain steadfast to the church community. Others may support the abusing clergyperson over the congregation that they perceive falsely accused him or her. Other disillusioned congregants may choose to leave the church completely or look for other church communities. This exodus can occur at any time during the congregation's attempt to deal with the crisis.

As disturbing as is the loss of members, the compromise of the spiritual climate can be even more disturbing. Like the victims, congregants have begun to wonder where God was when the abuse occurred. Feeling that God is "not there" can seriously erode the faith of individuals and of the congregation. Future clergy to that congregation may experience the fallout from this assault on their faith.

### *Response–Re-visioning Phase*

During the Response–Re-visioning Phase, the congregation begins to assess its initial response to the crisis of disclosure, and re-examines what the future might hold. In order to get to this point, some churches need intervention from a new pastor or an organization designed to help struggling churches. By this time the following has probably also begun to fall into place:

- The abuser is no longer at the church.
- Prosecution and/or treatment of the abuse is scheduled or has begun.
- The victims/families involved have been referred for counseling specific to the abuse.
- The denomination (and/or other governing body, depending upon the polity of the church) has responded to the vacant pulpit by assigning another pastor or pulpit supply temporarily.
- At some point an interim pastor should be sought who has some experience and training in working with congregations touched by clergy abuse.

The church community faces some specific tasks during this phase. First, they must firmly give up their denial and recognize that the abuse did occur. They must support the traumatized victim. Congregants must begin to accept that abuse does not occur in totally healthy communities. With this in mind, the members must work toward not only healing the congregation, but also setting up policies and procedures to prevent future abuse and outline a method of responding if it occurs. Finally, the members need to begin to look to the future, accepting that, although this abuse has happened, the church must find a way to find its spiritual core and attempt to go forward with a vision of doing God's work. This is a tall order, and some congregations struggle with these tasks for years before they are able to move on.

## *Reconstruction-Healing Phase*

To be authentic to the mission of a community dedicated to living out God's Word, the church must become a disciple-forming congregation. Discipleship requires that the congregation and each individual member look inward to discern God's place in the community and in individuals' lives. Ironically, healing from clergy abuse provides both the opportunity, based on the congregation's vulnerability, and the mandate, based on the need to return to a relationship in which God/Christ is at the head of the church, for beginning the work toward discipleship.

Discipleship is threefold, involving the deepening of our relationship with God, with ourselves, and with others; equipping, which involves recognizing our gifts, discerning the call to use them, and acquiring the skills and knowledge to support this ministry; and finally, ministering, the involvement in God's mission.[3] Each of these steps is discussed shortly.

The desire is to protect oneself from the scandal and the pain that the abuse causes both for the individual involved and the congregation; the tendency is to become inwardly centered. At this time, church members are rarely thinking benevolently about one another, much less the world outside the church. Remaining this way for too long may freeze them in a state of egocentrism which is far from the teachings of Christ.

Place yourself in the role of a clergyperson who has been sent to minister to a church wounded by clergy abuse. The members have weathered the prosecution of the perpetrator and have perhaps had an interim clergyperson who has taken them through the difficult months when they had begun to recognize how they had contributed to the abusive atmosphere. Now, they are ready to change.

> *We knew that we needed something, but we had no idea what would help us to find the spirituality that we had all but lost in the months we were consumed with avoiding the media and trying to figure out in our own minds what happened. Why hadn't we seen that our children were being abused right under our noses? As I began to emerge from that maze of confusion, I felt spiritually empty, thirsty for something more than the church was able to offer me. I knew that we, as a community, had to figure out what that something was, or people like me would seek it elsewhere.*

***Deepening the faith.*** When people are feeling at sea, one of the first steps is to ground them by reconnecting them with their spiritual roots. What would Jesus do in the face of a community that was disheartened and questioning its beliefs? Most likely, Jesus would encourage them to recognize that God was an ever present help in times of trouble. He used parables to let them know of the steadfast nature of God's presence.

One thought in helping congregants to rediscover their roots is to institute a series of groups on the teachings of Jesus and how they manifest themselves in our everyday lives. Group members might also be encouraged to look at their relationship with Christ. How did it begin? Has it faltered through the crisis? How and why? What threatened this relationship? How might they reconcile with Christ and bring him back into their lives? Often, discussing the relationship to Jesus in very tangible terms helps people to imagine how they might reconnect with their faith and deepen it.

Deepening one's faith also involves an acceptance of self as one of God's unique creations. This might be tied directly to the abuse situation, allowing individuals to forgive themselves when they feel that they have been complicit.

> *My husband and I were youth leaders at the time that Father Brian was abusing children in the parish. There were times, looking back, that I should have questioned more. Why did he insist upon taking certain children home, often alone? My husband and I couldn't even talk about it after he was arrested. I think that we each blamed ourselves and, at the same time, each other for not asking more questions or acting on our suspicions. I needed to forgive myself. I couldn't go on with the weight of the blame I had placed on my own shoulders.*

The discussion of self as a child of God may also address issues other than the abuse in the church. We all feel guilt over some pieces of our lives, and sometimes that guilt inhibits our ability to grow in spirituality.

Finally, deepening is about accepting one another and viewing each person as God's creation — someone who has within him or her the spark of divinity that makes them part of a community of believers. In fact, many faiths recognize the importance of saluting the divine spark in each individual. While I was in India, I was struck by the Hindu greeting of hands folded in reference and a slight bow. This greeting, called the *namastay,* conveys the message, "I salute the divinity within you!" I have sometimes used that salutation (after explaining it to the congregation) rather than shaking hands as people leave the church.

No matter how hard church members may try to leave the issue of abuse behind them, it will always be a part of their history. However, histories have a flip side — we can learn a great deal from them. This learning prepares us to meet the future better armed not to make the same mistakes again.

Abigail Johnson, in her book *Reflecting with God: Connecting Faith and Daily Life in Small Groups*,[4] suggests a procedure for dealing with a difficult event that might be applied to post-abuse situations. These steps may be difficult unless there is some distance and work that has already been done toward resolving the issues.

Johnson suggests that such reflection is best accomplished in small groups where everyone can express themselves with some degree of comfort. The first step is to *name the experience*. The members must be able to put aside their rationalizations and admit that this was a situation in which the pastor betrayed their trust and molested children. It often helps to develop a statement of what happened. The next step is for those involved in this reflection to *explore the experience and find another layer to the event*, a difficult exercise especially for those closest to the abuse. This is a time when feelings are named. How did it feel to have one's trust betrayed? What was especially challenging? What was happening to others in the situation? The third step requires one *to dig even deeper, and to expand one's thinking*. What values were compromised here? What were the power issues?[5]

The fourth of Johnson's steps is to *make faith connections*, which requires *finding God in the event*, also difficult to do in abuse situations. However, even in times of severe difficulty, God's presence can be discerned in the strength that individuals used to endure the events. A hymn or scripture passage that seems appropriate to the situation might be helpful. Theological themes or traditions in the church might also shed light on the circumstances. What was there about what transpired that has changed the beliefs or actions of the group?

It will be enlightening perhaps to *name the discoveries* that members have made about the events that so rocked the church. What have people learned about themselves and their fellow church members? Focus on the strengths and how members can support one another in the future. The focus should also be on God's ability to sustain and help to provide insight in the most incomprehensible circumstances. How can members build on this knowledge for the future?

The reflections *conclude with prayer* for the increased understanding if not of why the event occurred, then the strengths that emerged as people dealt with it, the benevolence of God in providing a refuge, and the hope for a future that will be free from such abusive events.[6]

Using a small group model and reflecting on the events of the past from the perspective of God's omnipresence and sustenance may also serve to deepen the connections between the members of these groups. At some point, there should also be a move to reunite people into a larger church community. Breaking down the task of reflection and then reconstituting can provide a powerful experience for a church body.

***Equipping the members.*** Any abuse situation involves an imbalance of power. As congregations look back, they might well discover that they depended too much on the leader — in this case, the pastor — and that person abused his or her power. To prevent such an event from occurring again, the laity needs to discover their own gifts and to be an integral part of the future church. Certainly there are many excellent reasons for equipping the laity, and preventing the further abuse of power is one of them.

Strengthening the involvement of the laity centers around helping members to recognize their gifts, their call to use them, and how they can do so. Paul refers to gifts several times in his writings. To the church in Corinth, he refers to one group of gifts (1 Cor. 12:7–11). Paul makes a similar statement to the Ephesians (4:11–13), and then to the Romans he mentions the gifts that are given to us by grace and encourages that they be used (Rom. 12:6–8). Although these gifts are references to qualities such as the ability to teach, heal, and prophesy, Stevens and Collins look at the concepts of gifts somewhat differently.

> Understood biblically and systemically, gifts are not something we possess, things that are implanted in us when we become Christians or have a deeper experience of God. Instead gifts are simply the persons we are in Christ and in relationships. *We* are the gifts. The bottom line is simply this: Gifts are ways in which people express their personhood in love in *concrete relationships.*[7]

These authors go on to say that it requires relationship for our gifts to be realized and that the "gift is a result of the interdependent relationship of members in the body of Christ."[8]

This interpretation of gifts may serve well when there is a history of abuse in the church. Members may need to rediscover positive relationships. Even if they have been supportive to one another through the crisis, there is still an erosion of trust. Seeing each person as the gift to the church community values the whole person, not just what he or she can contribute to the church. Ultimately individual members will feel more valued and less wounded by what transpired in the church, thus creating a closer church community.

One way to transform the future of a church as well as honoring the gifts that each member has to give is to invite the members to create a new mission statement. This offers three tangible forms of healing to a congregation. First, the very creation of a new mission statement, using a great deal of congregational input, can serve to strengthen congregational bonds. Second, creating a mission statement invites the church members to look forward instead of dwelling on the problems of the past. Also, members contribute so much to the process that they then feel committed to creating the church that they have envisioned.

Helping members to connect or reconnect, identifying and developing gifts to be used in relationship, and aiding in the process of knowing how and when to use these gifts provides a great deal of healing for a church community. It also encourages individuals to be other-directed, not just focusing on themselves and the hurt that they might be feeling. This prepares them for even further reaching out to others.

***Ministering to others.*** The last part of discipleship is ministering to others, either within the church or the wider community or world. The most obvious mission is to be present and available for those who have suffered directly from the abuse. However, one must also recognize the boundaries of your own and your congregation's abilities and expertise. Survivors and families need professional as well as church member help in their healing. When the victim uses a fellow congregant as a substitute for a professional counselor, neither party is well served. Even if the church member has expertise in counseling, there are ethical boundary issues involved in this individual providing therapy for the victim or family members. Church members can carry out other roles — by providing friendship and even encouraging a victim to seek help from a professional. Individual members might form a Care Committee to be of help to a victim (see Chapter 12) in conjunction and communication with a therapist skilled in working with abuse issues.

The second part of ministry is about mission to those outside the church. Typically, a church that experiences abuse by its leader will have a prominent place in the news for some time, often causing members to want to hide their membership in that community. To feel better about themselves the church members need to create a name for themselves within the community that overshadows the taint of abuse.

Once the congregants are helped to deepen their own faith and begin to value the gifts of one another, it is time to reach out to the community. One church did this by becoming involved in a mission that they understood well.

*Some of us began a support group for people whose lives had been touched by abuse and violence. We enlisted the help of a local mental health center that agreed to provide us with two consultants/facilitators. The group was open to anyone from any part of the community, and it grew to quite a few members. Some of those folks decided to come to church services as well. Those from other churches involved us in ecumenical worship and activities. Our church — the one that we felt people had pointed fingers at — was meeting a need for a whole community.*

Developing a mind-set that involves reaching out to others is not always easy to do, especially when a community has been inwardly directed. Sometimes it requires intentional reflection on how to do so. One way to do this is to invite members to consider what they would have liked from others when they were most in need of help. "I wanted others not to judge us," commented one woman. "Everyone was assuming the worst about us and our church community. The media added to the horror story. I would have loved just to talk to someone who had an open mind."

So, how can you help people to learn to be nonjudgmental? Suggests Luke's Gospel, "Do not judge, and you will not be judged; do not condemn and you will not be condemned. Forgive, and you will be forgiven" (Luke 6:36–37). Such a nonjudgmental attitude is preached by almost all religious traditions. Part of being nonjudgmental is the ability to listen to what another has to say without imposing one's own ideas or values on the words of the speaker. Many people would love to have someone to just listen to them openly and nonjudgmentally. As a therapist, I am struck by the number of people who seem to need just a listening ear when the rest of the world and those in it are moving so quickly that they do not have a moment to listen.

There are those in our communities who are discouraged and ready to give up. Several elders within a church volunteered time to help younger people to start their own businesses. The elders, many of whom had been successful businesspeople, were invaluable to the inexperienced new entrepreneurs. Encouraging others can take a very tangible perspective.

Appreciation is another commodity that many of us lack in this life. How good it feels to have someone tell us that we have done well. How validating it can be when someone recognizes how hard we have tried to do something even if it does not come out quite right.

Once the congregation has had a chance to consider the very personal question of what each of them would have liked when they needed others the most, it is time to consider how to involve them in the outside community — how to foster the spirit of reaching out to others. Again, problem solving or imagining groups might work well to join people in the effort. Two questions are important to consider: (1) What can we do to offer an open, accepting congregational atmosphere that will meet the needs and attract others? (2) How can we reach out into the greater community to further the mission of Christ?

Bringing together members to consider how they can reach out to others accomplishes several goals. It enhances communication and develops cooperation and collaboration, sharing responsibilities and making each person involved feel appreciated. It can teach conflict resolution, as certainly differences will arise. But they need to be worked through, keeping in mind the ideas of listening, being nonjudgmental and appreciating others. Above all, groups should be encouraged to remain Christ-centered and to see in each other the spark of divinity that binds us all. Finally, working together will help the congregants to once again develop trust in one another, something that is often destroyed by abuse within the church.

The exciting piece of discipleship forming is that each phase, thought, or behavior impacts others. For example, as the church members begin to see the impact that they can have in a wider community, they may feel more like the messengers of Christ, and consequently faith in themselves, in each other, and in God may be deepened.

Through this intentional revitalization, communities touched by abuse can truly heal — learning to communicate, trust, and forgive in the aftermath of what they have experienced.

## The Concept of Forgiveness

Rarely is the topic of abuse considered when someone does not bring up the concept of forgiveness. But forgiveness is a much misunderstood idea. What then is forgiveness, and how should it be addressed? The typical interpretation is to suggest that one forgive and forget, but that is not really what it is all about. First, a wrong has been done that has left significant scars on victims, families, and the congregation, and it cannot be just forgotten. Superficial forgiveness would only imply that the offender does not bear the burden of responsibility. Another cliché of sorts is to "just let it go." Forgiveness is not as simple as this either.

Forgiveness in the case of abuse within the church is based on the recognition that the abuse happened and that the abuser has the primary responsibility, while the church members also recognize their part in enabling. Once this has been fully processed and understood, the church must have completed any reorganization necessary to prevent the abuse from happening again. This last step includes some type of procedure to intervene if there is any question of abuse in the future. Once all this groundwork has been laid, with God very much a part of the process, it is time to talk about forgiveness.

In the treatment of families where sexual abuse has occurred, one prescription is for the offender to apologize to his or her victim. This step can have a very therapeutic effect both on the victims and on other family members and becomes an integral part of the offender's healing process. Certainly an apology from the offender to the congregation would also be beneficial when the abuse has taken place in a church setting, but rarely is the pastor able to return to offer this apology. A letter from him or her, read before the whole congregation, can be a substitute. Once members process their feelings after hearing this apology, they may be ready to begin to move on.

We spoke earlier about ministering to victims. Victims too must reconcile with the congregation and the congregation with them. Sometimes victims hold resentments because they feel that they were revictimized by the congregation not believing the reports of abuse. Other times the congregants resent the victims' accusations and hard feelings emerge. Reconciliation can be accomplished in a ritualized service of healing where God is called in as the healer of all. Other times, reconciliation can be part of a meeting where the congregation makes it known to victims that they support them and will walk with them on their journey toward healing. Since victims will most likely be children, care must be taken that this reconciliation is appropriate to their ages and development. Their families too may need this reconnection.

Reconciliation is also necessary with God. Some members, and not just victims, may have been angry with God, feeling that God abandoned the church in their time of trouble. It may be necessary to revisit the relationship with God and see how it might be strengthened.

Forgiveness then is undertaken when people in the church community have done the groundwork and can look to the future with hope. Forgiving is not forgetting or just letting go, but rather an acceptance that, although this crisis happened, it is part of the past and the church can move on, trusting in God that they will again learn to trust each other and work together. Forgiveness is moving on in peace, leaving behind resentments with others, so that members can forge new relationships together with God as the thread that binds them together.

With this vision in mind — a vision of God as the central force that joins people with one another and moves them toward the future — the pastor ministering to a church touched by abuse can make a real difference in the lives of the members.

## Chapter 12

# Adult Survivors in the Church

### Meeting the Adult Survivors in the Congregation

If sexual abuse is as abundant as experts believe, there is a good possibility that you are looking out over a number of sexual abuse survivors each Sunday without even knowing it. No accurate statistics are available about the percentage of people who grew up in homes with abuse, violence, or neglect. So how might you begin to recognize that there are adult survivors within the congregation with scars from a variety of childhood traumas? Some people are quite up front about their backgrounds and may tell you, some in more appropriate ways than others. When people tell you their experiences of abuse, it is important that you recognize that, unless you are trained specifically to counsel victims of childhood trauma, the best service you can provide is to refer them to a therapist who has such training.

Other survivors, with memories buried deep in their psyches, have never told anyone about their abuse. Why then might they choose a particular time to remember and or disclose what has happened to them?

### Why Adults Disclose

There are a variety of reasons, life stages, and events that might cause a survivor to finally tell someone about his or her abuse. These individuals may have disclosed their abuse or perceived that they did as children, but no one seemed to hear them.

For some survivors, *developmental tasks* cause them to remember or disclose. For example, the first boyfriend or girlfriend with the hint of sexual activity to come often stimulates anxiety and causes a former victim to seek help. For others, the promise of marriage and the expectations of being a spouse and parent bring back the memories. For others still, middle age and the expectation that one should be successful even when one feels out of control prompts them to seek help in dealing with these incongruities. Old age and the preparation for death can prompt a review and revelation as well.

For yet others, *relationships* cause them to break their silence. Sometimes they find someone with whom they want to spend their lives and worry that this person cannot be accepting if the secret of the abuse is revealed.

Some survivors are reminded of their abuse or neglect by *losses* in their lives — the death of the abuser or someone with whom they have shared confidences. The loss of a relationship, the loss of treasured things, and the loss of physical abilities may also bring up old feelings. *Additional traumas* may also result in reviving memories that have long been buried or ignored.

*Psychological triggers* often cause a survivor to talk about abuse or neglect that he or she suffered. The psyche stores memories in various forms, some in words and others in sensations. Sometimes encountering an event, hearing a word or phrases, or having other senses perceive a smell, a type of touch, or a sight can bring back the feelings attached to those memories and necessitate processing by the survivor. Sometimes these body sensations trigger flashbacks of the abuse or neglect, while at other times just the feelings surface. When Mattie smelled the distinctive odor of a particular type of soap, she would feel nauseous and anxious, and perspire with fear. As she processed these feelings in therapy, she began to have images of being sexually abused by an uncle. Only much later did she remember that the uncle used this particular kind of soap.

Some survivors reach out for help never knowing that abuse or neglect has played a significant role in their life. Sophie and Eric went to their pastor because they felt that their marriage was in trouble. After several sessions, the pastor began to suspect that their issues were deeper than she realized and she referred them to a trained marriage counselor. What eventually emerged was that Eric's sexual abuse as a child was impeding his ability to have a healthy sexual relationship. Without violence or anal stimulation he could not become aroused, and his somewhat naive wife was horrified by his needs.

## Residual Scars for Survivors

When someone has been abused or neglected as a child, it is often the residual scars that become obvious and may lead him or her to seek help. The scars that plague the lives of survivors can be many, some seeming relatively benign while others diminish the survivor's ability to lead a happy and fulfilled life. The residual effects may differ according to the type of maltreatment, the degree of trauma, and whether the abuse was perpetrated by a family member or someone outside the family. These residual effects may be divided into several areas that affect the way that the adult survivor sees the world around her or him. These areas are (1) mastery and control, (2) boundaries and self-definition, (3) reality testing and judgment, and (4) attachment and autonomy.

### *Mastery and Control*

One of the tasks that we learn throughout childhood is to gain a sense of mastery over ourselves and our environment. Ronnie Janoff-Bulman, in her book *Shattered Assumptions,*[1] proposes that most people hold three assumptions about life: that the world is meaningful, that the world is benevolent, and that the self is worthy. When these assumptions are dashed by our experiences in childhood, the individual has an uphill battle to regain control of his or her life. There is a *sense of powerlessness* that accompanies the trauma of shattered assumptions, and often *anger on the part of the survivor* over the fact that he or she did not have a childhood that equipped him or her to gain control over life. In fact, anger seems to be a universal effect of familial abuse. Feeling that he or she has been robbed of a childhood, betrayed by those who were supposed to love and protect him or her, and powerless over what has happened, the survivor's anger mounts. If it is turned inward it can result in behavior that can be self-injurious, or if turned outward is directed against others. Inwardly directed anger results in depression, self-mutilation, substance abuse, eating disorders, promiscuity, and other such behaviors. Outwardly directed anger may produce antisocial behaviors, aggression, or, in milder forms, just being a difficult person.

In addition to anger, many survivors of childhood trauma have *difficulty trusting* the world around them. If one cannot trust one's own parents, so survivors reason, whom can one trust? This trust may also extend to oneself and one's own abilities. Thus, it is not uncommon for survivors to sabotage their own efforts or question their own accomplishments.

Some survivors give up their control altogether when they become *addicted to drugs or alcohol.* These substances numb the pain but also rob survivors of the ability to face the real underlying issues. *Dissociation that becomes pathological* plagues some who were abused as children. Normal dissociation includes daydreaming in a boring meeting, or discovering that we are on a much traveled route when our intention had been to travel in another direction. For most of us, these happenings are just mildly annoying and soon forgotten. Pathological dissociation is different: it is a means to cope with one's abuse.

> *When my father sexually abused me, I used to "zone out." I'd pretend that my body wasn't there and I was somewhere else. It wasn't anything I consciously planned to do; it just happened. Then when he'd lock me in the closet, I sometimes wouldn't even realize I was there. I think that ability of my mind to go elsewhere kept me sane.*

Though such dissociation may help the survivor to cope with the trauma when it is occurring, this tendency to split off from reality may become problematic in later life. Melanie's husband complained that she never seemed to "be there" during their sexual intimacy. Melanie admitted that her mind automatically "left her body" during sexual relations, just as it had when her father abused her as a child.

The degree of dissociation can also become problematic. Trudie Chase in her book *When Rabbit Howls* writes of her ninety-three "personalities" that developed as a result of her ritualistic and sadistic abuse when she was a child.[2] Such severe dissociation, referred to as multiple personality disorder (or, more recently, dissociative identity disorder), where the personality divides into sometimes fully functioning aspects of one individual, is relatively rare but can be seen in survivors of severe abuse.

The feeling that one cannot control or master one's own life can also result in *depression, feeling numb or disinterested in the world* around one, *being fearful or hypervigilant,* or having *somatic complaints.* Physical reactions may also be flashbacks from the trauma itself. For example, some survivors who have been exposed to oral sexual activity complain of difficulties in swallowing or breathing in adulthood.

### Boundaries and Self-Definition

Mastery and control are closely related to boundaries and the definition of one's self. Some types of abuse promote confusion about where the self begins and the abuser ends. The mother who abuses her daughter is someone who has never sorted out her own identity sufficiently, viewing her daughter as an extension of herself. The pathological manifestation is that her abuse of her daughter becomes an almost masturbatory activity. As a result, the daughter may have difficulty with her own self-definition.[3] The *inability to trust* also creates in the survivor a question about whom she can trust and who can be let into the close perimeter of self. Some survivors cling to the family of the past, *unable to build boundaries as an adult,* and continually open themselves to renewed hurt. They often replicate this inability to separate by *becoming involved in relationships that perpetuate the abuse.*

Many survivors have been so conditioned to overbearing parental figures that they are unable to exert their own will. Some do not even know how to develop their own opinions or support them. "I let everybody walk all over me," commented one survivor. "I wouldn't even know how to stop them!" *Unable to be assertive,* survivors are often ripe to *become enmeshed in the controlling relationships* that they sought to avoid.

Boundaries have to do not only with the psyche but also with the body. Many survivors have difficulty with body issues, feeling that their *bodies are evil.* When they remember feeling pleasant physiological sensations in the midst of the abuse, they may feel that their body betrayed them and practice self-abuse of some type. This may take the form of *self-mutilation* (e.g., burning or cutting), *extreme overeating,* or *other types of eating disorders.* There is a very high correlation between eating disorders of all types and child sexual abuse. Some survivors of sexual abuse, feeling that their bodies are already damaged, become *sexually indiscriminate* or turn to promiscuous behaviors or even prostitution. The most extreme punishment of the body and the psyche is total self-destruction. Some survivors will attempt or commit *suicide.*

### *Reality Testing and Judgment*

The shattering of positive assumptions about the world and confusion about trust can also impair the survivor's ability to discern what is safe and dangerous within the world. Once, in a group of college students trying to support a young coed who had been raped the previous semester, one student commented: "You went out alone at night with a guy who you knew was being investigated for assault on a woman. What were you thinking?" While most of us learn not to expose ourselves to situations that would put us at risk for abuse, a survivor cannot always determine what is dangerous and what is not and does not always react appropriately.

During my research for my book *Secret Scars,*[4] I interviewed a young woman, Dolores, who had been raped by a group of men. She, her husband, and two other couples had been swimming in a deserted area of woods when a gang of men came upon them. The assailants had knives, but the two other women managed to scream and run away while the men tried to overpower the husbands. Dolores stood frozen on the spot where she had been when the group first emerged from the woods. When two of the husbands had gotten away and her husband was knocked out, the group turned to Dolores and all four of them raped her. She never uttered a sound.

Later, after the assailants went off and the victims had gotten help, Dolores's husband berated her for her lack of response. "You just let them!" he accused. "Why didn't you run or fight back!" Dolores admitted honestly that the sadistic abuse that she had experienced in childhood at the hands of her father had robbed her both literally and figuratively of her ability to scream.

Many survivors find that their ability to reality test is hampered, leaving them with *impaired judgment*. This inability to discern and react to danger may result in multiple victimization, one of the most distressing and puzzling aftereffects of being abused as a child, especially sexually. *Multiple victimization* occurs when a once-victimized child is victimized again and again throughout her or his life. For example, it is not uncommon for victims of rape as adults to have been sexually abused as children.

Only by understanding these symptoms can some survivors cope with the memories of the past.

### *Attachment and Autonomy*

Recent studies in the area of child abuse and trauma have found that a significant piece of the residual problems for survivors is that there has been an impediment in their ability to attach or bond with a caretaker in childhood. For most people, this bonding occurs naturally as parents meet the needs of their children, nurturing and loving them, and the children begin to recognize that the world is not a bad place in which to live. On this early attachment we build our expectations of and ability to form relationships throughout the remainder of our lives. Poor attachment results in individuals who have difficulty with socialization in general and relationships in particular.

Inconsistency or the lack of parenting in a child's early years can take its toll to a greater or lesser degree. This results in the *difficulty with or inability to form healthy relationships*. Not being used to touch or having been touched in abusive ways, survivors of physical and sexual abuse may have *difficulty with being touched*. Most survivors have never learned the normal tasks of childhood and as adults have *an inability to play*. Certainly, survivors of sexual abuse may battle with *sexual problems* that affect their ability to become intimate with others.

When one cannot attach properly to others, one also *does not develop a healthy sense of one's own autonomy*. The development of autonomy and a healthy self-concept is based on all the areas previously discussed as well.

Survivors of nonfamilial sexual abuse may have some of the same symptoms as those abused within families. Unless the offender is someone that the individual as a child knew well, however, there may not be the same sense of betrayal.

## Issues of God, Faith, and Self

When a survivor of clerical sexual abuse has been abused again by someone within the church, especially by a member of the clergy, issues of faith become paramount. That this survivor has even returned to a religious setting is a positive sign, as many who are abused by clergy understandably lose their desire to be associated with the church. Survivors of clergy abuse also tell us of their *confusion regarding God.* God is supposed to be all-loving and all-powerful. Therefore, why would God allow abuse to happen to a small child?

Survivors remember complying with the abuse and keeping the perpetrator's secret because that priest or minister was God's representative. In the eyes of the child, that clergyperson often seemed like God himself or herself. That this God-like person could be abusing understandably causes many survivors as adults to leave the church.

Sometimes domestic abuse seems to survivors to be sanctioned by the church. For example, said one survivor, "After being abused by my father, who used to tell me that I had to 'honor my father and mother' (from Exod. 20:12), I ended up being abused by the minister of our church. He too asked me if I loved God and when I said that I did, he began to recite a lot of biblical phrases that told me that what he was doing was in the Bible. Now I look back at those same passages and wonder that they could have been used in such a manner."

Many survivors of clergy abuse or those whose abusive parents connect them strongly with the church begin to *feel abandoned by God* as well. Because God has traditionally been characterized as male, survivors of abuse by male clerics or even fathers find significant interruption in their ability to maintain their faith in God and the church. But survivors of female abuse may also have faith issues. Survivors of physical and emotional abuse likewise associate what was done to them with some of the teachings of the church. Reports one of them, "My father, who was a really sadistic man, told me that he would sacrifice me as Abraham was going to do to Isaac, but that God wouldn't stop him. I think my father thought that it was funny, but the effect on me was that I had terrible nightmares. I hated Sunday school, and as soon as I could, I stopped going to church. Fortunately, I later met someone who helped me recognize that my father's interpretation of the Bible was a part of his abuse."

## Addressing the Needs of Adult Survivors

Armed with the knowledge about some of the ways in which past abuse or neglect might manifest itself in the lives of survivors, you may actually begin to recognize more of these folks within the congregation than you had previously realized. It is important to know what might be the most helpful responses for them.

While we may reach out to children who we feel are being abused, the picture may be somewhat different with adults. Even if you recognize the signs, I would recommend that you never tell an adult that you believe that he or she was abused. Many a lawsuit has been based on a therapist's suggesting to a survivor that he or she is a victim of sexual abuse. Certainly, if you are counseling an adult, it is legitimate, in fact advisable, to ask if they have ever been abused or victimized sexually, but the actual disclosure should be theirs. Survivors will come to you if they perceive that you are receptive to hearing their experiences.

There are ways that you can demonstrate that you are receptive to hearing from survivors. Involving the church in a safe church program and initiating the creation of a reporting protocol is one obvious way to bring the subject of abuse to the table. Another is to preach one or more sermons, specifically addressing the issue of abuse. One church planned a Bible study focused on "Healing the Hurt from the Past." The six-week program guided participants through their past abuses and helped them to recognize how God is present for them. There are also books about abuse and neglect that might be offered for people to borrow or added to the church library (see also Appendix 2). You might invite a speaker to discuss child abuse and neglect and how your church might become involved in prevention.

Before survivors seek you out, you should consider how you will respond. The first response to a victim telling his or her story is *to believe him or her no matter what your feelings*, the identity of the perpetrator, or the seeming questionable nature of what happened. Those who have heard survivors tell about abuse by cults will report that the survivor's story seemed like a page out of a demonic fantasy, so bizarre were the events. At this point it does not matter what the truth is. What matters is the narrative that the survivor feels compelled to tell.

When a survivor reaches out he or she may still not be sure if you can be fully trusted. The *survivor's trust is something that you must earn* through care, consistency, and understanding. This is a person who was abused as a child by an authority figure. Even for adults, your position as a clergyperson casts you in the role of an authority figure. Victims of clergy abuse will be working with their own set of conflicts about another clergyperson, even one of a different gender than the abuser.

Similar to hearing about abuse from a child victim, it is important to *monitor your own feelings* and *offer a calm and supportive presence.* Shock, embarrassment, or disbelief may be interpreted by survivors as rejection of them or betrayal. It can be particularly difficult when the survivor coming to you is the son or daughter of a church member, especially one whom you like and respect. At that moment, you simply need to be there for the survivor, though it is also important not to be critical of the perpetrator. Survivors may have very warm, as well as angry and resentful, feelings toward those who have abused them. Criticizing the abuser may shut down the survivor's ability to talk about that person and the abuse.

*Allow the survivor to tell the story at his or her own pace,* not interrupting for other than supportive words or gestures. It is also important to refer this individual to someone who is skilled in dealing with abuse and childhood trauma issues. If you are the survivor's pastor, the in-depth counseling required will not be possible given your role. *A different type of boundary is also required. For the most part, it is better to refer this survivor.*

Referral requires two things: first, that you have previously researched and have the names of professionals to whom you can refer, and second, that you are aware that parameters should be put around the telling of the narrative to you. If you know that you are going to refer an individual, allowing him or her to tell you all of the in-depth secrets will actually undermine his or her relationship with this future counselor. It might be better to say something like: "I can see how deeply you have been affected by this and understandably so. I am glad that you felt comfortable in telling me this, and I am concerned about you. But since this is not really my area of expertise, I'd like to see you make an appointment with this counselor. I think that she [or he] can be of the most help to you. Once you have seen a counselor, I will be glad to talk with you about how this has affected your faith."

Certainly the ideal is to be able to *collaborate with the counselor and the survivor* as they do their work together. When this is not possible, the survivor may still want to talk with you. However, these meetings should address faith issues. In the meantime, you might want to talk with the counselor (with the survivor's written permission).

Healing is not an easy process, nor is it a quick one. Some parishes are able to arrange for *support groups or individuals for survivors* as they progress along the road to recovery. This provides the survivor with acceptance and lessens the isolation that he or she might feel.

When working with adult survivors, we often feel that we would like to see the offender come to justice, but it is important that *the call for justice comes from the survivor.* Some survivors are ready to call for the offender to answer for the abuse, often legally. It is important to know the statute of limitations on prosecution of perpetrators as each state will differ. For this step, *survivors may also need a referral* as most clergy are probably not in the position to know the legal statutes or procedures. A good place to begin may be the district attorney's office in that area. There are also organizations that specialize in helping survivors seek justice (see Appendix 4). If the survivor was victimized by someone who could still be victimizing children, the issue becomes even more crucial.

Although clergy may be mandated reporters in your particular state, CPS may not be able to respond to a report if there is no indication of current abuse by a perpetrator. However, if an adult survivor comes forward, suggesting that the abuser may still be targeting children, CPS is more likely to look for ways to respond. In addition, the adult survivor may be able to take civil or initiate legal action for his or her own abuse that would then begin an investigation. It is rare that an abuser who has not been apprehended will cease his or her abusive lifestyle.

Although it is necessary for a survivor seeking legal recourse to do so though an attorney or district attorney, this can be a frightening step. The *survivor will need a great deal of support.* Facing the perpetrator again and recounting the abuse may cause the survivor to relive the abuse in a manner that brings up old feelings and conflicts. I always recommend that survivors seek therapy during this time. But spiritual support is also important, and a team of a therapist and a pastor and/or support group from the church can make all the difference in how the survivor is able to cope with the process of prosecuting the offender.

A survivor may want to confront an offender personally about the abuse of the individual. *I cannot state strongly enough the importance of having the help of a trained therapist for a survivor who wants to confront her or his perpetrator.* Therapists skilled in dealing with childhood abuse will prepare the survivor by taking her or him through the possible scenarios that might occur. We would like to believe that when an adult survivor confronts one's perpetrator, the latter will express shame and even apologize. However, this response is the exception rather than the rule and the survivor must be prepared for being told that she or he imagined the abuse or even caused it. Sometimes other family members get into the act, and the survivor can feel scapegoated.

Sometimes education is also required as survivors become more comfortable talking about their abuse. It is important for survivors to learn to choose their context and their audience for talking about their experiences. When individuals first realize that it is acceptable to discuss what has happened to them, they may tell others indiscriminately. Have you ever been among strangers—and not in your clerical garb or identified as clergy—and found that a complete stranger begins to tell you the most intimate details of his or her life? The reaction of many people is probably to back off and wonder why this individual is so inappropriate. Those in helping professions might not be as quick to react in this manner, but we still recognize that, in our culture, this behavior can isolate the individual and not gain the support or understanding that he or she so desperately wants.

Thus, survivors may need help in knowing who and when to tell about their abuse. While a support group or even an in-depth Bible study that talks about our own discipleship might be an appropriate place, a vestry or committee meeting would not be. So I tend to ask the survivors with whom I work, "What do you hope will happen when you tell your story?" Most agree that they want support and understanding. I then suggest that in the process of being abused they have learned well how to read the people around them. "So before you tell people," I tell them, "figure out who they are and how they might respond."

Not all survivors can discern the appropriateness of the people or situation, but many can. Those who have difficulty can also benefit from guidance in this area. If the survivor is seeing a therapist, these issues will probably also be discussed.

The key concepts in how clergy might respond to survivors in a supportive manner are as follows:

- Believe survivors' stories and value their feelings.
- Do not judge them for the way they have handled their lives.
- Allow survivors to set their own pace in their telling of their story and their healing.
- Know your limits. You should not counsel beyond your level of expertise.
- Even if you have expertise, know your role and your boundaries. Refer out.

- Empower survivors to take charge of their decisions and their lives, but do not push them beyond their ability to do so.
- Get support for yourself![5]

## Addressing the Needs of Family Members

Survivors of childhood abuse do not exist in a vacuum. They have family, and those family members may be a part of your congregation as well. They too may be in pain. In cases in which the abuse was in the home, the family members may be denying the abuse, feeling guilt about it, or feeling anger toward the victim for exposing the abuse to the world, even blaming the victim. Sometimes, siblings who have grown up in the same household express anger at the victim for talking about it. Nonabusing parents feel guilty that they did not see the abuse or intervene, or this parent may still be protecting the abuser and reject the survivor. When the victim has been abused outside the home, the family may also express guilt at not having been able to prevent it. Depending on the identity of the abuser and other family issues, they may not even support the victim.

*Kathleen had been abused by the family priest, who spent a good deal of time at the O'Malley's home. When, as an adult, Kathleen began to talk about the abuse, her family members were quite angry. Father Brendon had died several years before, and Mrs. O'Malley accused her daughter of "trying to tarnish the good Father's memory"! Her brothers and sisters admonished her for being so ungrateful after all the gifts that the priest had given them and all the outings he had taken them on. Kathleen wondered if they could possibly imagine what had gone on when he had taken her on outings.*

Be careful not to become too entangled in family disputes over abuse, especially when you are the spiritual leader for all of them. However, you might encourage them to seek help in sorting out their feelings about the abuse.

## Effects on the Helper

Confronting any type of abuse can have an impact on the helper, whether the helper is a clinician or clergy. This can be especially true when one is working with another adult who has an abusive background. On some level, there is the feeling of "there but for the grace of God go I." If your childhood was a relatively happy one, you begin to feel grateful when you see the devastation that an abusive childhood can wreak on some of its victims. But you may also feel a sense of *survivor's guilt.* "I was lucky; this individual wasn't." If your own childhood was abusive, you may find that *old conflicts arise for you.* It is important to recognize what your reality is and what is that of the survivor, and to have a place to go when the feelings that this person's experiences engender in you become too overwhelming.

Working with survivors of childhood trauma may well stimulate a variety of other feelings in those who seek to help and support them. Initially, as you begin to learn of the survivors' past you may feel *horror* or *dread.* How could a child possibly be treated in this manner? If the story feels too overwhelming, *denial* may set in. No, it can't possibly have happened that way! You may begin to avoid opportunities to hear more of the details (*avoidance*). You may also feel the survivor's *shame,* or become *disgusted* at what one human being could do to another. You may *pity* the past victim who had to endure such abuse. Having heard too much of the story, you may feel angry, even *rageful,* at the perpetrator or at the nonabusive parents who were not able to protect their children.[6]

As you talk with a survivor, you may also feel yourself taking on his or her feelings. The *anger, helplessness, powerlessness,* and *sense of being a child* again may be natural results of empathizing with the victim. As survivors grieve over lost childhoods, helpers too may feel this *grief.*

Helpers working with survivors of abuse may also feel what is sometimes referred to as vicarious victimization or the experience of developing many of the symptoms present in posttraumatic stress, like *fears, nightmares, hyperalertness,* and being *quick to startle.* It might seem that the world is not as safe or meaningful as you once believed, and you may seem to see victimization all around you.[7] Once again, this is a good time to seek to center yourself in your life outside of seeing the survivor. You may also need to talk with a spiritual director or even a therapist about these feelings (see also Chapter 14).

Survivors of sexual abuse may have difficulty keeping sexuality from permeating their lives. Therefore, this survivor may tend to sexualize therapeutic relationships. For this reason, appropriate boundaries must be maintained so that you do not put yourself in a position where your behavior can be questioned. Office doors with windows, or areas that are visible to others while protecting the privacy of the conversation, may provide some protection.

Despite the pitfalls of encountering the ravages of childhood trauma, the rewards for both the survivor and the clergy helper can be great. The spiritual aspect of healing is an extremely important one and one that can enhance other types of healing to a great degree. One of the most inspiring survivors I know is a woman who was the victim of neglect, abandonment, and sexual abuse by several different perpetrators. In adolescence, she acted out, abusing both her own body and those around her, but today she is a dedicated Christian who is not only active in her church and community but ministers to abused children in her career as a social worker. What brought her from a turbulent childhood was a strong faith and the help of several dedicated pastors and other spiritual people. She is an excellent example of the power of discernment and deepening faith that can bring healing to a survivor.

# PART THREE

# A Church and Community Look at Prevention

## Chapter 13

# Developing a Church Reporting Protocol

Recognizing that it may happen, the wise church will be prepared to respond before the need arises. A well-thought-out protocol of policies and procedures will give us support when we need to confront the church member who is beating his wife, intervene when a family abuses a child, or recognize that a child in Sunday school has been touched inappropriately. A protocol can even prevent abuse from happening within the church community. As one pastor commented, "I believe that the fact that we know the engagement process that sexual abusers use, are aware of the symptoms that abused children exhibit, and have procedures in place to protect both the adults and the children in our church will send a clear message to would-be offenders that they can't get away with abuse here!"

Before suggesting some steps for designing a church protocol, congregations need to consider a number of factors, as this chapter shows.

## The Influence of Polity

Different churches are influenced by the type of polity that governs them. Polity — or the structure of church governance — determines "how rules and procedures are developed, sustained and sanctioned."[1] In addition, one cannot begin to outline the chain of authority through which reports of abuse need to be channeled and acted upon without considering the polity of a denomination and how that polity impacts the individual church.

Churches can be divided into three basic governance structures or polities: episcopacy, eldership, and congregationalism.[2] In turn, each of these categories can be broken into individualized categories (see Table 13-1 on the following page for the placement of specific denominations within this framework). Episcopacy or governance by bishops can be further divided into monarchial episcopacy and managerial episcopacy. In *monarchial episcopacy,* bishops who govern have symbolic stature and are looked to as

## Table 13-1
## CHURCHES WITHIN SPECIFIC GOVERNANCE STRUCTURES

| | ***Episcopacy*** | |
|---|---|---|
| Monarchial | Managerial | Pastoral |
| Roman Catholic | United Methodist | Episcopal |

| | ***Eldership*** | |
|---|---|---|
| Representative | By Appointment/Seniority | By Discernment |
| Presbyterian<br>Reformed | Mormon<br>(Church of Jesus Christ of the Latter-day Saints) | Mennonite<br>Quaker<br>(Society of Friends) |

| | ***Congregationalism*** | |
|---|---|---|
| Connective | Associational | Without Over-Structures |
| *Lutheran | United Church of Christ<br>Congregational<br>Baptist | Christian<br>(Disciples of Christ) |

*Varies according to history, branch, and location; shows some aspects of episcopacy, but primary values appear to be congregationally based.

Chart adapted from E. L. Long, *Patterns of Polity: Varieties of Church Governance* (Cleveland: Pilgrim Press, 2001).

having full responsibility for the management and integrity of the church institution. *Managerial episcopacy* is dedicated to seeing that the church functions effectively. The bishop is similar to a superintendent of schools who oversees a system of connected smaller organizations to ensure that they function properly.

Despite the variations, all types of episcopacy require that protocol be written with recognition that there are channels of authority that go beyond the individual church governance. Churches represented by this type of polity must know how the central ecclesiastical organization responds to abuse situations. Frequently, these efforts to outline the approved response also have levels. In other words, central offices may have a protocol and the diocese, conference, or local governing body may have its own set of guidelines that interface with the national guidelines. The individual churches may rely on those guidelines. In some instances, especially in the types of episcopacies, there may be more room for individual churches to construct their own guidelines within those provided by the higher denominational offices.

Churches governed by elders, appointees, and other types of designated leaders, as well as those that have congregational polity, may need more guidance in knowing how to respond to abuse issues. Some of these denominations, on a central level, have developed recommended guidelines or made suggestions to parishes about how to respond. Others have left the issue totally to the discretion of the parishes or congregations.

Thus, one's denominational polity will be a significant factor in how an individual church goes about developing policies to respond to abuse issues within its walls.

## Wider Church Resources

It is also important to research whether the denomination to which your church belongs has a protocol or suggestions for devising one within churches. When I began this book, I assumed that churches would know if their denominations had any guidelines on abuse issues. Not only do most individual church communities not know the requirements or suggestions of the denomination, but finding these wider guidelines is not always an easy task.

For some time, I have been working with the Archdiocese of Boston as it attempts to deal with the crisis of sexual abuse within the Catholic Church and that diocese in particular. Part of the response has been to develop a diocese-wide protocol.[3] Once that task was completed, all of the parishes within the diocese were trained not only in the protocol but in child abuse prevention in general. I have watched the painful process of helping individual churches recognize the need for such protocol and training. People prefer not to face abuse. Sermons have been preached that cast stones at the trainers and developers of policies. People are frightened. There has been much resistance to the training and implementation of protocol and at this writing the efforts are continuing.

Knowing the resistance that people feel to dealing with abuse, some denominations have taken a stand on it (it is wrong) but have left the development of the specific procedures to deal with it to the individual church communities. Some denominations have offered guidelines but nothing more. Thus, as you begin your journey, it is important to discover what resources are offered by the wider church.

## Resources Available within the Church Community

*No one knew quite where to start when our small committee began the task of developing policies that could protect our children from child abuse. Then one man spoke up saying:*

*"My wife is a teacher, and I think her school just developed some kind of policies. Maybe I can talk with her."*

*We soon realized that the principal of this very same school was in our congregation. Someone else pointed out that a woman who taught Sunday school was a social worker for the child protection agency, and another committee member's husband was a lawyer. She was pretty sure he would agree to look over our final product from a legal perspective. Before we were finished discussing the issue, we realized that we had a myriad of talented folk right in our congregation who could offer valuable expertise as we designed our policies. It also gave the rest of the congregation input and made us feel that this was everyone's project.*

It is important to have direction in developing the protocol, as provided in this chapter, before you use your internal resources, but that is what this chapter is intended to provide. Once you have some ideas about how you should proceed, it is time to bring in the consultants.

## Categories of Protocol

Protocol can be divided into two categories: *response protocol*, or a set of policies and procedures that should be followed when there is evidence of an abuse situation that has already occurred, and *prevention protocol,* or the steps that the church will take to reduce the risk of abuse happening within the church or the church family. In my experience, most agencies, schools, and other institutions have combined these two types of protocol into one document.

In addition, there must be prescribed procedures outlined to address abuse situations that occur in the greater community and which come to the attention of church staff, as well as abuse of children or teens in the congregation by clergy or other church personnel. Again, these types of situations may be addressed as part of one protocol or document.

## Designing a Protocol

I have used several terms interchangeably, but it is useful to separate them at this point. *Policies* refers to "rules" or guidelines that one is expected to follow. For example, it might be a policy that no adult should be alone with a child. *Procedures* are action steps that must be taken to ensure that the policy is met. For example, if you are working with children and find yourself in a room alone with a child, you should make sure that the door is left open and you are in full view of other adults, or join with another class of adults and children. These, then, would be procedures. *Protocol* refers to the system of policies and procedures that enable something to get accomplished.

A protocol should respond to familial abuse, as well as abuse within the church. What should be included in such a document? Protocol for church settings should include:

- Provision for training that acquaints staff with the tools necessary to recognize the symptoms of abuse and neglect in children and the effects of domestic violence.
- A well-thought-out set of policies and procedures for the recognition and reporting of suspected abuse to child protection authorities, as well as protecting the confidentiality of victims and families.
- A clear-cut chain of authority that indicates responsibilities in dealing with abuse/neglect situations.
- Procedures for supporting the family once a report has been made.
- A policy statement clearly indicating conduct considered unethical for clergy or church staff.
- Procedure for making complaints with a specific person within the congregation designated to receive them.
- Procedures that provide for due process in assessing the validity of a complaint.
- Procedures to disclose previous complaints, findings, and actions at the denominational level.[4]

The most advantageous way to present a protocol is by generating a document or handbook that will be made available to all church members, but especially those coming into contact with children.

## Why Do We Need a Protocol?

Anticipating the questions that will undoubtedly arise about the necessity of protocol helps us to address them. We need protocol for the following reasons:

- To protect children from all types of abuse
- To protect clergy, staff, and volunteers who work with children from false accusations
- To protect the church from liability
- Because failure to respond to abuse within a church setting can affect an individual's faith

But the role of the church is not simply to prevent abuse within its walls. For no matter where it occurs, when one is harmed, it will affect the others. So churches must respond because:

- The effects of abuse are detrimental to a child's ability to learn.
- Abuse has residual effects that can be lifelong.
- The church may play a significant part in a child's life and, other than school and family, can be in the most pivotal position to help that child. If the abuse is within the family, that is especially important.

It is also important to have written protocol in place because churches experience a frequent turnover in leadership. When policies are made known to the entire congregation and a handbook of these policies and procedures is available to all, training of new church leaders becomes a much easier task.

Finally, secular authorities increasingly recognize that churches play an integral role in the lives of people who need help. With the inclusion of clergy in reporting laws, there is increased emphasis on church involvement in recognizing and intervening in the case of child abuse and neglect. Not only do protocols suggest how we might respond to this new responsibility, but most mandate training that promotes security in that role.

Who should have access to the protocol handbook once it is developed? The quick answer is everyone. The handbook should be made readily available to anyone within the church. However, particular individuals should be required to receive a protocol handbook and also be given training. These people include: all clergy, directors of Christian education, youth ministry staff, Sunday school personnel, and all other volunteers or staff who work with children or youth. Church officials and members of church governing committees should also have copies and be familiar with them. A protocol that is well known within a church community will facilitate appropriate responses when that difficult situation of having to respond to child abuse finally does arise.

## What Should Be Included in a Protocol?

A protocol handbook should include the following:

- A description of training of staff and others working with children, as well as the dissemination of the protocol
- Discussion of how to form a safety response team
- A description of prevention policies and procedures
- Procedures for reporting abuse or neglect suspected in the child's home situation
- Procedures for reporting abuse in the church setting
- Procedures following the report

### *Training*

It is vital that significant individuals (mentioned above) and ideally the whole congregation be trained about maltreatment and the church's response. There are some questions that need to be considered about this training. First, *what content should be included?* The following are important content areas:

- Definition of abuse, neglect, and sexual abuse, and the effects of domestic violence
- Symptoms of these different types of maltreatment that victims might demonstrate
- Policies/procedures (i.e., the protocol) that govern work with children within the parish

This book provides a beginning to familiarizing church staff with some of these areas, but there is not sufficient room in any text to cover everything. Most people learn more effectively by *doing* rather than just reading. Therefore, training would be better accomplished in a series of steps. *Anyone who comes in contact with children within the parish should be required to be trained in the above areas.* This can be accomplished by several training seminars — conducted by someone with expertise in child abuse and neglect — that staff and volunteers are expected to attend. Such resources are available within communities by contacting the child protection agency. In some areas other agencies provide information and/or training. Many district attorneys' offices have a child abuse unit that provides resources to the community. The Office for Child Advocacy (see *www.nationalchildrensalliance.com*) or the Children's Trust Fund (see *http://nccanch.af.hhs.gov/pubs/organization/trust.cfm*) in your area may provide information. (See the Appendixes for additional resources.) This is also another place where central denominational offices may be of help as many denominations have developed their own training materials.

In addition to the informational training mentioned above, all staff and volunteers must be trained in the protocol that your church develops or chooses to adopt. There should also be informational sessions for the entire congregation so that everyone knows the church's stand on abuse issues.

Specialized training should also be provided for staff and volunteers who work with children. Included in such training would be guidelines for working with children safely, including the church's stance on touching. Staff should also be schooled in how to make a child abuse report. This will be part of the total protocol, but those working closely with children need more in-depth training.

The discussion of a topic as weighty as child maltreatment can be anxiety-provoking for many people, so use various methods to raise consciousness. One such way is through sermons, and preachers will find an increasing number of sermon aids online and through written materials, such as McClure and Ramsay's *Telling the Truth: Preaching about Sexual and Domestic Violence*, which provides several model sermons in addition to giving pointers on what to consider when writing a sermon about such a potentially controversial topic.

### *Safety Response Team*

One innovation in responding to child protection issues is the development of safety response teams, referred to hereafter as SRTs. An SRT is a team developed within the church that responds to allegations of child abuse, both those that are perpetrated within the child's home and those within the church community. The SRT members avail themselves of as much additional training as they are able, through conferences, college courses, and workshops, so that they feel competent in handling most child maltreatment situations. Teams might meet regularly or only when there is a need.

Initially used in schools, this child protection team model is now being used by some churches. The advantages of such a team are multiple. First, an SRT provides a *group of individuals who are trained to respond to a crisis.* Though we often find ourselves paralyzed when facing such a crisis, we also know that a speedy resolution is the best response. An SRT can move quickly because the members are trained and prepared.

In addition, the SRT *provides multiple perspectives.* There is not just one person whose role it is to decide if this child abuse situation must be reported to a child protection agency, but a group of individuals who have conferred and find strength in the opinions of colleagues. The members of the SRT also *offer support* to the person who brings forth the concerns about child abuse.

When a suspicion is brought before an SRT, the members and the reporter discuss it and determine if it should be taken further. If the consensus is that the situation requires a report to someone beyond the church setting, usually the child protection agency, many SRTs take responsibility for making the report. SRTs *also see that the original reporter is kept abreast of what is happening* when appropriate. And this team *oversees the training of the church members* in issues of child maltreatment.

How should a safety response team be formed? Such a team may be appointed, be elected, or come forward as volunteers, but there should be some criteria for membership. Criteria for membership might be:

- a sincere interest in children and their well-being without feeling punitive toward parents who become abusers. Although abusers are responsible for what they do to their children, there are always underlying factors that make them also in need of understanding.
- an interest in having additional training in the area of child maltreatment and domestic violence.
- a willingness to make themselves available when necessary, either in person or via the phone.
- respect from the church community and being seen as approachable.

An appropriate number of members for a safety response team might be between three and five, depending on the size of the church. (The uneven number helps prevent tied votes.) Who should be on the safety response team? The minister, pastor, priest, or rabbi or his or her assistant might be appropriate, as well as the director of religious education, the Sunday school superintendent, or whoever is in charge of the children and youth. There should be at least one or two people who have no immediate involvement with the children's or youth programs.

Once the safety response team is formed, there will be several questions about its operation, including:

- When, where, and how often will the SRT meet?
- What role will the SRT take?
- To whom will the SRT report?
- If a report must be made to the child protection agency, will the SRT take on this responsibility?
- Will there be records of the meetings of the SRT? Where will these be kept? Who will have access?
- Will the composition of the SRT change? How often? How will new members be chosen?
- What additional training will SRT members be required to have?[5]

How often the team meets will depend on the members' availability and the needs of the church, but it is wise to meet periodically rather than just in the face of a crisis. Periodic meetings, like once a month, help members to become a team. If there are no reports to consider, these meetings might be spent arranging churchwide training, updating protocol content, or assessing the existing climate in regard to the safety of children.

The team members need to make themselves visible within the church community in a positive manner, so that when an issue arises, parishioners are willing to seek them out. For example, one church's safety response team sponsored a coffee hour at which they had pamphlets that they had created about the safety of children within the church. They also had games for the children and gave out little prizes, so that they would seem accessible to the children of the church. Another team planned a supper at which a speaker talked about child protection issues. The more identifiable the members of the team, the more approachable they are for church members.

Since SRT members will have the most training of any other church members, this team will make any necessary reports to CPS. The team will be familiar with the requirements of the central office of your denomination to determine if this office must be notified either before a child abuse report is made or simultaneously.

Record keeping is an important issue to consider. On one hand, there is continuity in keeping track of what has been discussed in meetings in reference to particular cases. On the other hand, the confidentiality of the victims, the alleged offender, and the families involved must be protected from the general membership of the church. Minutes of the SRT meetings or other such records should be kept in a locked cabinet, and authorization for access to that cabinet should be clearly articulated.

The composition of the SRT will change over time. It is advisable to determine at the onset how SRT members will be replaced. Swift resolution of replacement issues will ensure that the team continues to run smoothly. It should also be determined what types of training initial SRT members will need to have and how new members will be trained.

Although congregations have a great deal to consider in the formulation of a safety response team, the advantages over time far outweigh the effort involved in the up-front input.

### *Prevention Policies to Create a Safe Environment*

Much has been written recently about the policies and procedures that are needed to promote a safe church environment for children. One such document is Melton's *Safe Sanctuaries: Reducing the Risk of Child Abuse in the Church*.[6] This author suggests that there are some basic procedures that will go a long way toward reducing the risk of abuse within the church setting. Let me summarize these briefly.

The "two-adult rule" requires that there be two unrelated adults in any program area with children. Since child abusers thrive on secrecy and isolation, having two adults provides protection for children as well as more security for adults against the possibility of false accusations. Melton recommends that having two adults who are not related, even by marriage, assures that there is no collusion between them. This may be a burden on smaller churches that do not have the same number of available staff and volunteers. In these situations, another adult might be a "roamer," looking in on classrooms or meetings that are forced to have only one adult.

In addition to encouraging the use of two adults, the age of other youth leaders can become an issue. It is common, especially in smaller churches, to use teenagers in various roles with younger children. As a rule, this is not advisable when introducing a child-safe policy. Teens may not be mature enough to set appropriate boundaries or be fully responsible. Melton suggests that older youth leaders (e.g., twenty or twenty-one) should be at least five years older than the youth with whom they work.[7] Again, boundaries can become an issue if young people are too close in age.

Another issue related to supervision is the recommendation that all doors have windows through which one might be observed. If they do not have windows, then the doors might be made into half doors or left

**Table 13-2**
**SAMPLE PREVENTION POLICIES**

- No adult who has been convicted of any type of child abuse shall be allowed to work with children or youth in the church.
- Adult staff and volunteers shall observe the "two-adult rule" at all times. No adult shall ever be left alone with a child.
- Those working with children should have been members of the congregation for a minimum of six months prior to becoming involved with children's or youth ministries.
- Adult staff and volunteers shall be required to attend regular training.
- All classrooms or rooms for children's or youth work must be observable either through a windowed door, a half door, or an open door.
- No youth under eighteen will be allowed to supervise children unless in the company of an adult.
- All youth workers must be at least five years older than the oldest youth.

---

open when children and adults are in a room together. In fact, even in counseling situations with children or youth, doors should be left open not only to provide for the safety of children but to protect adults from false accusations.

Policies that include parents in their children's activities or at least notify them of the activities are important. Whenever a child is asked to or allowed to participate in an activity that is not part of the routine of Sunday school or other youth programs, parents should be furnished with a permission slip. In some larger churches parents of nursery-age children are provided with beepers, so that when the child needs attention or becomes upset or agitated, the parent can be called. In addition, parents can receive an orientation to the children's activities and classrooms along with being made aware of the safety policies that involve their children (see Table 13-2). Still other churches require that church ministry staff wear picture name tags so that parents know who is responsible for their children.

The screening and training of staff and volunteers are also vital to a safe program for children. Zarra emphasizes the need for screening all those who are in positions of dealing with children, but also agrees that this step might meet with a good deal of resistance. For this reason, he suggests that churches institute this on a step-by-step basis as follows:

## TIMETABLE FOR SCREENING

| | | |
|---|---|---|
| Month 1 | Weeks 1–2 | Announce a move to screen children's ministries workers and give reasons for doing so. Begin selecting screening committee members. |
| | Weeks 3–4 | Hold churchwide question-and-answer meetings. |
| Month 2 | Week 1 | Allow congregation to review screening forms. |
| | Week 2 | Hold another churchwide question-and-answer meeting. |
| | Week 3 | Introduce the screening committee. Have workers give testimonies in support of screening. |
| | Week 4 | Have a special recognition Sunday to honor children and children's ministries workers. |
| Month 3 | | Begin screening workers who are already involved in children's ministries and any new applicants. Give priority to those working with the youngest children and work up.[8] |

The question of who will be on the screening team must be considered. If there is limited resistance to the idea of screening, the safety response team may begin its duties by taking charge of screening. However, if there is a great deal of resistance in the church community, a special screening committee must be formed.

What is involved in screening those who work with children and youth? Zarra recommends that churches use the following:

- An application form that elicits general information, outlines specific ministry positions that have been or are being held, details experience with children, and provides the names and contact information of two references.
- A liability waiver that is signed by the applicant.[9]

Applicants must also be interviewed and their references contacted. In most churches, those who wish to work with children are now being asked to undergo a criminal records check (CORI) by completing a Criminal Records Check Authorization Form. (These forms are available through local police departments or sheriff's offices.) These checks determine if an individual has a criminal record.

The question of substitutes and occasional volunteers is often raised when screening is suggested. Many churches screen and train a pool of substitutes and volunteers that can be called upon when necessary.

The supervision of children is another important consideration. Some churches require that parents fill out registration cards for children at the beginning of each year. This registration also designates who is authorized to pick up the child after Sunday school. No child will be released to anyone who is not authorized. When children are brought to church, they may be brought to the sanctuary where they will be met by teachers or the director of Christian education. No child is left unattended in a classroom. These simple precautions further protect the safety of children and prevent children from wandering unattended in church building halls.

Some churches feel that there is a need to have policies on touching children and youth. Schools have battled with the controversy over touching for some time, and some have unfortunately prohibited touching children. Children need loving, appropriate touching and should not be deprived of this human contact. However, there may be a need for parameters. The touching should be done in public, related to the child's needs for care, and be age-appropriate. Children should be trained that they can refuse touch that does not feel right to them. Adults who work with children need to take responsibility for monitoring one another in terms of physical contact with children.

Well-thought-out policies for the protection of children will eventually become an integral part of the culture of the church. While some may argue that there is no need for them, the protection of children is an important part of ministry.

### *Procedures for Reporting Familial Abuse*

In Chapter 2, we considered how maltreatment might come to the attention of clergy or others within the church who work with children. A child may tell someone that he or she is being abused or tell another child, who reports it to an adult. Or an adult may suspect that a child is being abused at home because of the symptoms that that adult has learned to recognize that point to, or at least suggest, abuse or neglect. Chapters 5 and 6 discuss the mechanics of reporting and what will occur after the report has been made. But there must be policies and procedures to create a process that moves smoothly to avoid a minimum of trauma to the victim and all others involved. What should these policies look like?

First, we have to assume that your church has done some basic groundwork.

- Have you researched your own denomination to determine whether there is a policy in place at the central level?
- Have you determined the chain of authority (dependent upon your church polity) beyond the level of the individual church?
- Have you considered the formation of a safety response team—who will be on it and so on?
- Have you arranged for some type of training that will acquaint those who work with children and youth with the symptoms of abuse?

The next step is to research your state's requirements for reporting abuse situations. These are available through the local child protection agency (see Appendix 3 for listings by state). These guidelines usually outline the procedure for bringing a situation to the attention of CPS, and these agencies will supply you with the forms necessary. These forms should be kept in a central area at the church so that they are readily accessible when needed. It never hurts to develop a relationship with the local CPS office. Many CPS personnel are happy to speak with you if you have questions about whether or not a particular situation must be reported, and the CPS agency can also provide valuable training. At the very least, the church's safety response team should avail itself of CPS training.

Be sure to inquire about how reports should be made on weekends. Most CPS offices operate from Monday through Friday but have an emergency number that can be accessed on a weekend if a child is in imminent danger.

Policies should now be designed to guide those who need to make a report. If there is a safety response team, the procedure will be facilitated more efficiently because the team has already been trained. To develop these policies and procedures, think about what someone might do if an abuse situation is encountered. Consider the following scenario:

*Seven-year-old Betsy comes to her Sunday school class in obvious pain. She has difficulty sitting, and when she takes off her sweater her shirt rides, up displaying a large bruise in the area of her kidneys. From the appearance of it, the teacher worries that there may be some bleeding under the skin. She asks Betsy how she was hurt, but the child quickly pulls down her shirt. As the lesson progresses, the assistant teacher watches Betsy, who is crying silently. The assistant goes to her and asks if she can help. Betsy begins to cry harder, and the assistant takes her into one corner of the room to talk. Betsy admits that her father beat her. She is afraid to go home and was afraid to tell anyone lest she be hurt more. Her father had left the home after the abuse and has not returned, but Betsy is afraid that he will soon. What should the teachers do with this information?*

Policy and procedures here would indicate to whom the teachers must report this situation. An example of such policy might be the following:

*Anyone who observes a child displaying symptoms of abuse or neglect or to whom a child reports being abused or neglected must notify a member of the safety response team and the pastor immediately*. If there is no SRT, the minister might be the appropriate person to tell. However, in this situation, a service might be in progress and the minister is not likely to be able to leave. Therefore, there needs to be someone else who can be notified, if not immediately, at least as soon as the service is over. In this scenario, Betsy is likely to be picked up after church and may be in more danger.

The SRT should then convene as soon as possible. In this situation, it is likely that a report will need to be made to the child protection weekend hotline. Your policy should specify who makes that call.

What happens to Betsy during all this? Perhaps there is a coffee hour or something else that will naturally delay the need for her to go home. Chapter 5 reminds us that a child cannot be detained by anyone but the child protection agency. This fact should be included in the policy — that no one may detain a child after a church service and any other usual church activity (e.g., coffee hour).

There should also be a policy about notifying the family, but it is not always clear cut. Given that the church is the family of God, it is important to reach out to families and help them through their turmoil. Some will not understand why the church has acted in this manner until they are helped to recognize that they are in need of assistance and that the church's intervention will aid them in getting that. However, speaking with the family before the report has been made can jeopardize a child's safety.

### *Procedures for Reporting Abuse within the Church Community*

Policies that affect abuse within the church community are more often difficult to write and very difficult to act upon, but are absolutely necessary to protect children. Having clear policy allows abuse to be addressed in a timely manner that is more likely to protect children.

Allegations of abuse by church members must go through several channels. If the report is against the pastor, the safety response team should be in charge. This can be difficult for all involved, as can a case in which a member of the SRT could be the accused. Having policies in place provides a more objective handling of a very subjective situation. For sample policies related to reporting, see Table 13-3.

Part of the policy for both familial abuse and abuse within the church should be a statement with regard to record keeping. Although records should be maintained about the report, these should be kept locked and not available to the wider community. Remember too that only facts should be

---

**Table 13-3**
**SAMPLE INTERVENTION POLICIES**

- Anyone who observes a child displaying symptoms of abuse or neglect or to whom a child reports being abused or neglected must notify a member of the safety response team and the pastor immediately.
- The safety response team should then convene as soon as possible. If the SRT and the reporter determine that abuse or neglect should be reported to the child protection agency, the call shall be made immediately by the team designee or the pastor.
- No child shall be detained at other than a church service, Sunday school, or other usual church activity (e.g., coffee hour). If there is concern about the child's safety, CPS should be notified of this concern and asked how to proceed.
- The pastor or SRT designee will talk with the family of the child in question either while the call is being made to CPS or after.
- Clergy and church staff will give full cooperation to the civil authorities (CPS, police, or the district attorney's office) during any investigation that might ensue.
- The information of the abuse/neglect report will be kept confidential among the pastor, the SRT, and any others who are immediately involved in order to protect the privacy of the child and the family.
- All records of such reports should be kept in a locked cabinet, and the protocol should outline who has access.

included. Under recent laws in most states, an individual does have access to records pertaining to him or her. Hearsay information included in these records may be grounds for suit. The church's attorney may provide insight into what may be included in records.

### *Policies Regarding Known Offenders within a Church Family*

Churches are typically seen as loving and accepting communities, and therefore are frequently a place where known child abusers will seek support, help, and understanding. No matter what we may think of their

---

**Table 13-4**
**SAMPLE POLICIES REGARDING PAST OFFENDERS**

- Any known or previously convicted sexual offender shall not be allowed to work with children or youth in any capacity within the church community.
- Any known sexual offender must obtain permission from the Minister, safety response team, or the designated church body to serve on any committee within the church.
- Any known sexual offender will not be permitted to have a key to the premises.
- Any known offender will not be allowed to serve as a church officer.
- The name of any known offender shall be made known to the following:
  - Minister
  - Chairperson of the Nominating Committee
  - Chairperson of any committee on which he/she serves
  - Director of religious education and members of the Sunday school Staff
  - Head of the church governing body (e.g., vestry, board of deacons, trustees, etc.)
- All restrictions should be made known to the sexual offender in a discreet manner by the minister or safety response team. The offender will sign a written statement that he/she agrees to the terms. This statement will be kept confidential.

(Adapted from First Congregational Church, U.C.C. Policy, 1998)

offenses, they need to be accepted. However, it is important to set some limits in order that children are protected. The First Congregational Church of East Longmeadow policy offers some suggestions.[10] These are adapted in Table 13-4. For more information on returning offenders, see Chapter 8.

## Additional Policies

The policies suggested here are not necessarily exhaustive, but rather are meant to provide impetus to begin the process of developing a protocol that is tailored for your particular church. Explore what other churches have done, and research various texts and websites, including

- American Lutheran Church, "Families and Violence: The Church's Role," at *www.elca.org/jle/alc/alc.families_violence.html*
- *When Child Abuse Comes to Church,* by Bill Anderson (Minneapolis: Bethany House, 1992)
- Archdiocese of Boston, *Policies and Procedures for the Protection of Children*
- *Taking Care,* by Helen Armstrong (London: National Children's Bureau, 1997)
- Evangelical Lutheran Church in America, "Safe Havens for Children," at *www.elca.org/init/safehaven/packet/how.html* (2004)
- *Creating Safe Congregations: Toward an Ethic of Right Relations,* edited by Patricia Hoertdoerfer and William Sinkford (Boston: Unitarian Universalist Association, 1997)
- *Creating Safe and Sacred Places,* by Gerard J. McGlone and Mary Shrader, with Laurie Delgatto (Winona, MN: Saint Mary's Press, 2003)
- *Safe Sanctuaries: Reducing the Risk of Child Abuse in the Church,* by Joy T. Melton (Nashville: Discipleship Resources, 1998)
- *Preventing Child Abuse (Ages 9–12),* by Kathryn R. Reid with Marie Fortune (Cleveland: United Church Press, 2002)
- *It Should Never Happen Here,* by Ernest J. Zarra (Grand Rapids: Baker Books, 1997)

# Chapter 14

# Clergy Self-Care

The pastor's ability to be emotionally present for victims, families, and perpetrators is largely dependent upon his or her ability to remain in the flow of divine energy. To do this, we must be open and not so caught up in our own conflicts that we are unable to be conduits for God's grace.

## Seeing for the First Time

Encountering the destructive elements of human relationships is something that is quite familiar to clergy. But when you are thrust into the ugliness of child maltreatment or domestic violence, unable to deny the graphic details, it may become especially difficult to keep things in perspective.

The typical reactions when faced with the recognition of child abuse or domestic violence are disbelief, anger, helplessness, and denial. In the face of abusive situations, clergy often experience what is known in clinical circles as countertransference.

## Countertransference and the Clergy Helper

*Countertransference* can be defined as the transfer of feelings "from the helper's own past relationships with significant people to the present relationship.... The helper's needs are expressed in behaviors such as dominating, overprotecting, loving, pleasing, seducing, or manipulating helpees."[1]

How does one recognize and deal with countertransference issues? First, those in helping professions should explore, understand, and find comfort with their own values and attitudes. This may necessitate exploring the past and putting to rest some of the old demons that may lie buried there. Conflicts with parents left unresolved, for example, make one more vulnerable to becoming enmeshed in the conflicts between other parents and children and less able to be of real help to counselees or parishioners.

Second, and less tangible, one can often trust one's gut to discern when a victim's issues are pushing old buttons from our past.

> *As I listened to the child before me talk about the abuse he had experienced, I knew that I would need to refer him to another helper. At first, I wasn't sure why. Then I began to feel short of breath, weak, and helpless. I felt like I was suffocating, trapped in between walls that were closing in. It took me some time to process before I remembered why I might have felt that way. My father's extreme control over the family, his rages that sent us fleeing to our rooms, his yelling at anyone who got in his way when he was angry, had always made me feel like I was trapped. We had never been physically abused and when he was not drinking, ours was a relatively uneventful home life. But, as I thought about it, I realized that this child's story had loosed the caged and strategically forgotten dragons of my childhood.*

Initially, for this young minister, the feeling was one of discomfort. Not until later did she realize that her issues were those of countertransference.

Finally, having a healthy support system, those with whom you can discuss feelings and other issues, might help to gain recognition that you are in the realm of countertransference.

## As the Process Continues

We have been discussing the possible initial reactions that clergypersons might have to confronting abuse and neglect situations. Perhaps you have already recognized that it is time to call in reinforcements in the form of child protective services or law enforcement. It would be nice if one could then breathe a deep sigh and rest, knowing that all was being taken care of, but it doesn't always work that way. Not only might the abused, the abuser, or family members still seek your support, but many in clergy positions discover that they cannot let go.

Kirk Jones, in his book *Rest in the Storm,* uses the metaphor presented in the Synoptic Gospels (Matt. 8:23–27, Mark 4:35–41, and Luke 8:22–25) when Jesus is described as going to the back of the boat to sleep. Explaining that clergy should take the cue that they, like Jesus, need to rest on occasion, Jones goes on to identify several factors that make it difficult for clergy to take needed rest, or what he terms "blockades to the back of the boat."[2] These factors apply particularly to clergy who are embroiled in cases involving child maltreatment or domestic violence. The first of these factors is the "myth of our own indispensability." Ministers, priests, and rabbis often feel that they must be constantly on duty taking care of the needs of their church members as only they (in their perception) can do. Yet it is not possible to be all things to all people no matter how hard we try.

The second factor that Jones refers to is a feeling of invincibility in clergy that causes them to believe that they have limitless reservoirs of energy and resources. Because clergy are seen as professionals who can help others with "matters of deepest meaning and importance,"[3] they are often drawn into the murky waters surrounding abusive families. Because they are perceived to be close to God, families may feel that figuratively touching the robe of the holy person will bring them healing. This deep dependence and lofty expectation can be seductive and can lure us into believing that we can do the best for victims, abusers, and families. But by setting yourself up as constantly on-call and as an invincible healer, you may actually be doing the family a disservice. Let me suggest an example.

> *When Midge Roberti approached Father Sean about her suspicion that her husband, Mario, was sexually abusing their daughter, Gina, the priest hardly knew how to respond. He had seen Mario in church and could not believe that he could be abusing his daughter. Having had little experience with this type of situation, he counseled Midge as best he could. When Midge pleaded that he talk to eleven-year-old Gina, he agreed. Gina tearfully confirmed her mother's fears by disclosing that her father had been sexually abusing her for several years. Father Sean then approached Mario, who vehemently denied the allegations. Convinced that Gina was the one telling the truth and aware that he should be reporting the situation to Child Protection, Father Sean told Midge that he would go with her to report. Midge became hysterical and said that she could never "do that to Mario." She pleaded with Father Sean to counsel her daughter and her to "get us through this." Hoping that he could eventually convince them to seek help, Father Sean agreed. At the same time, worried about how he would counsel them, the priest sought the advice of another priest.*
>
> *"You have no choice but to report the situation," his colleague told him. "We are now mandated by law to do so."*
>
> *Father Sean told Midge what he had discovered. At first she was angry, saying that he would be betraying her trust. Finally she broke down and told him how much his counsel meant to her. She did not*

*feel that she could get through this difficult time without his support. At last, she said that she could never go to CPS, but he could call them provided he would continue to counsel Gina and her. Father Sean again agreed.*

*He called CPS and reported the situation. He did not think to mention that he had agreed to continue to see Midge and her daughter. Nor did he give the intake worker any more than the skeleton facts necessary to file a report. CPS began an investigation. Midge came into Father Sean's office three times during the week after he had made the report. One was a scheduled visit, and during the other two she just dropped in saying that she needed to talk to him. Between her second and third visits, Midge dropped off Gina and insisted that he talk to her. Feeling that it would help the girl to talk, Father Sean encouraged Gina to tell him more about the abuse she had suffered, which she did. During Midge's visits more history emerged. Mario had actually abused an older daughter as well. That daughter had eloped at seventeen, and did not have contact with the family. Midge described her older daughter as "confused and a bit seductive" and did not feel that the abuse had been Mario's fault. Now she feared that Gina was taking after her sister. Midge then begged that he "keep all this a secret" and reminded him that talking to him was "like confession," and he was obligated to tell no one.*

*Several nights after she had visited Father Sean for the third time, Midge called the priest at 3 a.m., hysterically explaining that she thought that Mario would soon be arrested. She said that he had threatened suicide and had left the house. She was frantic and begged Father Sean to come over immediately to "pray with her." Father Sean went to the house to be confronted by a sobbing and irrational Midge, who said that Gina had locked herself in the bathroom. He finally talked the girl into unlocking the door and discovered that she had tried to slit her wrists. Not knowing what else to do, Father Sean called an ambulance. Midge did not want her daughter to be hospitalized and angrily told him that he had made everything worse and "what kind of a priest was he anyway?!" Several nights later, the priest confessed to his colleague that he was feeling "out of his depth."*

By trying to be the sole support of and confidant for mother and daughter, this well-meaning priest actually muddied the waters. Had he told CPS what he knew early on and provided support rather than actual counseling for Midge, the investigating worker would have had an easier time of discovering the true facts of the case and taking steps to protect the family members from harm. Families where abuse is present are embroiled in secrets, and by becoming enmeshed in their web of intrigue, well-meaning clergy make it more difficult for the secrets to be uncovered and for the family to receive help. This priest's ministrations to the nonprotective parent, Midge, made Gina feel even more abandoned and may have contributed to the motivation for her suicide attempt. And Father Sean's probing Gina for details contaminated the district attorney's case against Mario so that he was never prosecuted. Father Sean emerged from the experience feeling battered and unsure of himself. He had thought that he could help, and his disillusionment was acute.

What might this clergyman have done differently? First, as a mandated reporter he should have brought the situation to the attention of CPS at the outset, explaining to the family that he was obligated to do so. Had Father Sean reported the situation to CPS, and suggested to the worker that he support Midge and her family through the investigation, not allowing the disclosure of intimate details, but facilitating their disclosure to and cooperation with the CPS investigation, the Roberti family and Father Sean might have come out of the experience less traumatized.

It is natural given our training to feel that we as clergy can offer hurting individuals comfort and healing. In many cases that may be all they need. But in such specialized areas as family violence, some expertise is necessary. A team approach of trained as well as caring professionals gives the family a better opportunity to benefit from help. Leave investigation and in-depth counseling to those trained in abuse intervention. Instead, clergy can offer the spiritual support that families so desperately need during a time when many feel that God has forsaken them.

## When Abuse Has Been Close to Home

In the last few years, the media has been filled with reports of abuse by clergy. It is no longer an uncommon experience to suspect or know that a child is being abused by a fellow clergy member. Newly developed or developing protocols and procedures tell us how to respond logistically, but what about the *feelings* that the discovery of abuse by a colleague engenders? One minister described how he felt when he discovered that his colleague from another denomination within the same town had been abusing children.

> *I had known Pastor Pete for years. We had served together at ecumenical functions, provided chaplain services at the local hospital, called each other for support, and even shared a dinner or two together. When I read in the paper that he had been arrested for abusing boys in his parish, I was sure that there had been some mistake. When more victims came forward, many of whom were now men who had been abused by Pete years earlier, I began to wonder if there was some type of a conspiracy. But when a close friend of my wife's and mine told us what had happened to her son, I could no longer deny the reality. I literally sat down and cried. Why did he do such a thing? What was he thinking? I remembered all our times together. And then I began to feel dirty myself. I thought back over all the ecumenical youth trips we had cosponsored, wondering if I had ever been inadvertently involved. My wife helped me to realize that it was not my problem but Pete's. Then I blamed myself because I did not see what was happening. Weren't there signs? Was I blind? I tortured myself with sleepless nights of wonder and self-chastisement. Had it not been for a concerned, supportive wife, I do not think I would have made it through those first days.*

McDonough discusses the effects that abuse has on the nonoffending clergy. He suggests that the self-image of clergy often suffers.

> Many clergy members grew up in families and communities in which the profession of ordained ministry was held in exceptional high regard.... Clergy have perceived their profession as uniquely trustworthy and valuable to society.... The misconduct scandal of the past decade has caused many clergy members to question the trustworthiness of their vocational field. Clergy speak of a sense of shame at their own ordination and a hesitancy to wear distinctive dress and other signs of office in public.[4]

Like the above pastor, many clergy members also blame themselves for not recognizing or acting more quickly when they had suspicions that abuse might be taking place. Some begin to think back to discover or be embarrassed about their own past boundary violations. McDonough also suggests that the reports of abuse by fellow clergy may actually join with other factors to become a catalyst for the departure of nonoffending clergy from ministry.

Clergy members have also scrutinized and in some cases altered their own behaviors. "I used to think nothing of hugging little children in my parish," explained one priest. "Now, I am cautious. I don't want to give anyone fuel for misunderstanding my motives. I feel like I always have to be on guard." Other clergy members admit to being much more careful about how they handle youth activities. One minister told me that he will never conduct a youth trip or outing without at least two other adults, and he never allows any of them to be alone with a child who is not their own son or daughter.

It is sad that such an atmosphere now exists. Perhaps in time, greater awareness of the problem of abuse and more effective prevention will allow clergy to feel more relaxed and less fearful.

## Reporting One's Colleagues

In Chapter 10, we discussed the fact that there is no more difficult task than being the first one to recognize impropriety on the part of a colleague and knowing that one must report it for the sake of his or her parishioners. "I knew that it had to be done," explained one minister, "but it was one of the most painful things I have ever experienced. I don't think that Jed's wife will ever forgive me, even though I know that she was already considering divorce."

Marie Fortune, well known for her speaking out against abuse by clergy, explains why she feels that abuse must be reported. She explains that abusers will reoffend if they do not receive specialized treatment. Those who sexually abuse children deny, minimize, and lie to protect themselves. It is important not to get caught up in these defensive mechanisms. Even though offenders may seem remorseful, they will usually not follow through getting help without being compelled to do so. Since child maltreatment is actually an abuse of power, such treatment is more effective when it is mandated by another form of authority, like the court. Fortune makes the point that clergy do not have the skills or the resources to treat offenders or assist victims. She concludes that "quick forgiveness is likely to be cheap grace and unlikely to lead to repentance."[5]

All these facts aside, there is little that will make it easy when a fellow clergy person has taken on the role of offender. There are some very natural reactions when you suspect abuse by a colleague. These mirror in some instances how we feel about the recognition of abuse in general, but are intensified by the closeness to ourselves and our vocation. Initially, there may be the disbelief and the denial. As you become more convinced of the reality of your colleague's misconduct, you may feel agony about what to do. To report the situation to the proper authorities may feel similar to Judas fingering the pieces of silver at the last minute before he plants that betraying kiss. But there is a major difference. Not to intervene in the situation of abuse is to sentence other victims to betrayal.

*I suspected that the senior minister was inappropriate with the children he seemed to have constantly around him. I told my husband of my fears, thinking that he would talk me out of doing anything about it. But he surprised me by saying that he had also had concerns. He also told me that he had faith in my perceptions and if I had such strong suspicions, I was probably onto something. That was not what I wanted to hear. I felt that even confronting my superior about his actions was a betrayal. He had been good to me, and I owed him a great deal. But then I watched the children... how innocent they were. And I remembered the ones who had stopped coming to church and wondered if this had anything to do with it. Finally I knew that I had to do something to at least ease my mind that children were not being harmed.*

This young minister went to her bishop, who had also had his suspicions about the minister in charge of her church. What followed was a painful time of disclosure and revelation. "I had nightmares about whether I had ruined his life," she continued. "But I finally realized that I had protected other children in the church as well as enabling this minister to get some help."

Even if you are forced to report a fellow clergy member, you may be left with doubts. But remember that being a spiritual leader is to help others grow in their search toward truth. Harming others, as an abuser inevitably does, is not in keeping with spiritual wholeness. Only through intervention can this colleague be helped to regain a positive direction spiritually. Growth may be accompanied by pain, as much as we would like to avoid it.

## Wrestling with Old Dragons

In this day when statistics tell us that a significant number of adults were abused or neglected, or were witnesses to domestic violence in their own childhoods, it should not be surprising that a fair number of these adults become clergy. The helping professions attract those who have their own childhood dragons and want to help others slay theirs. Most of the time our past dragons can be made to behave and kept in their dens, but dealing with other people's abuse problems tends to waken them and call them out. If you have suffered abuse in your own childhood, you may find it difficult to cope with your memories and feelings from the past.

Survivors from childhood abuse often feel that their perception is distorted. Some past victims, due to their heightened awareness, see abuse everywhere. Therefore when they are confronted with an actual abuse situation, they may assume that they are just imagining it. Conversely, other survivors are convinced that what happened to them was unique and therefore deny the presence of abuse in the families or lives of others, even if it seems obvious. In neither case do many survivors feel they can trust their own judgment. If you have had any of these feelings, it is even more important that you share your concerns with someone in your support system. Their perceptions might help you to sort out reality.

Abusive childhoods leave one with scars, often hidden ones. When you are confronted with abuse situations in your current life, it may create anxiety for you. Old fears and phobias may re-emerge. Nightmares and flashbacks may reappear. Old feelings of paralysis, guilt, or helplessness may emerge. You may feel yourself consumed with feelings of rage against the perpetrator or nonprotecting parent or even anger at the victim for his or her inability to act. This feeling can also cause a great deal of guilt in you as you may know well how paralyzed the victim feels. All of these feelings may motivate you to seek help through professional counseling. Even if you have been in therapy in the past, the healthiest survivors recognize that an occasional counseling tune-up is necessary, especially when life has placed too-familiar traumas in their paths.

In addition to such deeply personal reactions, you, as past victim, may remember how ineffective the helping system (e.g., CPS, the police, or the courts) may have been in your own case and hesitate to involve them now. But the reality is that the systems working with childhood abuse have been updated no matter how negatively the media sometimes portrays them. Training for CPS, police, and court personnel is more prevalent, and there is an emphasis on more humane treatment of victims and families as well as offenders. No longer are children removed from their homes as a *first* resort. Instead, social workers try to work with families to keep them together if they are able to protect the child from further abuse or neglect. And as other professionals, like clergy, are designated as mandated reporters and begin to join the helping team, the prognosis for healing is better than it was in years past.

## Taking Care of Ourselves

This chapter is dedicated to helping clergy members who deal with abuse situations to practice self-care in the face of a disturbing and emotionally draining task. Part of coping with this emotional drain is naming and being prepared for feelings that may arise. But the minister, priest, or rabbi must also take steps to protect himself or herself from the burnout that can result from intervening in abuse situations.

Whether the abuse comes from the home, the community, or within the church itself, the effects on clergy who confront it can be profound. Therefore, it is vital that clergy practice *intentional* self-care. The first part of this is attitudinal and has been alluded to earlier in the chapter. Recognizing that one is neither indispensable nor invincible is vital. As clergy, we may believe that we have the gift of healing, yet if you are not trained specifically to deal with abuse situations, you could do more harm than good if you try to be the primary helper. You can provide invaluable support to victims, perpetrators, and family members while still cooperating with child protection and/or law enforcement. In fact, this support can provide a conduit for families to get the help they need.

There is no more important time to spend time in "the back of the boat" (to use Jones's image mentioned earlier) than when confronting abuse situations. Jones suggests some important steps to taking the responsibility for self-care. First, one must *accept the reality that such self-care time is needed.* Then *learning to refuse responsibilities* that may be pressed on one is important.[6] For example, a family member in pain may want to confess all and see you at any time of the night or day, but you are of more help to yourself, as well as to them, if you set some limits. The facts of the abuse need to be told to the investigating agency, not to you in a confidence that you do not feel you can break. And you will be better able to support this needy individual if you see her or him during regular hours rather than at times that rob you of your own rest.

It is especially important when going through a difficult time like supporting people in abuse situations that clergy plan downtime for themselves. Once you have involved other professionals, they can pick up the slack when you are away or "off duty." This downtime should be spent in truly relaxing pursuits that will mobilize your energy and give you the resources to be effective when you return to work. Prayer is also important in times of crisis. But prayer, although extremely powerful, may also need physical manifestations. For example, one pastor told me that she prayed that everything would work out well for a family that had come to her attention. She prayed, but she made no report nor did she offer physical help in any way. Coupling prayers with action would have been more effective.

Jones also mentions the importance of pacing oneself.[7] When we are caught up in busyness and add the anxiety of a crisis situation, we greatly diminish not only our effectiveness but also our own endurance. There is much to be said for what many of my generation learned from the technique taught in natural childbirth classes. One piece of those lessons that I still use is the "cleansing breath." To do this one takes a deep breath in through the nose and breathes out through the mouth. At the same time, I find concentrating on the breath centers my whole being. I often use this in times of stress. A succession of such breaths gives one an opportunity not only to center but to calm down and quietly plan how to pace oneself.

In addition to such self-care techniques we need vital support systems when working with abuse situations. The isolation and secret keeping so characteristic of abusive families can be contagious. To be truly effective in dealing with them, helpers must surround themselves with their own supportive people with whom they can be open and honest. Although the constraints of confidentiality may make it impossible to discuss the specifics of cases, we can use support systems to vent about our own feelings or to relax. Whether it is a supportive spouse or partner or close friends, we all need the comfort of someone who is there for us, particularly during crises.

We are much better able to make a difference to those in trouble if we recognize our own vulnerability and need for self-care. Then, attending to these needs will make the difference between offering true help or burning ourselves out in the process.

## Chapter 15

# Hope for the Future

The best way to respond to child abuse and neglect is to prevent it. Clergy can have an integral role in that prevention. What can we learn from past efforts that will help us in providing assistance ourselves?

## Prevention Efforts to This Point

To date, there have been three areas of prevention in the field of child abuse and neglect. *Primary prevention* refers to the efforts that have been made to educate people about ways to prevent maltreatment in general. This education has mainly been centered around training children in schools in areas that may protect them from abuse. For example, we know from studies of abusive parents that they are deficient in certain skills. One well-known child advocate broke these skills into five tasks that abusive parents never learned: to make decisions, to take responsibility for their own actions, to delay gratification, to get their needs met appropriately, and to separate feelings from actions.[1] The lack of these important skills makes these parents at higher risk to abuse their children. Therefore, teaching children all these tasks holds promise for interrupting the cycle and making them healthier adults.

In addition, schools now strive to teach children important life skills and help bolster children's self-esteem. Considering that the maltreatment of children is often based on the parents' feeling of inadequacy and poor self-image, the hope is that better equipped children will be better parents.

Today, schools often teach children self-protection in sexual abuse situations. The three key components are: that their bodies are their own; that it is therefore acceptable for them to ask adults not to touch them, especially when it does not feel right; and that they must tell a trusted adult when this touching does happen. Schools also educate children about healthy sexuality and some even talk about parenting skills. These are all positive steps in helping children prepare for the future as well as helping them to protect themselves as much as possible.

There is also an increasing effort on the part of agencies to educate the general public about abuse and neglect. Certainly we as a society are more conscious of the dynamics of abuse than we were in our parents' generation. As a result of this raised consciousness, parents are more likely to be able to talk with their children about the dangers of abuse.

*Secondary prevention* refers to services that have been offered to populations that are considered at high risk to abuse their children if there is not some education or intervention before the fact. Agencies that serve children have been active in providing services for at-risk parents. For example, an increasing number of programs are available for teen parents to help them to better care for their children. In addition, some programs provide support for new mothers of any age, especially those who may not have had adequate models for mothering. One of the best known of these programs is Healthy Start, a program begun in Hawaii that has now become widespread. This program offers long-term in-home services for parents until their children are three years old.

Medical facilities have also become better at recognizing and referring parents who might need help in their parenting. In addition, early screening in schools may identify children who are having difficulty at home and whose parents are in need of additional supports. And there is more recognition that parents from other cultures may be in need of specialized, culturally sensitive intervention.

Finally, *tertiary prevention* is designed to prevent abuse from happening again once it has been identified. Many of the suggestions that have been made throughout this book represent ways that the abuse cycle can be interrupted and children can be protected from further abuse or neglect.

## Becoming an Advocate for Children and Their Families

Churches are in an excellent position to be advocates for children, and clergy are important advocates for social change. The efforts that you and your congregants make can be on several levels, locally, statewide, and nationally. The following are just a few suggestions. You may well find other ways to advocate for children and their families.

### *On the Local Level*

Although there are many areas in which one can be active in advocating for abused and neglected children in the local community, there is often more power in numbers. Ecumenical efforts can afford greater results. Even if the service is provided by your particular church, having the support of other worship communities strengthens the whole. So, for example, churches within a community might well raise the consciousness of the whole geographical area by sponsoring informational meetings on family violence or the needs of children.

*One June, our church invited speakers from various types of agencies that serve families where there is violence. The panel of professionals discussed how each agency helped people and how we could strengthen their efforts. They outlined what families experienced and how children may even end up in foster care for a time. The agency representative emphasized that they are always looking for people to apply to be foster parents. She also suggested that we might contribute to foster children's school supplies or other needs for the next school year. The CPS social worker reported that, although they have lots of donations at Christmas, there are other times — like the beginning of the new school year — when kids need things as well. As a result, we launched a school bag campaign. We got lists of the school needs of kids who were in CPS care and asked parishioners for donations of school supplies, money, and school bags. It took us a good part of the summer to collect the supplies and the bags and match them with our list of the needs of particular children. We are a community with a great number of summer people, and we even got them involved. And the two other churches in our community also wanted to be a part of the campaign. Although we are a relatively small church (at least in the off-season months) we managed to fill over one hundred school bags for the CPS agency. It made us feel great that we could help in this small way. It also brought us together as a community.*

Another possible project for churches is to make contact with the local women and children's shelter and offer to aid them with donations of toiletries for people in the shelter and supplies that these women and their children might need to set up house away from their batterer. Or the shelter might appreciate specific food donations or money to buy supplies. One small office offered to buy and donate winter coats, boots, and mittens for children. Such efforts not only serve to educate church members about child abuse and domestic violence, but also help them to know the individuals involved.

CPS agencies cannot always provide for the needs of the children they service. It may help them to have extra funds or person power available. One suggestion is to connect with the local CPS office and offer to set up a fund for those needs that their budget cannot accommodate. At one time, the erstwhile Office for Children in Massachusetts had a fund through its Community Council called "Individual Kid Money." These funds were used for needs that CPS could not meet. For example, the child who is graduating from high school might want a special outfit that CPS cannot furnish. Another child might be particularly skilled in music and would love to take lessons to play an instrument, or this child could be a part of the school music program if he or she was able to rent an instrument. Providing these small extras for children whose parents cannot afford to do so would be a welcome gift.

Since one contributor to abuse and neglect is parental stress, a church community might also sponsor an after-school or parental respite program. For these projects one might need to enlist the help of trained professionals who deal with abused and neglected children. Often the lack of physical space prevents such programs from happening. Check this idea with the church's insurance carrier, but arrangements can often be made if there is a real desire on the part of church members.

Making the church available for meetings such as Parents Anonymous (a self-help group for overwhelmed parents), parenting workshops, or other such groups may meet a significant community need. As I have traveled to different churches to hold training for clergy, I have become aware that many churches now charge for community groups to use their facilities, and some of these fees are quite substantial. This fee usually goes to upkeep, heat, electricity, and wear and tear on the building, which is understandable. But perhaps part of the church's mission on behalf of abused and neglected children could be to offer the facilities to such groups free of charge.

Earlier, we discussed familiarizing yourself with professional services within the community that serve children and their families. Your church might collect pamphlets and information about available community resources and display these both in the church somewhere and at community functions.

Some people have difficulty accessing services because they are intimidated by the obligatory forms that they must complete. Perhaps a group of volunteers from your church would be willing to make their services available to parents who need help accessing services and completing forms.

### On the State or National Level

A computer search of your area might turn up a number of worthy causes or important programs in which a church might want to become involved. You might try such phrases as "advocacy for abused and neglected children" and add the name of your state to find services in your regional area.

Nationally, numerous agencies work for child abuse prevention. Almost all states have a Children's Trust Fund. These agencies, originally founded by pediatrician and child abuse expert Ray Helfer, are dedicated to providing a wide array of child abuse prevention and training. In addition, Child Advocacy Centers across the country are involved in similar activities. Search for these by name with the name of your state.

Organizations such as the Children's Defense Fund, the National Children's Alliance (formerly the National Network for Children's Advocacy Centers), Prevent Child Abuse America, the National Center for Missing and Exploited Children, and the Child Abuse Prevention Network might have ideas and suggestions. In June of 2006, the Children's Bureau of the U.S. Department of Health and Human Services developed the Information Gateway, a website that has consolidated the information from a variety of the above named agencies and others to provide resources for those interested in all types of child welfare, including child abuse and neglect. This is a website well worth checking out. It can be accessed at *www.childwelfare.gov.*

Whether your contributions to prevention efforts are local, state, or national, they can be effective and will give the church members a sense that they can do something concrete to help children and their families.

## Supporting Societal Changes

To more fully stem the tide of violence in families and toward children, the efforts must be seen in societal changes as well as contributions of time and energy to agencies and organizations. In our churches and our faith we can find the insight, the energy, and the courage to seek change throughout the culture.

Through our faith teachings and especially those of Christ, we are taught *respect and compassion* for one another. Earlier, I suggested that we learn to view the divinity in each and every individual, recognizing his or her uniqueness and his or her importance as one of God's own. This may begin by very small steps — for example, by opting to respect one another even when we are under significant stress.

Violence permeates our society, and until we have had enough of it, it will continue to do so. Movies and television shows that promote violence as a way to solve problems are not helping either us or our children to develop a mind-set of cooperation and negotiation. Sometime, when you have just watched a particularly violent movie, monitor your own reactions. Is your pulse rate elevated? Do you feel cranky or fearful? Are you ready to act aggressively? When you watch something that promotes a peaceful and cooperative theme, especially a love story, how are your feelings different?

Increasing numbers of programs in schools are successfully teaching children to negotiate in an attempt to prevent violence — something we could all do with learning. The same is true of mediation. When two or more people disagree, it is sometimes necessary to help them to see the value of negotiation and cooperation. Increasingly, court programs have set up mediation programs designed to prevent lengthy lawsuits and help people come to more equitable accommodations with one another. Mediation is a necessary tool in today's world where the stakes — both personally and professionally — can be high.

Respect, negotiation, and mediation lead naturally to *mutuality and cooperation* — people working together for a common cause. Congregations have a head start in this area if they just recognize it. As congregants, we have come together to worship and to strive to remain faithful to the teachings of God. When we consider commandments such as love your neighbor and do unto your neighbor as you would have him or her do to you, we are led naturally to respect, negotiate, and cooperate with that neighbor.

## Children, the Church, and a New Millennium

Society has been likened to a large battleship. It may change direction, but the change will be slow and must be deliberate. But children cannot wait until the "battleship" turns in a manner that protects and nurtures them as well as lessening the violence in which they live. As we go forward in this new millennium, churches may be the hope for children in the here and now. But we must be intentional in our attention to children and their needs. How do we do this?

First, we can listen to what children need and listen when they are being harmed. We can prepare a safe place for children by developing church protocol to prevent the abuse that might otherwise harm them. We can be a refuge for violent and conflict-ridden families who cannot nurture their children as they should. We can reach out a hand to them and bring them into a safe and loving environment. At the same time, we can connect them with other professionals who can help them to turn their lives around. Finally, as we are caring for the children and seeking to make their world safe and more nurturing, we can advocate that others do likewise.

The writer of the Gospel of John tells us that Jesus came so that we might have life and have it more abundantly (John 10:10). It is up to us to see that children are given this right by being kept safe from harm and by being given a brighter future. As we advocate for abused and neglected children, we live out Jesus' teachings, for "it is to such as these that the kingdom of heaven belongs" (Luke 18:16b).

# *Appendix 1*

# Clergy as Mandated Reporters

| | Privilege granted but limited to "pastoral communications" | Privilege denied in cases of suspected child abuse or neglect | Privilege not addressed in the reporting laws |
|---|---|---|---|
| *Clergy enumerated as mandated reporters* | Alabama, Arizona, Arkansas, California, Colorado, Illinois, Louisiana, Maine, Massachusetts, Michigan, Minnesota, Missouri, Montana, Nevada, New Mexico, North Dakota, Oregon, Pennsylvania, South Carolina, Vermont, Wisconsin | New Hampshire, West Virginia | Connecticut, Mississippi |
| *Clergy not enumerated as mandated reporters but may be included within "any person" designation* | Delaware, Florida, Idaho, Kentucky, Maryland, Utah, Wyoming | North Carolina, Rhode Island, Texas | Indiana, Nebraska, New Jersey, Oklahoma, Tennessee, Puerto Rico |
| *Neither clergy nor "any person" enumerated as mandated reporters* | Washington | Not applicable | Alaska, American Samoa, District of Columbia, Georgia, Guam, Hawaii, Iowa, Kansas, New York, Northern Mariana Islands, Ohio, South Dakota, Virgin Islands, Virginia |

Privileged communications for clergy refers to their right to maintain confidentiality in "pastoral communications." In some cases these communications may be exempt from reporting laws and may be addressed in the reporting statute. If it is not addressed specifically in the statute, exemption may or may not be granted. The individual state statute should be consulted.

From the Information Gateway of the Children's Bureau, Administration for Children and Families, U.S. Department of Health and Human Services at *www.childwelfare.gov/systemwide/laws_policies/statutes/clergymandated.cfm.*

# Appendix 2

# Suggested Reading

## General Reading on Child Maltreatment

Bancroft, Lundy, and Jay G. Silverman. *The Batterer as Parent*. Thousand Oaks, CA: Sage, 2002.

Crosson-Tower, Cynthia. *Understanding Child Abuse and Neglect*. Boston: Allyn and Bacon, 2005.

Danzig, Rivka A. "The Battered Jewish Family: Social and Clinical Implications," in *Crisis and Continuity: The Jewish Family in the 21st Century*, ed. Norman Linzer, Irving N. Levitz, and David J. Schnall, 39–53. Hoboken, NJ: KTAV Publishers, 1995.

Featherman, Joan. "Jews and Child Abuse." In *Sexual Abuse in Nine American Cultures*, ed. Lisa Fontes. Thousand Oaks, CA: Sage, 1995.

Hampton, Robert L. *Black Family Violence*. Lexington, MA: Lexington Books, 2003.

Shelman, Eric, and Stephen Lazoritz. *Out of the Darkness: The Story of Mary Ellen Wilson*. Lake Forest, CA: Dolphin Moon Publishing, 1998.

Stone, Robin. *No Secrets, No Lies: How Black Families Can Heal from Sexual Abuse*. New York: Broadway Books, 2004.

vanDam, Carla. *Identifying Child Molesters: Preventing Child Sexual Abuse*. New York: Haworth Press, 2001.

## Child Sexual Abuse and the Internet

Jenkins, Phillip. *Beyond Tolerance: Child Pornography and the Internet*. New York: New York University Press, 2001.

Rice Hughes, Donna. *Kids Online: Protecting Your Children in Cyberspace*. Grand Rapids: Fleming H. Revell, 1998.

Taylor, Max, and Ethel Quayle. *Child Pornography: An Internet Crime*. New York: Brunner-Routledge, 2003.

## Child Maltreatment, Domestic Violence, and Church Communities

Fortune, Marie M. *Sexual Violence: The Sin Revisited*. 2nd ed. Cleveland: Pilgrim Press, 2005.

Kearney, R. Timothy. *Caring for Sexually Abused Children: A Handbook for Families and Churches*. Downers Grove, IL: InterVarsity Press, 2001.

Kroeger, Catherine Clark, and Nancy Nason-Clark. *No Place for Abuse: Biblical and Practical References to Counteract Domestic Violence*. Downers Grove, IL: InterVarsity Press, 2001.

McClure, John S., and Nancy J. Ramsay, eds. *Telling the Truth: Preaching about Sexual and Domestic Violence*. Cleveland: United Church Press, 1998.

Miles, Al. *Domestic Violence: What Every Pastor Needs to Know.* Minneapolis: Augsburg Fortress, 2000.

———. *Violence in Families: What Every Christian Needs to Know.* Minneapolis: Augsburg Fortress, 2002.

## *Sexual Abuse by Clergy*

Benyei, Candace R. *Understanding Clergy Misconduct in Religious Systems.* New York: Haworth Press, 1998.

Berry, Jason. *Lead Us Not into Temptation.* New York: Doubleday, 2000.

Bruni, Frank, and Elinor Burkett. *A Gospel of Shame.* New York: Perennial, 2002.

Fortune, Marie M., and W. Merle Longwood, eds. *Sexual Abuse in the Catholic Church.* New York: Haworth Press, 2003.

Investigative Staff of the *Boston Globe. Betrayal: The Crisis in the Catholic Church.* Boston: Little, Brown, 2002.

O'Grady, Ron. *The Hidden Shame of the Church.* Geneva: World Council of Churches, 2001.

## *First-Person Accounts of Sexual Abuse*

Allan, Joyce. *Because I Love You: The Silent Shadow of Child Sexual Abuse.* Charlottesville: Virginia Foundations for the Humanities Press, 2002.

Bergeron, Gary. *Don't Call Me Victim: Faith, Hope and Sexual Abuse in the Catholic Church.* Lowell, MA: ArcAngel Publishing, 2005.

Theodore, Wayne, with Leslie Alan Horvitz. *Wayne: An Abused Child's Story of Courage, Survival and Hope.* Gig Harbor, WA: Harbor Press, 2003.

Wiklund, Patricia. *Sleeping with a Stranger: How I Survived Marriage to a Child Molester.* Holbrook, MA: Adams Publishing, 1995.

## *Resources for Adult Survivors, Their Partners, and Those Who Help Them*

Bilich, Marion, Susan Bonfiglio, and Steven Carlson. *Shared Grace: Therapists and Clergy Working Together.* New York: Haworth Press, 2000.

Blume, Sue. *Secret Survivors: Uncovering Incest and Its After-Effects on Women.* New York: Ballantine, 1997.

Cameron, Grant. *What about Me: A Guide for Men Helping Female Partners Deal with Childhood Sexual Abuse.* Canada: Creative Bound, Inc., 2002.

Lev, Rachael. *Shine the Light: Sexual Abuse and Healing in the Jewish Community.* Boston: Northeastern University Press, 2002.

Lew, Mike. *Victims No Longer: The Classic Guide for Men Recovering from Child Sexual Abuse.* New York: HarperCollins, 2004.

## *Resources for Parents*

Angelica, Jade Christine. *We Are Not Alone: A Guidebook for Helping Professionals and Parents Supporting Adolescent Victims of Sexual Abuse.* New York: Haworth Press, 2002.

Bancroft, Lundy. *When Dad Hurts Mom: Helping Your Children Heal the Wounds of Witnessing Abuse.* New York: G. P. Putnam's Sons, 2004.

Brohl, Kathryn, and Joyce Case Potter. *When Your Child Has Been Molested: A Parent's Guide to Healing and Recovery.* New York: Wiley, 2004.

## Resources on Prevention

Friberg, Nils C., and Mark R. Laaser. *Before the Fall: Preventing Pastoral Sexual Abuse.* Collegeville, MN: Liturgical Press, 1998.

Goering Reid, Kathryn, with Marie Fortune. *Preventing Child Sexual Abuse: A Curriculum for Children Ages Nine through Twelve.* Cleveland: United Church Press, 2002.

Hammer, Richard R., Steven W. Klipowicz, and James F. Cobble Jr. *Reducing the Risk of Child Sexual Abuse in Your Church.* Matthews, NC: Christian Ministry Resources, 1993.

Hoertdoerfer, Patricia, and William Sinkford. *Creating Safe Congregations: Toward an Ethic of Right Relations.* Boston: Unitarian Universalist Association, 1997.

McClintock, Karen A. *Preventing Sexual Abuse in Congregations: A Resource for Leaders.* Herndon, VA: Alban Institute, 2004.

McGlone, Gerard J., and Mary Shrader with Laurie Delgatto. *Creating Safe and Sacred Places: Identifying, Preventing and Healing Sexual Abuse.* Winona, MN: Saint Mary's Press, 2003.

Zarra, Ernest J. III. *It Should Never Happen Here.* Grand Rapids: Baker Books, 1997.

## *Appendix 3*

# Reporting Hotlines

Abuse must be reported within the state in which it occurs. In addition,

1. Not every state has a reporting hotline
2. Not every hotline is accessible twenty-four hours a day
3. If the state does have a hotline, it may be accessible only within that state

Since hotlines may change periodically, it is best to find out your up-to-date hotline number by going to ChildHelp USA at *www.childhelpusa.org/get_help*. This should be done *before* a crisis arises.

The following are the most recent hotline numbers:

**Alabama:** Report by county — 334-242-9500

**Alaska:** 907-269-3900 (out of state)
800-478-4444 (in state)
or Division of Family & Youth Services Regional Office

**Arizona:** 888-SOS-CHILD (888-767-2445)

**Arkansas:** 800-482-5964

**California:** Report by county
916-445-2832 (out of state)

**Colorado:** Report by county
303-866-3003 (nationwide)

**Connecticut:** 800-842-2288 (nationwide)
800-624-5518 (TDD/hearing impaired, in state)

**Delaware:** 800-292-9582
302-577-6550 (out of state)

**District of Columbia:** 202-671-7233 (nationwide)

**Florida:** 800-962-2873 (nationwide)

**Georgia:** Report by county

**Hawaii:** Report by Island
808-832-5300 (Oahu)

**Idaho:** Report by regional office

**Illinois:** 800-252-2873 (in state)
217-524-2606 (out of state)

**Indiana:** 800-800-5556 (in state)
Out of state: report by regional office

**Iowa:** 800-362-2178 (nationwide)

**Kansas:** 800-922-5330
785-296-0044 (out of state)

**Kentucky:** 800-752-6200
502-595-4550 (out of state)

**Louisiana:** Report by parish/county
225-342-6832 (out of state, during business hours)

**Maine:** 800-452-1999
207-287-2983 (out of state)
207-287-3492 (TTY)

**Maryland:** 800-332-6347 (in state)
Out of state: report by county

**Massachusetts:** 800-792-5200
617-232-4882 (out of state)

**Michigan:** 800-942-4357
517-373-3572 (out of state)

**Minnesota:** Report by county

**Mississippi:** 800-222-8000
601-359-4991 (out of state)

**Missouri:** 800-392-3738
573-751-3448 (out of state)

**Montana:** 800-332-6100
406-444-5900 (out of state)

**Nebraska:** 800-652-1999
402-595-1324 (out of state, during business hours)

**Nevada:** 800-992-5757
775-684-4400 (out of state, during business hours)

**New Hampshire:** 800-894-5533 (in state)
800-852-3388 (in state, after hours)
603-271-6563 (out of state)
603-225-9000 (out of state, after hours)

**New Jersey:** 800-792-8610 (nationwide, 24 hours)
800-835-5510 (TDD/hearing impaired)

**New Mexico:** 800-797-3260 (24 hours)
505-841-6100 (out of state, 24 hours)

**New York:** 800-342-3720
518-474-8740 (out of state)

**North Carolina:** Report by county

**North Dakota:** Report by regional office
701-328-2316 (nationwide, 8:00 a.m.–5:00 p.m.)
800-245-3736 (in state, 8:00 a.m.–5:00 p.m.)

**Ohio:** Report by County
614-466-9824 (nationwide, during business hours)

**Oklahoma:** 800-522-3511 (nationwide, 24 hours)

**Oregon:** 800-854-3508 ext. 2402 (in state, during business hours)
503-378-5414 (TTY, hearing impaired)
503-378-6704 (nationwide, during business hours)

**Pennsylvania:** 800-932-0313 (in state)
717-783-8744 (in and out of state)

**Rhode Island:** 800-RI-CHILD (800-742-4453) (nationwide, 24 hours)

**South Carolina:** Report by county (in state)
803-898-7318 (out of state, during business hours)

**South Dakota:** Report by county
605-773-3227 (nationwide, during business hours)

**Tennessee:** Report by county
615-532-3545 (nationwide, during business hours)
After hours: contact county Department of Human Services

**Texas:** 800-252-5400
512-834-3784 (out of state, during business hours)
512-832-2020 (out of state, after hours)

**Utah:** 800-678-9399 (nationwide)

**Vermont:** Report by county (during business hours)
800-649-5285 (in state)

**Virginia:** 800-552-7096
804-786-8536 (out of state)

**Washington:** 800-562-5624 (nationwide)

**West Virginia:** 800-352-6513
304-558-7980 (out of state, during business hours)

**Wisconsin:** Report by county
608-266-3036 (nationwide, during business hours)

**Wyoming:** 800-457-3659 (in state, report by county)

## *Appendix 4*

# Resources for Domestic Violence, Adult Survivors, and Information

**National Coalition Against Domestic Violence**
P.O. Box 18749, Denver, CO 80218
Phone: 303-839-1852
Fax: 303-831-9251
*www.ncadv.org*

**National Domestic Violence Hotline**
800-799-SAFE (7233) 24-hour referral service

**Survivors Network of those Abused by Priests (SNAP)**
P.O. Box 6416, Chicago, IL 60680-6416
Toll-Free: 877-SNAPHEALS (877-762-7432)
*www.snapnetwork.org*

**Voices in Action, Inc.**
P.O. Box 148309, Chicago, Illinois 60614
800-7-VOICE-8
312-327-1500
*www.voices-action.org*

**Center for the Prevention of Sexual and Domestic Violence (CPSDV)**
2400 N. 45th Street #10, Seattle, WA 98103
Office: 206-634-1903
Fax: 206-634-0115
*www.cpsdv.org*
(An interreligious educational resource addressing religious issues associated with sexual and domestic violence, with books and videos available to religious leaders and communities.)

**ChildHelp USA–National Child Abuse Hotline**
National Headquarters, 15757 N. 78th Street, Scottsdale, AZ 85260
Office: 480-922-8212
Fax: 480-922-7061
Hotline: 800-4-A-Child (800-422-4453)
*www.childhelpusa.org*
(The ChildHelp National Child Abuse Hotline serves the United States, Canada, U.S. Virgin Islands, Puerto Rico, and Guam. The hotline is staffed 24 hours, 7 days a week.)

**The Awareness Center, Inc.: Jewish Coalition Against Sexual Abuse/Assault (JCASA)**
P.O. Box 65273
Baltimore, MD 21209
443-857-5560
*www.theawarenesscenter.org*
(This organization provides information and resources to Jewish survivors, family members, and perpetrators of sexual violence. Provides good information from a Jewish perspective.)

**Faith Trust Institute**
2400 N. 45th Street #10
Seattle, WA 98103
Office: 206-634-1903
Fax: 206-634-0115
*www.faithtrustinstitute.org*
(A multi-faith organization working to end sexual and domestic violence. Provides training and a variety of resources.)

## *Appendix 5*

# Useful Websites Providing Resources to Develop Protocol or Prevention Programs

A variety of churches have developed prevention and protocol materials. Although they may be listed under a specific denomination, most are useful for multiple denominations. The following is a partial list:

*www.elca.org/init/safehaven/packet/called.html* (Evangelical Lutheran Church)

*www.crcna.org/pages/preventionresources.cfm* (Christian Reformed Church)

*www.virtus.org* (Roman Catholic)

*www.myyaya.org/youth/yth_resources-cap-01.htm* (Episcopal Church)

*www.ucc.org/ministries/safe/safebook.pdf* (United Church of Christ)

*www.uua.org/cde/education/safecong.html* (Unitarian Universalist)

*www.gnjumc.org/safe.html* (United Methodist Church)

*www.shalomctr.org/node/910* (Jewish) gives a sample protocol developed by the Kehilla Community Synagogue in Oakland, California.

*www.theawarenesscenter.org* (Jewish) Although not protocol specifically, there is a wealth of information there that might help to develop one from a Jewish perspective.

# Notes

## Introduction

1. Carol J. Adams and Marie M. Fortune, *Violence against Women and Children* (New York: Continuum, 1995), 11.

## Chapter 1: Maltreatment Comes in Many Forms

1. Categories differ depending upon the source. These categories are a compilation of the following: Cynthia Crosson-Tower, *Understanding Child Abuse and Neglect* (Boston: Allyn and Bacon, 2005); Hendrika B. Cantwell, "The Neglect of Child Neglect," in *The Battered Child,* ed. Mary E. Helfer, Ruth S. Kempe and Richard D. Krugman (Chicago: University of Chicago Press, 1997), 347–73; and Harold Dubowitz, ed., *Neglected Children: Research, Practice, and Policy* (Thousand Oaks, CA: Sage Publications, 1999).

2. For an interesting and detailed story of Mary Ellen's plight, see Eric A. Shelman and Stephen Lazoritz, *Out of the Darkness: The Story of Mary Ellen Wilson* (Lake Forest, CA: Dolphin Moon Publishing, 1998).

3. Robert W. ten Bensel, Marguerite M. Rheinberger, and Samuel X. Radbill, "Children in a World of Violence: Roots of Child Maltreatment," in *Battered Child,* 23–26.

4. David Finkelhor, *Child Sexual Abuse* (New York: Free Press, 1984).

5. Crosson-Tower, *Understanding Child Abuse and Neglect.*

6. See especially Dorota Iwaniec, *The Emotionally Abused and Neglected Child* (West Sussex, UK, and Hoboken, NJ: John Wiley and Sons, 2006), 28.

7. See the following website for more information: *www.childwitnesstoviolence.org/care_givers_for_caregivers_facts.html.*

8. Ibid.

9. Al Miles, *Domestic Violence: What Every Pastor Needs to Know* (Minneapolis: Augsburg Press, 2000), 38.

## Chapter 2: Recognizing Child Maltreatment

1. See also Crosson-Tower, *Understanding Child Abuse and Neglect,* 63–91; Mark D. Joffe, "Child Neglect and Abandonment," in *Recognition of Child Abuse for Mandated Reporters,* ed. Angelo P. Giardino and Eileen R. Giardino (St. Louis: G. W. Medical Publishing, 2002), 39–54.

2. Crosson-Tower, *Understanding Child Abuse and Neglect,* 102.

3. See also Peter G. Jaffee and Linda L. Baker, eds., *Protecting Children from Domestic Violence* (New York: Guilford Press, 2004), and Audrey Mullender, Ellen Malos, Umme Iman, Linda Regan, and Liz Kelly, *Children's Perspective on Domestic Violence* (Thousand Oaks, CA: Sage Publications, 2003).

4. Lundy Bancroft and Jay G. Silverman, *The Batterer as Parent* (Thousand Oaks, CA: Sage Publications, 2002), 41.

## Chapter 3: A Look at the Dysfunctional Family

1. James Garbarino and Cyleste C. Collins, "Child Neglect: The Family with a Hole in the Middle," in *Neglected Children,* ed. Howard Dubowitz (Thousand Oaks, CA: Sage Publications, 1999), 3.

2. See Garbarino and Collins, "Child Neglect," and Patricia McKinsey Crittenden, "Child Neglect: Causes and Contributors," in *Neglected Children,* ed. Howard Dubowitz (Thousand Oaks, CA: Sage Publications, 1999), 48–49.

3. Crittenden, "Child Neglect," 47.

4. See ibid. for more information on this type of family.

5. See ibid., 57–62.

6. See ibid., 62–66.

7. For a summary of these models, see Harvey Wallace, *Family Violence: Legal, Medical and Social Perspectives* (Boston: Allyn and Bacon, 2005), 9–24.

8. Raymond Helfer, lecture given in New Bedford, Massachusetts, March 1979, as cited in Cynthia Crosson-Tower, *When Children Are Abused: An Educator's Guide to Intervention* (Boston: Allyn and Bacon Company, 2002), 62–64.

9. Bancroft and Silverman, *The Batterer as Parent,* 64–97.

10. Sharon D. Herzberger, *Violence in the Family* (Boulder, CO: Westview Press, 1996); Richard L. Davis, *Domestic Violence: Facts and Fallacies* (Westport, CT: Praeger, 1998).

## Chapter 4: The Sexual Abuser and the Family

1. Based on the work of David Finkelhor, *Child Sexual Abuse* (New York: Free Press, 1984), 54–58.

2. Ibid., 58–61.

3. Based on the work of A. Nicholas Groth, "The Incest Offender," in *Handbook of Clinical Intervention in Child Sexual Abuse,* ed. Suzanne M. Sgroi (Lexington, MA: Lexington Books, 1982), 99–104.

4. Jacqui Saradjian and Helga G. I. Hanks, *Women Who Sexually Abuse Children: From Research to Clinical Practice* (New York: John Wiley & Sons, 1996).

5. Ibid., 146–47.

6. Ibid.

7. See Suzanne M. Sgroi, Linda Canfield Blick, and Frances Sarnacki Porter, "A Conceptual Framework for Sexual Abuse," in *Handbook of Clinical Intervention in Child Sexual Abuse,* ed. Suzanne M. Sgroi (Lexington, MA: Lexington Books, 1982), 13–27, and Groth, "Incest Offender."

8. The dynamics of progression in sexual abuse are originally credited to Sgroi, Blick, and Porter, "Conceptual Framework for Sexual Abuse," 10–12.

9. Ibid.

10. These categories are based on the work of Toni Cavanaugh Johnson with Joanne Ross Feldmeth, "Sexual Behaviors: A Continuum," in *Sexualized Children,* ed. Eliana Gil and Toni Cavanaugh Johnson (Rockville, MD: Launch Press, 1993), 41–52.

11. Jane F. Gilgun, "Factors Mediating the Effects of Childhood Maltreatment," in *The Sexually Abused Male,* ed. Mic Hunter (New York: Lexington Books, 1991), 177–90.

12. Virginia C. Strand, *Treating Secondary Victims: Intervention with the Non-Offending Mother in the Incest Family* (Thousand Oaks, CA: Sage Publications, 2000).

13. Barbara Rosencrans, *The Last Secret: Daughters Sexually Abused by Mothers* (Brandon, VT: Safer Society Press, 1997).

14. Marcus Erooga and Helen Masson, eds., *Children and Young People Who Sexually Abuse Others* (New York: Routledge, 1999).

## Chapter 5: The Dilemma of Reporting and How It Works

1. Adapted from Crosson-Tower, *When Children Are Abused,* 117.

2. See Deborah Anderson, Martha Finne, and Jeanette Swofford (illustrator), *Margaret's Story: Sexual Abuse and Going to Court* (Glenville, IL: Silver Burdett Press, 1996).

3. Kathryn Brohl and Joyce Case Potter, *When Your Child Has Been Molested: A Parent's Guide to Healing and Recovery* (New York: Wiley, 2004); Aphrodite Matsakis, *When the Bough Breaks: A Helping Guide for Parents of Sexually Abused Children* (Oakland, CA: New Harbinger Press, 1991); Leigh Baker, *Protecting Your Child from Sexual Predators* (New York: St. Martin's Press, 2002).

4. Based on Kee MacFarlane, "Helping Parents Cope with Extrafamilial Molestation," in Kee MacFarlane and Jill Waterman, *Sexual Abuse of Young Children* (New York: Guilford Press, 1988), 299–311, 304–7.

## Chapter 6: Responding When There Is Domestic Violence

1. Lenore Walker, "Spouse Abuse: A Basic Profile," in *Abuse and Religion: When Praying Is Not Enough*, ed. Anne L. Horton and Judith Williamson (New York: Lexington Books, 1990), 13–20; Christina M. Dalpiaz, *Breaking Free, Starting Over: Parenting in the Aftermath of Family Violence* (Westport, CT: Praeger, 2004); Lundy Bancroft, *When Dad Hurts Mom: Helping Children Heal the Wounds of Witnessing Abuse* (New York: G. P. Putnam and Sons, 2004); Al Miles, *Violence in Families: What Every Christian Needs to Know* (Minneapolis: Augsburg Fortress, 2002).

2. Bancroft and Silverman, *The Batterer as Parent*; James Newton Poling, *Understanding Male Violence: Pastoral Care Issues* (St. Louis: Chalice Press, 2003).

3. See Catherine Clark Kroeger and Nancy Nason-Clark, *No Place for Abuse: Biblical and Practical Resources to Counteract Domestic Violence* (Downers Grove, IL: InterVarsity Press, 2001).

4. Bancroft, *When Dad Hurts Mom,* 82–83.

## Chapter 7: Being the Good Shepherd While the System Does Its Work

1. Bancroft, *When Dad Hurts Mom,* 177–85.

2. Marion Bilich, Susan Bonfiglio, and Steven Carlson, *Shared Grace: Therapists and Clergy Working Together* (New York: Haworth Press, 2000).

## Chapter 8: Helping the Congregation Be a Supportive "Family"

1. Leroy Howe, *A Pastor in Every Pew: Equipping Laity for Pastoral Care* (Valley Forge, PA: Judson Press, 2000).

2. Edwin H. Friedman, *Generation to Generation: Family Process in Church and Synagogue* (New York: Guilford Press, 1985), 27.

3. Donald Smarto, *Keeping Ex-Offenders Free: An Aftercare Guide* (Grand Rapids: Baker Books, 1994).

4. W. Brad Johnson and William L. Johnson, *The Pastor's Guide to Psychological Disorders and Treatments* (New York: Haworth Pastoral Press, 2000).

5. John S. McClure and Nancy J. Ramsay, eds., *Telling the Truth: Preaching about Sexual and Domestic Violence* (Cleveland: United Church Press, 1998).

## Chapter 9: When the Shepherd Strays

1. A. W. Richard Sipe, *Sex, Priests and Power* (New York: Brunner/Mazel, 1995), 10; S. Laeuchli, *Power and Sexuality: The Emergence of Canon Law at the Synod of Elvira* (Philadelphia: Temple University Press, 1972), 47.

2. Sipe, *Sex, Priests and Power.*

3. See Jason Berry, *Lead Us Not into Temptation* (New York: Doubleday, 2000).

4. Elinor Burkett and Frank Bruni, *Gospel of Shame* (New York: Viking, 1993).

5. G. Lloyd Rediger, *Beyond the Scandals* (Minneapolis: Fortress Press, 2003).

6. Phillip Jenkins, *Pedophiles and Priests: Anatomy of a Contemporary Crisis* (New York: Oxford University Press, 2001).

7. Sipe, *Sex, Priests and Power,* 61.

8. Ibid., 70.

9. Adapted from Crosson-Tower, *Understanding Child Abuse and Neglect,* 191.

10. Investigative Staff of the Boston Globe, *Betrayal: The Crisis in the Catholic Church* (Boston: Little, Brown, 2002), 16.

11. Ibid., 18.

12. Ibid.

13. James F. McLaughlin, "Technophilia: A Modern Day Paraphilia," *Knight Stick* 51 (1998): 47–51; Crosson-Tower, *Understanding Child Abuse and Neglect.*

14. James F. McLaughlin, "Cyber Child Sexual Offender," *Knight Stick* 55 (2000): 39–42; Crosson-Tower, *Understanding Child Abuse and Neglect,* 188.

15. Gerard J. McGlone and Mary Shrader with Laurie Delgatto, *Creating Safe and Sacred Places* (Winona, MN: Saint Mary's Press, 2003), 28.

16. Len Sperry, *Sex, Priestly Ministry and the Church* (Collegeville, MN: Liturgical Press, 2003), 136.

## Chapter 10: Responding to Abuse by Clergy

1. Investigative Staff of the *Boston Globe, Betrayal,* 3.

2. Stanley J. Grenz and Roy D. Bell, *Betrayal of Trust: Confronting and Preventing Clergy Sexual Misconduct* (Grand Rapids: Baker Books, 1995), 28–29.

3. Ibid.

4. Ibid., 120–26.

5. Ibid.

6. Ibid., 126–28.

7. Neil and Thea Ormerod, *When Ministers Sin: Sexual Abuse in the Churches* (Alexandria, Australia: Millennium Books, 1995), 76–91.

8. See Investigative Staff of the *Boston Globe, Betrayal,* 43.

## Chapter 11: Helping the Church after Clergy Abuse

1. Adapted from the family systems work of Beverly James and Maria Nasjleti, *Treating Sexually Abused Children and Their Families* (Palo Alto, CA: Consulting Psychologists Press, 1983).

2. Chilton Knudsen, "Understanding Congregational Dynamics," in *Restoring the Soul of the Church*, ed. Nancy Myer Hopkins and Mark Laaser (Collegeville, MN: Liturgical Press, 1995), 75–101.

3. Jeffrey D. Jones, *Traveling Together: A Guide for Disciple-Forming Congregations* (Bethesda, MD: Alban Institute, 2005).

4. Abigail Johnson, *Reflecting with God: Connecting Faith and Daily Life in Small Groups* (Herndon, VA: Alban Institute, 2004).

5. Ibid.

6. Ibid.

7. R. Paul Stevens and Phil Collins, *The Equipping Pastor: Systems Approach to Congregational Leadership* (Bethesda, MD: Alban Institute, 1993), 3.

8. Ibid., 35.

## Chapter 12: Adult Survivors in the Church

1. Ronnie Janoff-Bulman, *Shattered Assumptions: Towards a New Psychology of Trauma* (New York: Free Press, 1992).

2. Trudie Chase and the Troops, *When Rabbit Howls* (New York: Berkley Trade, 2002).

3. Bobbie Rosencrans, *The Last Secret: Daughters Abused by Mothers* (Brandon, VT: Safer Society Press, 1997).

4. Cynthia Crosson-Tower, *Secret Scars: A Guide for Survivors of Child Sexual Abuse* (New York: Viking/Penguin, 1988).

5. Loosely adapted from Chris Servaty, "Support Counseling with Victims of Sexual Assault," in *Sexual Assault and Abuse: A Handbook for Clergy and Religious Professionals,* ed. Mary D. Pellauer, Barbara Chester, and Jane A. Boyajian (San Francisco: HarperSanFrancisco, 1987), 138–39. This can also be generalized to other types of childhood trauma.

6. Christine A. Courtois, *Healing the Incest Wound* (New York: W. W. Norton, 1996). Although these characteristics are based on Courtois's findings with the therapists of incest survivors, they can be generalized to those who help past victims of a variety of types of child maltreatment.

7. Ibid.

## Chapter 13: Developing a Church Reporting Protocol

1. E. L. Long Jr., *Patterns of Polity: Varieties of Church Governance* (Cleveland: Pilgrim Press, 2001), 5.

2. Ibid.

3. See Archdiocese of Boston, *Policies and Procedures for the Protection of Children* (Boston: Author, 2003).

4. Adapted from Patricia Hoertdoerfer and Gretchen Thomas, "It Takes a Whole Congregation to Raise a Child," in *Creating Safe Congregations: Toward an Ethic of Right Relations,* ed. Patricia Hoertdoerfer and William Sinkford (Boston: Unitarian Universalist Association, 1997), 59–60.

5. Adapted from Cynthia Crosson-Tower, *When Children Are Abused: An Educator's Guide to Intervention* (Boston: Allyn and Bacon, 2002).

6. Joy T. Melton, *Safe Sanctuaries: Reducing the Risk of Child Abuse in the Church* (Nashville: Discipleship Resources, 1998).

7. Ibid.

8. Ernest J. Zarra, *It Should Never Happen Here* (Grand Rapids: Baker Books, 1997), 32–33.

9. Ibid.

10. The First Congregational Church, United Church of Christ, *Policy Handbook for Child Safety and Protection* (Longmeadow, MA: Author, 1998).

## Chapter 14: Clergy Self-Care

1. Lawrence M. Brammer and Ginger MacDonald, *The Helping Relationship* (Boston: Allyn and Bacon, 2002), 40.

2. Kirk Byron Jones, *Rest in the Storm: Self-Care Strategies for Clergy and Other Caregivers* (Valley Forge, PA: Judson Press, 2001).

3. Ibid., 32.

4. Kevin McDonough, "The Effects of the Misconduct Crisis on Non-Offending Clergy," in *Restoring the Soul of the Church*, ed. Nancy M. Hopkins and Mark Laaser (Collegeville, MN: Liturgical Press, 1995), 102–15.

5. Marie M. Fortune, "Confidentiality and Mandatory Reporting: A Clergy Dilemma," in *Sexual Assault and Abuse*, ed. Mary D. Pellauer, Barbara Chester, and Jane A. Boyajian (San Francisco: HarperSanFrancisco, 1987), 198–208, 202.

6. Jones, *Rest in the Storm.*

7. Ibid.

## Chapter 15: Hope for the Future

1. See the work of Ray Helfer as quoted in Crosson-Tower, *Understanding Child Abuse and Neglect,* 110–11.